FreeBSD Porter's Handbook

The FreeBSD Documentation Project

FreeBSD Porter's Handbook

by

Revision: 51411

2018-02-09 17:19:21 by mat.

Copyright © 2000, 2001, 2002, 2003, 2004, 2005, 2006, 2007, 2008, 2009, 2010, 2011, 2012, 2013, 2014, 2015, 2016, 2017 The FreeBSD Documentation Project

Table of Contents

List of Tables

List of Examples

Chapter 1. Introduction

The FreeBSD Ports Collection is the way almost everyone installs applications ("ports") on FreeBSD. Like everything else about FreeBSD, it is primarily a volunteer effort. It is important to keep this in mind when reading this document.

In FreeBSD, anyone may submit a new port, or volunteer to maintain an existing unmaintained port. No special commit privilege is needed.

Chapter 2. Making a New Port

Interested in making a new port, or upgrading existing ports? Great!

What follows are some guidelines for creating a new port for FreeBSD. To upgrade an existing port, read this, then read Chapter 11, *Upgrading a Port*.

When this document is not sufficiently detailed, refer to /usr/ports/Mk/bsd.port.mk , which is included by all port Makefiles. Even those not hacking Makefiles daily can gain much knowledge from it. Additionally, specific questions can be sent to the FreeBSD ports mailing list.

 Note

Only a fraction of the variables (*VAR*) that can be overridden are mentioned in this document. Most (if not all) are documented at the start of /usr/ports/Mk/bsd.port.mk ; the others probably ought to be. Note that this file uses a non-standard tab setting: Emacs and Vim will recognize the setting on loading the file. Both vi(1) and ex(1) can be set to use the correct value by typing :set tabstop=4 once the file has been loaded.

Looking for something easy to start with? Take a look at the list of requested ports and see if you can work on one (or more).

Chapter 3. Quick Porting

This section describes how to quickly create a new port. For applications where this quick method is not adequate, the full "Slow Porting" process is described in Chapter 4, *Slow Porting*.

First, get the original tarball and put it into DISTDIR, which defaults to /usr/ports/distfiles .

Note

These steps assume that the software compiled out-of-the-box. In other words, absolutely no changes were required for the application to work on a FreeBSD system. If anything had to be changed, refer to Chapter 4, *Slow Porting*.

Note

It is recommended to set the DEVELOPER make(1) variable in /etc/make.conf before getting into porting.

```
# echo DEVELOPER=yes >> /etc/make.conf
```

This setting enables the "developer mode" that displays deprecation warnings and activates some further quality checks on calling make.

3.1. Writing the Makefile

The minimal Makefile would look something like this:

```
# $FreeBSD$

PORTNAME= oneko
DISTVERSION= 1.1b
CATEGORIES= games
MASTER_SITES= ftp://ftp.cs.columbia.edu/archives/X11R5/contrib/

MAINTAINER= youremail@example.com
COMMENT= Cat chasing a mouse all over the screen

.include <bsd.port.mk>
```

Note

In some cases, the Makefile of an existing port may contain additional lines in the header, such as the name of the port and the date it was created. This additional information has been declared obsolete, and is being phased out.

Try to figure it out. Do not worry about the contents of the $FreeBSD$ line, it will be filled in automatically by Subversion when the port is imported to our main ports tree. A more detailed example is shown in the sample Makefile section.

3.2. Writing the Description Files

There are two description files that are required for any port, whether they actually package or not. They are `pkg-descr` and `pkg-plist` . Their `pkg-` prefix distinguishes them from other files.

3.2.1. pkg-descr

This is a longer description of the port. One to a few paragraphs concisely explaining what the port does is sufficient.

 Note

This is *not* a manual or an in-depth description on how to use or compile the port! *Please be careful when copying from the README or manpage.* Too often they are not a concise description of the port or are in an awkward format. For example, manpages have justified spacing, which looks particularly bad with monospaced fonts.

On the other hand, the content of `pkg-descr` must be longer than the COMMENT line from the Makefile. It must explain in more depth what the port is all about.

A well-written `pkg-descr` describes the port completely enough that users would not have to consult the documentation or visit the website to understand what the software does, how it can be useful, or what particularly nice features it has. Mentioning certain requirements like a graphical toolkit, heavy dependencies, runtime environment, or implementation languages help users decide whether this port will work for them.

Include a URL to the official WWW homepage. Prepend *one* of the websites (pick the most common one) with WWW: (followed by single space) so that automated tools will work correctly. If the URI is the root of the website or directory, it must be terminated with a slash.

 Note

If the listed webpage for a port is not available, try to search the Internet first to see if the official site moved, was renamed, or is hosted elsewhere.

This example shows how `pkg-descr` looks:

```
This is a port of oneko, in which a cat chases a poor mouse all over
the screen.
 :
(etc.)

WWW: http://www.oneko.org/
```

3.2.2. pkg-plist

This file lists all the files installed by the port. It is also called the "packing list" because the package is generated by packing the files listed here. The pathnames are relative to the installation prefix (usually `/usr/local`).

Here is a small example:

```
bin/oneko
man/man1/oneko.1.gz
lib/X11/app-defaults/Oneko
lib/X11/oneko/cat1.xpm
lib/X11/oneko/cat2.xpm
```

```
lib/X11/oneko/mouse.xpm
```

Refer to the pkg-create(8) manual page for details on the packing list.

Note

It is recommended to keep all the filenames in this file sorted alphabetically. It will make verifying changes when upgrading the port much easier.

Tip

Creating a packing list manually can be a very tedious task. If the port installs a large numbers of files, creating the packing list automatically might save time.

There is only one case when pkg-plist can be omitted from a port. If the port installs just a handful of files, list them in PLIST_FILES , within the port's Makefile. For instance, we could get along without pkg-plist in the above oneko port by adding these lines to the Makefile:

```
PLIST_FILES= bin/oneko \
  man/man1/oneko.1.gz \
  lib/X11/app-defaults/Oneko \
  lib/X11/oneko/cat1.xpm \
  lib/X11/oneko/cat2.xpm \
  lib/X11/oneko/mouse.xpm
```

Note

Usage of PLIST_FILES should not be abused. When looking for the origin of a file, people usually try to grep through the pkg-plist files in the ports tree. Listing files in PLIST_FILES in the Makefile makes that search more difficult.

Tip

If a port needs to create an empty directory, or creates directories outside of ${PREFIX} during installation, refer to Section 8.2.1, "Cleaning Up Empty Directories" for more information.

The price for this way of listing a port's files and directories is that the keywords described in pkg-create(8) and Section 8.6, "Expanding Package List with Keywords" cannot be used. Therefore, it is suitable only for simple ports and makes them even simpler. At the same time, it has the advantage of reducing the number of files in the ports collection. Please consider using this technique before resorting to pkg-plist .

Later we will see how pkg-plist and PLIST_FILES can be used to fulfill more sophisticated tasks.

3.3. Creating the Checksum File

Just type make makesum. The ports framework will automatically generate distinfo. Do not try to generate the file manually.

3.4. Testing the Port

Make sure that the port rules do exactly what is desired, including packaging up the port. These are the important points to verify:

- `pkg-plist` does not contain anything not installed by the port.

- `pkg-plist` contains everything that is installed by the port.

- The port can be installed using the `install` target. This verifies that the install script works correctly.

- The port can be deinstalled properly using the `deinstall` target. This verifies that the deinstall script works correctly.

- The port only has access to network resources during the `fetch` target phase. This is important for package builders, such as ports-mgmt/poudriere.

- Make sure that `make package` can be run as a normal user (that is, not as `root`). If that fails, the software may need to be patched. See also Section 17.18, "`fakeroot`" and Section 17.84, "`uidfix`".

Procedure 3.1. Recommended Test Ordering

1. `make stage`

2. `make check-orphans`

3. `make package`

4. `make install`

5. `make deinstall`

6. `make package` (as user)

Make certain no warnings are shown in any of the stages.

Thorough automated testing can be done with ports-mgmt/poudriere from the Ports Collection, see Section 10.5, "Poudriere" for more information. It maintains `jails` where all of the steps shown above can be tested without affecting the state of the host system.

3.5. Checking the Port with `portlint`

Please use `portlint` to see if the port conforms to our guidelines. The ports-mgmt/portlint program is part of the ports collection. In particular, check that the Makefile is in the right shape and the package is named appropriately.

> **Important**
>
> Do not blindly follow the output of `portlint`. It is a static lint tool and sometimes gets things wrong.

3.6. Submitting the New Port

Before submitting the new port, read the DOs and DON'Ts section.

Once happy with the port, the only thing remaining is to put it in the main FreeBSD ports tree and make everybody else happy about it too.

Important

We do not need the `work` directory or the `pkgname.tgz` package, so delete them now.

Next, either create a patch(1), or a shar(1) file. Assuming the port is called oneko and is in the games category.

Example 3.1. Creating a `.diff` for a New Port

Add all the files with svn add. cd to the base of the ports tree so full paths to the changed files are included in the diff, then generate the diff with svn diff. For example:

```
% svn add .
% cd ../..
% svn diff games/oneko > oneko.diff
```

Important

To make it easier for committers to apply the patch on their working copy of the ports tree, please generate the `.diff` from the base of your ports tree.

Example 3.2. Creating a `.shar` for a New Port

cd to the directory above where the port directory is located, and use shar to create the archive:

```
% cd ..
% shar `find oneko` > oneko.shar
```

Submit one of oneko.shar or oneko.diff with the bug submission form. Use product "Ports & Packages", component "Individual Port(s)", and follow the guidelines shown there. Add a short description of the program to the Description field of the PR (perhaps a short version of COMMENT), and remember to add oneko.shar or oneko.diff as an attachment.

Note

Giving a good description in the summary of the problem report makes the work of port committers a lot easier. We prefer something like "New port: *category/portname short description of the port*" for new ports. Using this scheme makes it easier and faster to begin the work of committing the new port.

After submitting the port, please be patient. The time needed to include a new port in FreeBSD can vary from a few days to a few months. A simple search form of the Problem Report database can be searched at https://bugs.freebsd.org/bugzilla/query.cgi.

To get a listing of *open* port PRs, select *Open* and *Ports & Packages* in the search form, then click [Search].

After looking at the new port, we will reply if necessary, and commit it to the tree. The submitter's name will also be added to the list of Additional FreeBSD Contributors and other files.

Chapter 4. Slow Porting

Okay, so it was not that simple, and the port required some modifications to get it to work. In this section, we will explain, step by step, how to modify it to get it to work with the ports paradigm.

4.1. How Things Work

First, this is the sequence of events which occurs when the user first types make in the port's directory. Having bsd.port.mk in another window while reading this really helps to understand it.

But do not worry, not many people understand exactly how bsd.port.mk is working... :-)

1. The fetch target is run. The fetch target is responsible for making sure that the tarball exists locally in DISTDIR. If fetch cannot find the required files in DISTDIR it will look up the URL MASTER_SITES , which is set in the Makefile, as well as our FTP mirrors where we put distfiles as backup. It will then attempt to fetch the named distribution file with FETCH, assuming that the requesting site has direct access to the Internet. If that succeeds, it will save the file in DISTDIR for future use and proceed.

2. The extract target is run. It looks for the port's distribution file (typically a compressed tarball) in DISTDIR and unpacks it into a temporary subdirectory specified by WRKDIR (defaults to work).

3. The patch target is run. First, any patches defined in PATCHFILES are applied. Second, if any patch files named patch-* are found in PATCHDIR (defaults to the files subdirectory), they are applied at this time in alphabetical order.

4. The configure target is run. This can do any one of many different things.

    1. If it exists, scripts/configure is run.

    2. If HAS_CONFIGURE or GNU_CONFIGURE is set, WRKSRC/configure is run.

5. The build target is run. This is responsible for descending into the port's private working directory (WRKSRC) and building it.

6. The stage target is run. This puts the final set of built files into a temporary directory (STAGEDIR , see Section 6.1, "Staging"). The hierarchy of this directory mirrors that of the system on which the package will be installed.

7. The package target is run. This creates a package using the files from the temporary directory created during the stage target and the port's pkg-plist .

8. The install target is run. This installs the package created during the package target into the host system.

The above are the default actions. In addition, define targets pre-*something* or post-*something*, or put scripts with those names, in the scripts subdirectory, and they will be run before or after the default actions are done.

For example, if there is a post-extract target defined in the Makefile, and a file pre-build in the scripts subdirectory, the post-extract target will be called after the regular extraction actions, and pre-build will be executed before the default build rules are done. It is recommended to use Makefile targets if the actions are simple enough, because it will be easier for someone to figure out what kind of non-default action the port requires.

The default actions are done by the do-*something* targets from bsd.port.mk. For example, the commands to extract a port are in the target do-extract. If the default target does not do the job right, redefine the do-*something* target in the Makefile.

> **Note**
>
> The "main" targets (for example, `extract`, `configure`, etc.) do nothing more than make sure all the stages up to that one are completed and call the real targets or scripts, and they are not intended to be changed. To fix the extraction, fix `do-extract`, but never ever change the way `extract` operates! Additionally, the target `post-deinstall` is invalid and is not run by the ports infrastructure.

Now that what goes on when the user types `make install` is better understood, let us go through the recommended steps to create the perfect port.

4.2. Getting the Original Sources

Get the original sources (normally) as a compressed tarball (`foo.tar.gz` or *foo*`.tar.bz2`) and copy it into `DISTDIR`. Always use *mainstream* sources when and where possible.

Set the variable `MASTER_SITES` to reflect where the original tarball resides. Shorthand definitions exist for most mainstream sites in `bsd.sites.mk`. Please use these sites—and the associated definitions—if at all possible, to help avoid the problem of having the same information repeated over again many times in the source base. As these sites tend to change over time, this becomes a maintenance nightmare for everyone involved. See Section 5.4.2, "`MASTER_SITES`" for details.

If there is no FTP/HTTP site that is well-connected to the net, or can only find sites that have irritatingly non-standard formats, put a copy on a reliable FTP or HTTP server (for example, a home page).

If a convenient and reliable place to put the distfile cannot be found, we can "house" it ourselves on `ftp.Free-BSD.org`; however, this is the least-preferred solution. The distfile must be placed into `~/public_distfiles/` of someone's `freefall` account. Ask the person who commits the port to do this. This person will also set `MASTER_SITES` to `LOCAL/`*username* where *username* is their FreeBSD cluster login.

If the port's distfile changes all the time without any kind of version update by the author, consider putting the distfile on a home page and listing it as the first `MASTER_SITES`. Try to talk the port author out of doing this; it really does help to establish some kind of source code control. Hosting a specific version will prevent users from getting checksum mismatch errors, and also reduce the workload of maintainers of our FTP site. Also, if there is only one master site for the port, it is recommended to house a backup on a home page and list it as the second `MASTER_SITES`.

If the port requires additional patches that are available on the Internet, fetch them too and put them in `DISTDIR`. Do not worry if they come from a site other than where the main source tarball comes, we have a way to handle these situations (see the description of PATCHFILES below).

4.3. Modifying the Port

Unpack a copy of the tarball in a private directory and make whatever changes are necessary to get the port to compile properly under the current version of FreeBSD. Keep *careful track* of steps, as they will be needed to automate the process shortly. Everything, including the deletion, addition, or modification of files has to be doable using an automated script or patch file when the port is finished.

If the port requires significant user interaction/customization to compile or install, take a look at one of Larry Wall's classic Configure scripts and perhaps do something similar. The goal of the new ports collection is to make each port as "plug-and-play" as possible for the end-user while using a minimum of disk space.

> **Note**
>
> Unless explicitly stated, patch files, scripts, and other files created and contributed to the FreeBSD ports collection are assumed to be covered by the standard BSD copyright conditions.

4.4. Patching

In the preparation of the port, files that have been added or changed can be recorded with diff(1) for later feeding to patch(1). Doing this with a typical file involves saving a copy of the original file before making any changes using a `.orig` suffix.

```
% cp file file.orig
```

After all changes have been made, cd back to the port directory. Use `make makepatch` to generate updated patch files in the `files` directory.

4.4.1. General Rules for Patching

Patch files are stored in `PATCHDIR`, usually `files/`, from where they will be automatically applied. All patches must be relative to `WRKSRC`. Typically `WRKSRC` is a subdirectory of `WRKDIR`, the directory where the distfile is extracted. Use `make -V WRKSRC` to see the actual path. The patch names are to follow these rules:

- Avoid having more than one patch modify the same file. For example, having both `patch-foobar.c` and `patch-foobar.c2` making changes to `${WRKSRC}/foobar.c` makes them fragile and difficult to debug.

- When creating names for patch files, replace each underscore (_) with two underscores (__) and each slash (/) with one underscore (_). For example, to patch a file named `src/freeglut_joystick.c`, name the corresponding patch `patch-src_freeglut__joystick.c`. Do not name patches like `patch-aa` or `patch-ab`. Always use the path and file name in patch names. Using `make makepatch` automatically generates the correct names.

- A patch may modify multiple files if the changes are related and the patch is named appropriately. For example, `patch-add-missing-stdlib.h` .

- Only use characters `[-+._a-zA-Z0-9]` for naming patches. In particular, *do not use :: as a path separator,* use _ instead.

Minimize the amount of non-functional whitespace changes in patches. It is common in the Open Source world for projects to share large amounts of a code base, but obey different style and indenting rules. When taking a working piece of functionality from one project to fix similar areas in another, please be careful: the resulting patch may be full of non-functional changes. It not only increases the size of the ports repository but makes it hard to find out what exactly caused the problem and what was changed at all.

If a file must be deleted, do it in the `post-extract` target rather than as part of the patch.

4.4.2. Manual Patch Generation

> Note
>
> Manual patch creation is usually not necessary. Automatic patch generation as described earlier in this section is the preferred method. However, manual patching may be required occasionally.

Patches are saved into files named patch-* where * indicates the pathname of the file that is patched, such as patch-Imakefile or patch-src-config.h .

After the file has been modified, diff(1) is used to record the differences between the original and the modified version. -u causes diff(1) to produce "unified" diffs, the preferred form.

```
% diff -u file.orig file > patch-pathname-file
```

When generating patches for new, added files, -N is used to tell diff(1) to treat the non-existent original file as if it existed but was empty:

```
% diff -u -N newfile.orig newfile > patch-pathname-newfile
```

Do not add $FreeBSD$ RCS strings in patches. When patches are added to the Subversion repository with svn add, the fbsd:nokeywords property is set to yes automatically so keywords in the patch are not modified when committed. The property can be added manually with svn propset fbsd:nokeywords yes files....

Using the recurse (-r) option to diff(1) to generate patches is fine, but please look at the resulting patches to make sure there is no unnecessary junk in there. In particular, diffs between two backup files, Makefiles when the port uses Imake or GNU configure, etc., are unnecessary and have to be deleted. If it was necessary to edit configure.in and run autoconf to regenerate configure, do not take the diffs of configure (it often grows to a few thousand lines!). Instead, define USE_AUTOTOOLS=autoconf:261 and take the diffs of configure.in.

4.4.3. Simple Automatic Replacements

Simple replacements can be performed directly from the port Makefile using the in-place mode of sed(1). This is useful when changes use the value of a variable:

```
post-patch:
 @${REINPLACE_CMD} -e 's|for Linux|for FreeBSD|g' ${WRKSRC}/README
```

Quite often, software being ported uses the CR/LF convention in source files. This may cause problems with further patching, compiler warnings, or script execution (like /bin/sh^M not found .) To quickly convert all files from CR/LF to just LF, add this entry to the port Makefile:

```
USES= dos2unix
```

A list of specific files to convert can be given:

```
USES= dos2unix
DOS2UNIX_FILES= util.c util.h
```

Use DOS2UNIX_REGEX to convert a group of files across subdirectories. Its argument is a find(1)-compatible regular expression. More on the format is in re_format(7). This option is useful for converting all files of a given extension. For example, convert all source code files, leaving binary files intact:

```
USES= dos2unix
DOS2UNIX_REGEX= .*\.([ch]|cpp)
```

A similar option is DOS2UNIX_GLOB , which runs find for each element listed in it.

```
USES= dos2unix
DOS2UNIX_GLOB= *.c *.cpp *.h
```

The base directory for the conversion can be set. This is useful when there are multiple distfiles and several contain files which require line-ending conversion.

```
USES= dos2unix
DOS2UNIX_WRKSRC= ${WRKDIR}
```

4.4.4. Patching Conditionally

Some ports need patches that are only applied for specific FreeBSD versions or when a particular option is enabled or disabled. Conditional patches are specified by placing the full paths to the patch files in EXTRA_PATCHES.

Example 4.1. Applying a Patch for a Specific FreeBSD Version

```
.include <bsd.port.options.mk>

# Patch in the iconv const qualifier before this
.if ${OPSYS} == FreeBSD && ${OSVERSION} < 1100069
EXTRA_PATCHES= ${PATCHDIR}/extra-patch-fbsd10
.endif

.include <bsd.port.mk>
```

Example 4.2. Optionaly Applying a Patch

When an option requires a patch, use *opt*_EXTRA_PATCHES and *opt*_EXTRA_PATCHES_OFF to make the patch conditional on the *opt* option. See Section 5.13.3.11, "Generic Variables Replacement, *OPT_VARIABLE* and *OPT_VARIABLE_OFF*" for more information.

```
OPTIONS_DEFINE=    FOO BAR
FOO_EXTRA_PATCHES=  ${PATCHDIR}/extra-patch-foo
BAR_EXTRA_PATCHES_OFF= ${PATCHDIR}/extra-patch-bar.c \
   ${PATCHDIR}/extra-patch-bar.h
```

Example 4.3. Using EXTRA_PATCHES With a Directory

Sometime, there are many patches that are needed for a feature, in this case, it is possible to point EXTRA_PATCHES to a directory, and it will automatically apply all files named patch-* in it.

Create a subdirectory in ${PATCHDIR} , and move the patches in it. For example:

```
% ls -l files/foo-patches
-rw-r--r--  1 root  wheel    350 Jan 16 01:27 patch-Makefile.in
-rw-r--r--  1 root  wheel   3084 Jan 18 15:37 patch-configure
```

Then add this to the Makefile:

```
OPTIONS_DEFINE= FOO
FOO_EXTRA_PATCHES= ${PATCHDIR}/foo-patches
```

The framework will then use all the files named patch-* in that directory.

4.5. Configuring

Include any additional customization commands in the configure script and save it in the scripts subdirectory. As mentioned above, it is also possible do this with Makefile targets and/or scripts with the name pre-configure or post-configure.

4.6. Handling User Input

If the port requires user input to build, configure, or install, set IS_INTERACTIVE in the Makefile. This will allow "overnight builds" to skip it. If the user sets the variable BATCH in their environment (and if the user sets the variable INTERACTIVE, then *only* those ports requiring interaction are built). This will save a lot of wasted time on the set of machines that continually build ports (see below).

It is also recommended that if there are reasonable default answers to the questions, PACKAGE_BUILDING be used to turn off the interactive script when it is set. This will allow us to build the packages for CDROMs and FTP.

Chapter 5. Configuring the Makefile

Configuring the Makefile is pretty simple, and again we suggest looking at existing examples before starting. Also, there is a sample Makefile in this handbook, so take a look and please follow the ordering of variables and sections in that template to make the port easier for others to read.

Consider these problems in sequence during the design of the new Makefile:

5.1. The Original Source

Does it live in DISTDIR as a standard gzipped tarball named something like foozolix-1.2.tar.gz ? If so, go on to the next step. If not, the distribution file format might require overriding one or more of DISTVERSION , DISTNAME, EXTRACT_CMD, EXTRACT_BEFORE_ARGS, EXTRACT_AFTER_ARGS, EXTRACT_SUFX, or DISTFILES.

In the worst case, create a custom do-extract target to override the default. This is rarely, if ever, necessary.

5.2. Naming

The first part of the port's Makefile names the port, describes its version number, and lists it in the correct category.

5.2.1. PORTNAME

Set PORTNAME to the base name of the software. It is used as the base for the FreeBSD package, and for DISTNAME.

> **Important**
>
> The package name must be unique across the entire ports tree. Make sure that the PORTNAME is not already in use by an existing port, and that no other port already has the same PKGBASE. If the name has already been used, add either PKGNAMEPREFIX or PKGNAMESUFFIX.

5.2.2. Versions, DISTVERSION or PORTVERSION

Set DISTVERSION to the version number of the software.

PORTVERSION is the version used for the FreeBSD package. It will be automatically derived from DISTVERSION to be compatible with FreeBSD's package versioning scheme. If the version contains *letters*, it might be needed to set PORTVERSION and not DISTVERSION .

> **Important**
>
> Only one of PORTVERSION and DISTVERSION can be set at a time.

From time to time, some software will use a version scheme that is not compatible with how DISTVERSION translates in PORTVERSION .

Tip

When updating a port, it is possible to use pkg-version(8)'s **-t** argument to check if the new version is greater or lesser than before. See Example 5.1, "Using pkg-version(8) to Compare Versions.".

Example 5.1. Using pkg-version(8) to Compare Versions.

pkg version -t takes two versions as arguments, it will respond with <, = or > if the first version is less, equal, or more than the second version, respectively.

```
% pkg version -t 1.2 1.3
< ❶
% pkg version -t 1.2 1.2
= ❷
% pkg version -t 1.2 1.2.0
= ❸
% pkg version -t 1.2 1.2.p1
> ❹
% pkg version -t 1.2.a1 1.2.b1
< ❺
% pkg version -t 1.2 1.2p1
< ❻
```

❶   1.2 is before 1.3.
❷   1.2 and 1.2 are equal as they have the same version.
❸   1.2 and 1.2.0 are equal as nothing equals zero.
❹   1.2 is after 1.2.p1 as .p1, think "pre-release 1".
❺   1.2.a1 is before 1.2.b1, think "alpha" and "beta", and a is before b.
❻   1.2 is before 1.2p1 as 2p1, think "2, patch level 1" which is a version after any 2.X but before 3.

Note

In here, the a, b, and p are used as if meaning "alpha", "beta" or "pre-release" and "patch level", but they are only letters and are sorted alphabetically, so any letter can be used, and they will be sorted appropriately.

Table 5.1. Examples of DISTVERSION and the Derived PORTVERSION

DISTVERSION	PORTVERSION
0.7.1d	0.7.1.d
10Alpha3	10.a3
3Beta7-pre2	3.b7.p2
8:f_17	8f.17

Example 5.2. Using DISTVERSION

When the version only contains numbers separated by dots, dashes or underscores, use DISTVERSION .

```
PORTNAME=   nekoto
DISTVERSION= 1.2-4
```

It will generate a PORTVERSION of 1.2.4.

Example 5.3. Using DISTVERSION When the Version Starts with a Letter or a Prefix

When the version starts or ends with a letter, or a prefix or a suffix that is not part of the version, use DISTVERSIONPREFIX, DISTVERSION , and DISTVERSIONSUFFIX.

If the version is v1.2-4:

```
PORTNAME=         nekoto
DISTVERSIONPREFIX=  v
DISTVERSION= 1_2_4
```

Some of the time, projects using GitHub will use their name in their versions. For example, the version could be nekoto-1.2-4:

```
PORTNAME=         nekoto
DISTVERSIONPREFIX=  nekoto-
DISTVERSION= 1.2_4
```

Those projects also sometimes use some string at the end of the version, for example, 1.2-4_RELEASE:

```
PORTNAME=         nekoto
DISTVERSION= 1.2-4
DISTVERSIONSUFFIX=  _RELEASE
```

Or they do both, for example, nekoto-1.2-4_RELEASE:

```
PORTNAME=         nekoto
DISTVERSIONPREFIX=  nekoto-
DISTVERSION= 1.2-4
DISTVERSIONSUFFIX=  _RELEASE
```

DISTVERSIONPREFIX and DISTVERSIONSUFFIX will not be used while constructing PORTVERSION , but only used in DISTNAME.

All will generate a PORTVERSION of 1.2.4.

Example 5.4. Using DISTVERSION When the Version Contains Letters Meaning "alpha", "beta", or "pre-release"

When the version contains numbers separated by dots, dashes or underscores, and letters are used to mean "alpha", "beta" or "pre-release", which is, before the version without the letters, use DISTVERSION .

```
PORTNAME=   nekoto
DISTVERSION= 1.2-pre4
```

```
PORTNAME=   nekoto
DISTVERSION= 1.2p4
```

Both will generate a PORTVERSION of 1.2.p4 which is before than 1.2. pkg-version(8) can be used to check that fact:

```
% pkg version -t 1.2.p4 1.2
<
```

Example 5.5. Not Using DISTVERSION When the Version Contains Letters Meaning "Patch Level"

When the version contains letters that are not meant as "alpha", "beta", or "pre", but more in a "patch level", and meaning after the version without the letters, use PORTVERSION .

```
PORTNAME=   nekoto
PORTVERSION= 1.2p4
```

In this case, using DISTVERSION is not possible because it would generate a version of 1.2.p4 which would be before 1.2 and not after. pkg-version(8) will verify this:

```
% pkg version -t 1.2 1.2.p4
> ❶
% pkg version -t 1.2 1.2p4
< ❷
```

❶   1.2 is after 1.2.p4, which is *wrong* in this case.
❷   1.2 is before 1.2p4, which is what was needed.

For some more advanced examples of setting PORTVERSION , when the software's versioning is really not compatible with FreeBSD's, or DISTNAME when the distribution file does not contain the version itself, see Section 5.4.1, "DISTNAME".

5.2.3. PORTREVISION and PORTEPOCH

5.2.3.1. PORTREVISION

PORTREVISION is a monotonically increasing value which is reset to 0 with every increase of DISTVERSION , typically every time there is a new official vendor release. If PORTREVISION is non-zero, the value is appended to the package name. Changes to PORTREVISION are used by automated tools like pkg-version(8) to determine that a new package is available.

PORTREVISION must be increased each time a change is made to the port that changes the generated package in any way. That includes changes that only affect a package built with non-default options.

Examples of when PORTREVISION must be bumped:

- Addition of patches to correct security vulnerabilities, bugs, or to add new functionality to the port.

- Changes to the port Makefile to enable or disable compile-time options in the package.

- Changes in the packing list or the install-time behavior of the package. For example, a change to a script which generates initial data for the package, like ssh(1) host keys.

- Version bump of a port's shared library dependency (in this case, someone trying to install the old package after installing a newer version of the dependency will fail since it will look for the old libfoo.x instead of libfoo.(x+1)).

- Silent changes to the port distfile which have significant functional differences. For example, changes to the distfile requiring a correction to `distinfo` with no corresponding change to `DISTVERSION`, where a `diff -ru` of the old and new versions shows non-trivial changes to the code.

Examples of changes which do not require a `PORTREVISION` bump:

- Style changes to the port skeleton with no functional change to what appears in the resulting package.

- Changes to `MASTER_SITES` or other functional changes to the port which do not affect the resulting package.

- Trivial patches to the distfile such as correction of typos, which are not important enough that users of the package have to go to the trouble of upgrading.

- Build fixes which cause a package to become compilable where it was previously failing. As long as the changes do not introduce any functional change on any other platforms on which the port did previously build. Since `PORTREVISION` reflects the content of the package, if the package was not previously buildable then there is no need to increase `PORTREVISION` to mark a change.

A rule of thumb is to decide whether a change committed to a port is something which *some* people would benefit from having. Either because of an enhancement, fix, or by virtue that the new package will actually work at all. Then weigh that against that fact that it will cause everyone who regularly updates their ports tree to be compelled to update. If yes, `PORTREVISION` must be bumped.

Note

People using binary packages will *never* see the update if `PORTREVISION` is not bumped. Without increasing `PORTREVISION`, the package builders have no way to detect the change and thus, will not rebuild the package.

5.2.3.2. PORTEPOCH

From time to time a software vendor or FreeBSD porter will do something silly and release a version of their software which is actually numerically less than the previous version. An example of this is a port which goes from foo-20000801 to foo-1.0 (the former will be incorrectly treated as a newer version since 20000801 is a numerically greater value than 1).

Tip

The results of version number comparisons are not always obvious. `pkg version` (see pkg-version(8)) can be used to test the comparison of two version number strings. For example:

```
% pkg version -t 0.031 0.29
>
```

The > output indicates that version 0.031 is considered greater than version 0.29, which may not have been obvious to the porter.

In situations such as this, `PORTEPOCH` must be increased. If `PORTEPOCH` is nonzero it is appended to the package name as described in section 0 above. `PORTEPOCH` must never be decreased or reset to zero, because that would cause comparison to a package from an earlier epoch to fail. For example, the package would not be detected as out of date. The new version number, 1.0.1 in the above example, is still numerically less than the previous version, 20000801, but the ,1 suffix is treated specially by automated tools and found to be greater than the implied suffix ,0 on the earlier package.

Dropping or resetting PORTEPOCH incorrectly leads to no end of grief. If the discussion above was not clear enough, please consult the FreeBSD ports mailing list.

It is expected that PORTEPOCH will not be used for the majority of ports, and that sensible use of DISTVERSION , or that use PORTVERSION carefully, can often preempt it becoming necessary if a future release of the software changes the version structure. However, care is needed by FreeBSD porters when a vendor release is made without an official version number — such as a code "snapshot" release. The temptation is to label the release with the release date, which will cause problems as in the example above when a new "official" release is made.

For example, if a snapshot release is made on the date 20000917 , and the previous version of the software was version 1.2, do not use 20000917 for DISTVERSION . The correct way is a DISTVERSION of 1.2.20000917 , or similar, so that the succeeding release, say 1.3, is still a numerically greater value.

5.2.3.3. Example of PORTREVISION and PORTEPOCH Usage

The gtkmumble port, version 0.10, is committed to the ports collection:

```
PORTNAME= gtkmumble
DISTVERSION= 0.10
```

PKGNAME becomes gtkmumble-0.10.

A security hole is discovered which requires a local FreeBSD patch. PORTREVISION is bumped accordingly.

```
PORTNAME= gtkmumble
DISTVERSION= 0.10
PORTREVISION= 1
```

PKGNAME becomes gtkmumble-0.10_1

A new version is released by the vendor, numbered 0.2 (it turns out the author actually intended 0.10 to actually mean 0.1.0, not "what comes after 0.9" - oops, too late now). Since the new minor version 2 is numerically less than the previous version 10, PORTEPOCH must be bumped to manually force the new package to be detected as "newer". Since it is a new vendor release of the code, PORTREVISION is reset to 0 (or removed from the Makefile).

```
PORTNAME= gtkmumble
DISTVERSION= 0.2
PORTEPOCH= 1
```

PKGNAME becomes gtkmumble-0.2,1

The next release is 0.3. Since PORTEPOCH never decreases, the version variables are now:

```
PORTNAME= gtkmumble
DISTVERSION= 0.3
PORTEPOCH= 1
```

PKGNAME becomes gtkmumble-0.3,1

 Note

If PORTEPOCH were reset to 0 with this upgrade, someone who had installed the gtkmumble-0.10_1 package would not detect the gtkmumble-0.3 package as newer, since 3 is still numerically less than 10. Remember, this is the whole point of PORTEPOCH in the first place.

5.2.4. PKGNAMEPREFIX and PKGNAMESUFFIX

Two optional variables, PKGNAMEPREFIX and PKGNAMESUFFIX, are combined with PORTNAME and PORTVERSION to form PKGNAME as ${PKGNAMEPREFIX}${PORTNAME}${PKGNAMESUFFIX}-${PORTVERSION} . Make sure this conforms to our guidelines for a good package name. In particular, the use of a hyphen (-) in PORTVERSION is *not* allowed. Also, if the package name has the *language-* or the *-compiled.specifics* part (see below), use PKGNAMEPREFIX and PKGNAMESUFFIX, respectively. Do not make them part of PORTNAME.

5.2.5. Package Naming Conventions

These are the conventions to follow when naming packages. This is to make the package directory easy to scan, as there are already thousands of packages and users are going to turn away if they hurt their eyes!

Package names take the form of *language_region-name-compiled.specifics-version.numbers* .

The package name is defined as ${PKGNAMEPREFIX}${PORTNAME}${PKGNAMESUFFIX}-${PORTVERSION} . Make sure to set the variables to conform to that format.

language_region-
> FreeBSD strives to support the native language of its users. The *language-* part is a two letter abbreviation of the natural language defined by ISO-639 when the port is specific to a certain language. Examples are ja for Japanese, ru for Russian, vi for Vietnamese, zh for Chinese, ko for Korean and de for German.
>
> If the port is specific to a certain region within the language area, add the two letter country code as well. Examples are en_US for US English and fr_CH for Swiss French.
>
> The *language-* part is set in PKGNAMEPREFIX.

name
> Make sure that the port's name and version are clearly separated and placed into PORTNAME and DISTVERSION . The only reason for PORTNAME to contain a version part is if the upstream distribution is really named that way, as in the textproc/libxml2 or japanese/kinput2-freewnn ports. Otherwise, PORTNAME cannot contain any version-specific information. It is quite normal for several ports to have the same PORTNAME, as the www/apache* ports do; in that case, different versions (and different index entries) are distinguished by PKGNAMEPREFIX and PKGNAMESUFFIX values.
>
> There is a tradition of naming Perl 5 modules by prepending p5- and converting the double-colon separator to a hyphen. For example, the Data::Dumper module becomes p5-Data-Dumper .

-compiled.specifics
> If the port can be built with different hardcoded defaults (usually part of the directory name in a family of ports), the *-compiled.specifics* part states the compiled-in defaults. The hyphen is optional. Examples are paper size and font units.
>
> The *-compiled.specifics* part is set in PKGNAMESUFFIX.

-version.numbers
> The version string follows a dash (-) and is a period-separated list of integers and single lowercase alphabetics. In particular, it is not permissible to have another dash inside the version string. The only exception is the string pl (meaning "patchlevel"), which can be used *only* when there are no major and minor version numbers in the software. If the software version has strings like "alpha", "beta", "rc", or "pre", take the first letter and put it immediately after a period. If the version string continues after those names, the numbers follow the single alphabet without an extra period between them (for example, 1.0b2).
>
> The idea is to make it easier to sort ports by looking at the version string. In particular, make sure version number components are always delimited by a period, and if the date is part of the string, use the 0.0.*yyyy*.*mm*.*dd* format, not *dd*.*mm*.*yyyy* or the non-Y2K compliant *yy*.*mm*.*dd* format. It is important to prefix the version with 0.0. in case a release with an actual version number is made, which would be numerically less than *yyyy*.

Important

Package name must be unique among all of the ports tree, check that there is not already a port with the same `PORTNAME` and if there is add one of `PKGNAMEPREFIX` or `PKGNAMESUFFIX`.

Here are some (real) examples on how to convert the name as called by the software authors to a suitable package name, for each line, only one of `DISTVERSION` or `PORTVERSION` is set in, depending on which would be used in the port's `Makefile`:

Table 5.2. Package Naming Examples

Distribution Name	PKGNAMEPRE-FIX	PORTNAME	PKGNAMESUF-FIX	DISTVERSION	PORTVERSION	Reason or comment
mule-2.2.2	(empty)	mule	(empty)	2.2.2		No changes required
mule-1.0.1	(empty)	mule	1	1.0.1		This is version 1 of mule, and version 2 already exists
EmiClock-1.0.2	(empty)	emiclock	(empty)	1.0.2		No uppercase names for single programs
rdist-1.3alpha	(empty)	rdist	(empty)	1.3alpha		Version will be `1.3.a`
es-0.9-beta1	(empty)	es	(empty)	0.9-beta1		Version will be `0.9.b1`
mail-man-2.0rc3	(empty)	mailman	(empty)	2.0rc3		Version will be `2.0.r3`
v3.3beta021.s-rc	(empty)	tiff	(empty)		3.3	What the heck was that anyway?
tvtwm	(empty)	tvtwm	(empty)		p11	No version in the filename, use what upstream says it is
piewm	(empty)	piewm	(empty)	1.0		No version in the filename, use what upstream says it is
xvgr-2.10pl1	(empty)	xvgr	(empty)		2.10.pl1	In that case, `pl1` means patch level, so using DISTVERSION is not possible.

Distribution Name	PKGNAMEPRE-FIX	PORTNAME	PKGNAMESUF-FIX	DISTVERSION	PORTVERSION	Reason or comment
gawk-2.15.6	ja-	gawk	(empty)	2.15.6		Japanese language version
psutils-1.13	(empty)	psutils	-letter	1.13		Paper size hardcoded at package build time
pkfonts	(empty)	pkfonts	300	1.0		Package for 300dpi fonts

If there is absolutely no trace of version information in the original source and it is unlikely that the original author will ever release another version, just set the version string to 1.0 (like the piewm example above). Otherwise, ask the original author or use the date string the source file was released on (0.0.*yyyy*.*mm*.*dd*) as the version.

5.3. Categorization

5.3.1. CATEGORIES

When a package is created, it is put under /usr/ports/packages/All and links are made from one or more subdirectories of /usr/ports/packages . The names of these subdirectories are specified by the variable CATEGORIES. It is intended to make life easier for the user when he is wading through the pile of packages on the FTP site or the CDROM. Please take a look at the current list of categories and pick the ones that are suitable for the port.

This list also determines where in the ports tree the port is imported. If there is more than one category here, the port files must be put in the subdirectory with the name of the first category. See below for more discussion about how to pick the right categories.

5.3.2. Current List of Categories

Here is the current list of port categories. Those marked with an asterisk (*) are *virtual* categories—those that do not have a corresponding subdirectory in the ports tree. They are only used as secondary categories, and only for search purposes.

> **Note**
>
> For non-virtual categories, there is a one-line description in COMMENT in that subdirectory's Makefile.

Category	Description	Notes
accessibility	Ports to help disabled users.	
afterstep *	Ports to support the AfterStep window manager.	
arabic	Arabic language support.	
archivers	Archiving tools.	
astro	Astronomical ports.	
audio	Sound support.	
benchmarks	Benchmarking utilities.	
biology	Biology-related software.	

Category	Description	Notes
cad	Computer aided design tools.	
chinese	Chinese language support.	
comms	Communication software.	Mostly software to talk to the serial port.
converters	Character code converters.	
databases	Databases.	
deskutils	Things that used to be on the desktop before computers were invented.	
devel	Development utilities.	Do not put libraries here just because they are libraries. They should *not* be in this category unless they truly do not belong anywhere else.
dns	DNS-related software.	
docs *	Meta-ports for FreeBSD documentation.	
editors	General editors.	Specialized editors go in the section for those tools. For example, a mathematical-formula editor will go in math, and have editors as a second category.
elisp *	Emacs-lisp ports.	
emulators	Emulators for other operating systems.	Terminal emulators do *not* belong here. X-based ones go to x11 and text-based ones to either comms or misc, depending on the exact functionality.
finance	Monetary, financial and related applications.	
french	French language support.	
ftp	FTP client and server utilities.	If the port speaks both FTP and HTTP, put it in ftp with a secondary category of www.
games	Games.	
geography *	Geography-related software.	
german	German language support.	
gnome *	Ports from the GNOME Project.	
gnustep *	Software related to the GNUstep desktop environment.	
graphics	Graphics utilities.	
hamradio *	Software for amateur radio.	
haskell *	Software related to the Haskell language.	
hebrew	Hebrew language support.	
hungarian	Hungarian language support.	

Category	Description	Notes
ipv6 *	IPv6 related software.	
irc	Internet Relay Chat utilities.	
japanese	Japanese language support.	
java	Software related to the Java™ language.	The java category must not be the only one for a port. Save for ports directly related to the Java language, porters are also encouraged not to use java as the main category of a port.
kde *	Ports from the KDE Project.	
kld *	Kernel loadable modules.	
korean	Korean language support.	
lang	Programming languages.	
linux *	Linux applications and support utilities.	
lisp *	Software related to the Lisp language.	
mail	Mail software.	
math	Numerical computation software and other utilities for mathematics.	
mbone *	MBone applications.	
misc	Miscellaneous utilities	Things that do not belong anywhere else. If at all possible, try to find a better category for the port than misc, as ports tend to be overlooked in here.
multimedia	Multimedia software.	
net	Miscellaneous networking software.	
net-im	Instant messaging software.	
net-mgmt	Networking management software.	
net-p2p	Peer to peer network applications.	
news	USENET news software.	
palm	Software support for the Palm™ series.	
parallel *	Applications dealing with parallelism in computing.	
pear *	Ports related to the Pear PHP framework.	
perl5 *	Ports that require Perl version 5 to run.	
plan9 *	Various programs from Plan9.	
polish	Polish language support.	

Category	Description	Notes
ports-mgmt	Ports for managing, installing and developing FreeBSD ports and packages.	
portuguese	Portuguese language support.	
print	Printing software.	Desktop publishing tools (previewers, etc.) belong here too.
python *	Software related to the Python language.	
ruby *	Software related to the Ruby language.	
rubygems *	Ports of RubyGems packages.	
russian	Russian language support.	
scheme *	Software related to the Scheme language.	
science	Scientific ports that do not fit into other categories such as astro, biology and math.	
security	Security utilities.	
shells	Command line shells.	
spanish *	Spanish language support.	
sysutils	System utilities.	
tcl *	Ports that use Tcl to run.	
textproc	Text processing utilities.	It does not include desktop publishing tools, which go to print.
tk *	Ports that use Tk to run.	
ukrainian	Ukrainian language support.	
vietnamese	Vietnamese language support.	
windowmaker *	Ports to support the WindowMaker window manager.	
www	Software related to the World Wide Web.	HTML language support belongs here too.
x11	The X Window System and friends.	This category is only for software that directly supports the window system. Do not put regular X applications here. Most of them go into other x11-* categories (see below).
x11-clocks	X11 clocks.	
x11-drivers	X11 drivers.	
x11-fm	X11 file managers.	
x11-fonts	X11 fonts and font utilities.	
x11-servers	X11 servers.	
x11-themes	X11 themes.	
x11-toolkits	X11 toolkits.	

Category	Description	Notes
x11-wm	X11 window managers.	
xfce *	Ports related to the Xfce desktop environment.	
zope *	Zope support.	

5.3.3. Choosing the Right Category

As many of the categories overlap, choosing which of the categories will be the primary category of the port can be tedious. There are several rules that govern this issue. Here is the list of priorities, in decreasing order of precedence:

- The first category must be a physical category (see above). This is necessary to make the packaging work. Virtual categories and physical categories may be intermixed after that.

- Language specific categories always come first. For example, if the port installs Japanese X11 fonts, then the CATEGORIES line would read japanese x11-fonts .

- Specific categories are listed before less-specific ones. For instance, an HTML editor is listed as www editors, not the other way around. Also, do not list net when the port belongs to any of irc, mail, news, security, or www, as net is included implicitly.

- x11 is used as a secondary category only when the primary category is a natural language. In particular, do not put x11 in the category line for X applications.

- Emacs modes are placed in the same ports category as the application supported by the mode, not in editors. For example, an Emacs mode to edit source files of some programming language goes into lang.

- Ports installing loadable kernel modules also have the virtual category kld in their CATEGORIES line. This is one of the things handled automatically by adding USES=kmod.

- misc does not appear with any other non-virtual category. If there is misc with something else in CATEGORIES, that means misc can safely be deleted and the port placed only in the other subdirectory.

- If the port truly does not belong anywhere else, put it in misc.

If the category is not clearly defined, please put a comment to that effect in the port submission in the bug database so we can discuss it before we import it. As a committer, send a note to the FreeBSD ports mailing list so we can discuss it first. Too often, new ports are imported to the wrong category only to be moved right away.

5.3.4. Proposing a New Category

As the Ports Collection has grown over time, various new categories have been introduced. New categories can either be *virtual* categories—those that do not have a corresponding subdirectory in the ports tree— or *physical* categories—those that do. This section discusses the issues involved in creating a new physical category. Read it thouroughly before proposing a new one.

Our existing practice has been to avoid creating a new physical category unless either a large number of ports would logically belong to it, or the ports that would belong to it are a logically distinct group that is of limited general interest (for instance, categories related to spoken human languages), or preferably both.

The rationale for this is that such a change creates a fair amount of work for both the committers and also for all users who track changes to the Ports Collection. In addition, proposed category changes just naturally seem to attract controversy. (Perhaps this is because there is no clear consensus on when a category is "too big", nor whether categories should lend themselves to browsing (and thus what number of categories would be an ideal number), and so forth.)

Here is the procedure:

1. Propose the new category on FreeBSD ports mailing list. Include a detailed rationale for the new category, including why the existing categories are not sufficient, and the list of existing ports proposed to move. (If there are new ports pending in Bugzilla that would fit this category, list them too.) If you are the maintainer and/or submitter, respectively, mention that as it may help the case.

2. Participate in the discussion.

3. If it seems that there is support for the idea, file a PR which includes both the rationale and the list of existing ports that need to be moved. Ideally, this PR would also include these patches:

   - Makefiles for the new ports once they are repocopied

   - Makefile for the new category

   - Makefile for the old ports' categories

   - Makefiles for ports that depend on the old ports

   - (for extra credit, include the other files that have to change, as per the procedure in the Committer's Guide.)

4. Since it affects the ports infrastructure and involves moving and patching many ports but also possibly running regression tests on the build cluster, assign the PR to the Ports Management Team <portmgr@FreeBSD.org>.

5. If that PR is approved, a committer will need to follow the rest of the procedure that is outlined in the Committer's Guide.

Proposing a new virtual category is similar to the above but much less involved, since no ports will actually have to move. In this case, the only patches to include in the PR would be those to add the new category to CATEGORIES of the affected ports.

5.3.5. Proposing Reorganizing All the Categories

Occasionally someone proposes reorganizing the categories with either a 2-level structure, or some other kind of keyword structure. To date, nothing has come of any of these proposals because, while they are very easy to make, the effort involved to retrofit the entire existing ports collection with any kind of reorganization is daunting to say the very least. Please read the history of these proposals in the mailing list archives before posting this idea. Furthermore, be prepared to be challenged to offer a working prototype.

5.4. The Distribution Files

The second part of the Makefile describes the files that must be downloaded to build the port, and where they can be downloaded.

5.4.1. DISTNAME

DISTNAME is the name of the port as called by the authors of the software. DISTNAME defaults to ${PORTNAME}-${DISTVERSIONPREFIX}${DISTVERSION}${DISTVERSIONSUFFIX}, and if not set, DISTVERSION defaults to ${PORTVERSION} so override DISTNAME only if necessary. DISTNAME is only used in two places. First, the distribution file list (DISTFILES) defaults to ${DISTNAME}${EXTRACT_SUFX}. Second, the distribution file is expected to extract into a subdirectory named WRKSRC, which defaults to work/${DISTNAME}.

Some vendor's distribution names which do not fit into the ${PORTNAME}-${PORTVERSION} -scheme can be handled automatically by setting DISTVERSIONPREFIX, DISTVERSION, and DISTVERSIONSUFFIX. PORTVERSION will be derived from DISTVERSION automatically.

Important

Only one of `PORTVERSION` and `DISTVERSION` can be set at a time. If `DISTVERSION` does not derive a correct `PORTVERSION`, do not use `DISTVERSION`.

If the upstream version scheme can be derived into a ports-compatible version scheme, set some variable to the upstream version, *do not* use `DISTVERSION` as the variable name. Set `PORTVERSION` to the computed version based on the variable you created, and set `DISTNAME` accordingly.

If the upstream version scheme cannot easily be coerced into a ports-compatible value, set `PORTVERSION` to a sensible value, and set `DISTNAME` with `PORTNAME` with the verbatim upstream version.

Example 5.6. Deriving PORTVERSION Manually

BIND9 uses a version scheme that is not compatible with the ports versions (it has - in its versions) and cannot be derived using `DISTVERSION` because after the 9.9.9 release, it will release a "patchlevels" in the form of `9.9.9-P1`. DISTVERSION would translate that into `9.9.9.p1`, which, in the ports versioning scheme means 9.9.9 pre-release 1, which is before 9.9.9 and not after. So `PORTVERSION` is manually derived from an `ISCVERSION` variable to output `9.9.9p1`.

The order into which the ports framework, and pkg, will sort versions is checked using the `-t` argument of pkg-version(8):

```
% pkg version -t 9.9.9 9.9.9.p1
> ❶
% pkg version -t 9.9.9 9.9.9p1
< ❷
```

❶ The > sign means that the first argument passed to `-t` is greater than the second argument. `9.9.9` is after `9.9.9.p1`.

❷ The < sign means that the first argument passed to `-t` is less than the second argument. `9.9.9` is before `9.9.9p1`.

In the port `Makefile`, for example dns/bind99, it is achieved by:

```
PORTNAME= bind
PORTVERSION= ${ISCVERSION:S/-P/P/:S/b/.b/:S/a/.a/:S/rc/.rc/} ❶
CATEGORIES= dns net ipv6
MASTER_SITES= ISC/bind9/${ISCVERSION} ❷
PKGNAMESUFFIX= 99
DISTNAME= ${PORTNAME}-${ISCVERSION} ❸

MAINTAINER= mat@FreeBSD.org
COMMENT= BIND DNS suite with updated DNSSEC and DNS64

LICENSE= ISCL

# ISC releases things like 9.8.0-P1 or 9.8.1rc1, which our versioning does not like
ISCVERSION= 9.9.9-P6 ❹
```

❹ Define upstream version in `ISCVERSION`, with a comment saying *why* it is needed.

❶ Use `ISCVERSION` to get a ports-compatible `PORTVERSION`.

❷ Use `ISCVERSION` directly to get the correct URL for fetching the distribution file.

❸   Use ISCVERSION directly to name the distribution file.

Example 5.7. Derive DISTNAME from PORTVERSION

From time to time, the distribution file name has little or no relation to the version of the software.

In comms/kermit, only the last element of the version is present in the distribution file:

```
PORTNAME= kermit
PORTVERSION= 9.0.304
CATEGORIES= comms ftp net
MASTER_SITES= ftp://ftp.kermitproject.org/kermit/test/tar/
DISTNAME= cku${PORTVERSION:E}-dev20 ❶
```

❶   The :E make(1) modifier returns the suffix of the variable, in this case, 304. The distribution file is
     correctly generated as cku304-dev20.tar.gz.

Example 5.8. Exotic Case 1

Sometimes, there is no relation between the software name, its version, and the distribution file it is distributed in.

From audio/libworkman:

```
PORTNAME=      libworkman
PORTVERSION=   1.4
CATEGORIES=    audio
MASTER_SITES=  LOCAL/jim
DISTNAME=      ${PORTNAME}-1999-06-20
```

Example 5.9. Exotic Case 2

In comms/librs232, the distribution file is not versioned, so using DIST_SUBDIR is needed:

```
PORTNAME=      librs232
PORTVERSION=   20160710
CATEGORIES=    comms
MASTER_SITES=  http://www.teuniz.net/RS-232/
DISTNAME=      RS-232
DIST_SUBDIR= ${PORTNAME}-${PORTVERSION}
```

Note

PKGNAMEPREFIX and PKGNAMESUFFIX do not affect DISTNAME. Also note that if WRKSRC is equal
to ${WRKDIR}/${DISTNAME} while the original source archive is named something other than

> ${PORTNAME}-${PORTVERSION}${EXTRACT_SUFX}, leave DISTNAME alone— defining only DIST-
> FILES is easier than both DISTNAME and WRKSRC (and possibly EXTRACT_SUFX).

5.4.2. MASTER_SITES

Record the directory part of the FTP/HTTP-URL pointing at the original tarball in MASTER_SITES . Do not forget the trailing slash (/)!

The make macros will try to use this specification for grabbing the distribution file with FETCH if they cannot find it already on the system.

It is recommended that multiple sites are included on this list, preferably from different continents. This will safeguard against wide-area network problems.

Important

MASTER_SITES must not be blank. It must point to the actual site hosting the distribution files. It cannot point to web archives, or the FreeBSD distribution files cache sites. The only exception to this rule is ports that do not have any distribution files. For example, meta-ports do not have any distribution files, so MASTER_SITES does not need to be set.

5.4.2.1. Using MASTER_SITE_ * Variables

Shortcut abbreviations are available for popular archives like SourceForge (SOURCEFORGE), GNU (GNU), or Perl CPAN (PERL_CPAN). MASTER_SITES can use them directly:

```
MASTER_SITES= GNU/make
```

The older expanded format still works, but all ports have been converted to the compact format. The expanded format looks like this:

```
MASTER_SITES=  ${MASTER_SITE_GNU}
MASTER_SITE_SUBDIR= make
```

These values and variables are defined in Mk/bsd.sites.mk. New entries are added often, so make sure to check the latest version of this file before submitting a port.

Tip

For any MASTER_SITE_ *FOO* variable, the shorthand *FOO* can be used. For example, use:

```
MASTER_SITES= FOO
```

If MASTER_SITE_SUBDIR is needed, use this:

```
MASTER_SITES= FOO/bar
```

Note

Some MASTER_SITE_ * names are quite long, and for ease of use, shortcuts have been defined:

Table 5.3. Shortcuts for **MASTER_SITE_** * Macros

Macro	Shortcut
PERL_CPAN	CPAN
GITHUB	GH
GITHUB_CLOUD	GHC
LIBREOFFICE_DEV	LODEV
NETLIB	NL
RUBYGEMS	RG
SOURCEFORGE	SF
SOURCEFORGE_JP	SFJP

5.4.2.2. Magic MASTER_SITES Macros

Several "magic" macros exist for popular sites with a predictable directory structure. For these, just use the abbreviation and the system will choose a subdirectory automatically. For a port named Stardict, of version 1.2.3, and hosted on SourceForge, adding this line:

```
MASTER_SITES= SF
```

infers a subdirectory named /project/stardict/stardict/1.2.3 . If the inferred directory is incorrect, it can be overridden:

```
MASTER_SITES= SF/stardict/WyabdcRealPeopleTTS/${PORTVERSION}
```

This can also be written as

```
MASTER_SITES= SF
MASTER_SITE_SUBDIR= stardict/WyabdcRealPeopleTTS/${PORTVERSION}
```

Table 5.4. Magic **MASTER_SITES** Macros

Macro	Assumed subdirectory
APACHE_COMMONS_BINARIES	${PORTNAME:S,commons-,,}
APACHE_COMMONS_SOURCE	${PORTNAME:S,commons-,,}
APACHE_JAKARTA	${PORTNAME:S,-,/,}/source
BERLIOS	${PORTNAME:tl}.berlios
CHEESESHOP	source/${DISTNAME:C/(.).*/\1/}/ ${DISTNAME:C/(.*)-[0-9].*/\1/}
CPAN	${PORTNAME:C/-.*//}
DEBIAN	pool/main/${PORTNAME:C/^((lib)?.).*$/\1/}/ ${PORTNAME}
FARSIGHT	${PORTNAME}
FESTIVAL	${PORTREVISION}
GCC	releases/${DISTNAME}
GENTOO	distfiles
GIMP	${PORTNAME}/${PORTVERSION:R}/
GH	${GH_ACCOUNT}/${GH_PROJECT}/tar.gz/ ${GH_TAGNAME}?dummy=/

Macro	Assumed subdirectory
GHC	`${GH_ACCOUNT}/${GH_PROJECT}/`
GNOME	`sources/${PORTNAME}/${PORTVERSION:C/^([0-9]+` `\.[0-9]+).*/\1/}`
GNU	`${PORTNAME}`
GNUPG	`${PORTNAME}`
GNU_ALPHA	`${PORTNAME}`
HORDE	`${PORTNAME}`
LODEV	`${PORTNAME}`
MATE	`${PORTVERSION:C/^([0-9]+\.[0-9]+).*/\1/}`
MOZDEV	`${PORTNAME:tl}`
NL	`${PORTNAME}`
QT	`archive/qt/${PORTVERSION:R}`
SAMBA	`${PORTNAME}`
SAVANNAH	`${PORTNAME:tl}`
SF	`${PORTNAME:tl}/${PORTNAME:tl}/${PORTVERSION}`

5.4.3. `USE_GITHUB`

If the distribution file comes from a specific commit or tag on GitHub for which there is no officially released file, there is an easy way to set the right `DISTNAME` and `MASTER_SITES` automatically. These variables are available:

Table 5.5. `USE_GITHUB` Description

Variable	Description	Default
GH_ACCOUNT	Account name of the GitHub user hosting the project	`${PORTNAME}`
GH_PROJECT	Name of the project on GitHub	`${PORTNAME}`
GH_TAGNAME	Name of the tag to download (2.0.1, hash, ...) Using the name of a branch here is incorrect. It is also possible to use the hash of a commit id to do a snapshot.	`${DISTVERSIONPRE-FIX}${DISTVERSION}${DISTVERSIONSUF-FIX}`
GH_SUBDIR	When the software needs an additional distribution file to be extracted within `${WRKSRC}`, this variable can be used. See the examples in Section 5.4.3.1, "Fetching Multiple Files from GitHub" for more information.	(none)
GH_TUPLE	`GH_TUPLE` allows putting `GH_AC-COUNT`, `GH_PROJECT`, `GH_TAGNAME`, and `GH_SUBDIR` into a single variable. The format is *account:project:tag-name:group/subdir*. The */subdir* part is optional. It is helpful when there is more than one GitHub project from which to fetch.	

Important

Do not use `GH_TUPLE` for the default distribution file, as it has no default.

Example 5.10. Simple Use of `USE_GITHUB`

While trying to make a port for version 1.2.7 of pkg from the FreeBSD user on github, at https://github.com/freebsd/pkg, The `Makefile` would end up looking like this (slightly stripped for the example):

```
PORTNAME= pkg
DISTVERSION= 1.2.7

USE_GITHUB= yes
GH_ACCOUNT= freebsd
```

It will automatically have `MASTER_SITES` set to GH GHC and WRKSRC to `${WRKDIR}/pkg-1.2.7` .

Example 5.11. More Complete Use of `USE_GITHUB`

While trying to make a port for the bleeding edge version of pkg from the FreeBSD user on github, at https://github.com/freebsd/pkg, the `Makefile` ends up looking like this (slightly stripped for the example):

```
PORTNAME= pkg-devel
DISTVERSION= 1.3.0.a.20140411

USE_GITHUB= yes
GH_ACCOUNT= freebsd
GH_PROJECT= pkg
GH_TAGNAME= 6dbb17b
```

It will automatically have `MASTER_SITES` set to GH GHC and WRKSRC to `${WRKDIR}/pkg-6dbb17b` .

Tip

`20140411` is the date of the commit referenced in `GH_TAGNAME`, not the date the Makefile is edited, or the date the commit is made.

Example 5.12. Use of `USE_GITHUB` with `DISTVERSIONPREFIX`

From time to time, `GH_TAGNAME` is a slight variation from `DISTVERSION` . For example, if the version is `1.0.2`, the tag is `v1.0.2`. In those cases, it is possible to use `DISTVERSIONPREFIX` or `DISTVERSIONSUFFIX`:

```
PORTNAME= foo
```

```
DISTVERSIONPREFIX= v
DISTVERSION= 1.0.2

USE_GITHUB= yes
```

It will automatically set `GH_TAGNAME` to `v1.0.2`, while `WRKSRC` will be kept to `${WRKDIR}/foo-1.0.2` .

Example 5.13. Using USE_GITHUB When Upstream Does Not Use Versions

If there never was a version upstream, do not invent one like `0.1` or `1.0`. Create the port with a `DISTVERSION` of `gYYYYMMDD`, where `g` is for Git, and *YYYYMMDD* represents the date the commit referenced in `GH_TAGNAME`.

```
PORTNAME= bar
DISTVERSION= g20140411

USE_GITHUB= yes
GH_TAGNAME= c472d66b
```

This creates a versioning scheme that increases over time, and that is still before version `0` (see Example 5.1, "Using pkg-version(8) to Compare Versions." for details on pkg-version(8)):

```
% pkg version -t g20140411 0
<
```

Which means using `PORTEPOCH` will not be needed in case upstream decides to cut versions in the future.

Example 5.14. Using USE_GITHUB to Access a Commit Between Two Versions

If the current version of the software uses a Git tag, and the port needs to be updated to a newer, intermediate version, without a tag, use git-describe(1) to find out the version to use:

```
% git describe --tags  f0038b1
v0.7.3-14-gf0038b1
```

`v0.7.3-14-gf0038b1` can be split into three parts:

`v0.7.3`
>   This is the last Git tag that appears in the commit history before the requested commit.

`-14`
>   This means that the requested commit, `f0038b1`, is the 14th commit after the `v0.7.3` tag.

`-gf0038b1`
>   The `-g` means "Git", and the `f0038b1` is the commit hash that this reference points to.

```
PORTNAME= bar
DISTVERSIONPREFIX=  v
DISTVERSION= 0.7.3-14
DISTVERSIONSUFFIX=  -gf0038b1

USE_GITHUB= yes
```

This creates a versioning scheme that increases over time (well, over commits), and does not conflict with the creation of a `0.7.4` version. (See Example 5.1, "Using pkg-version(8) to Compare Versions." for details on pkg-version(8)):

```
% pkg version -t 0.7.3 0.7.3.14
<
% pkg version -t 0.7.3.14 0.7.4
<
```

Note

If the requested commit is the same as a tag, a shorter description is shown by default. The longer version is equivalent:

```
% git describe --tags  c66c71d
v0.7.3
% git describe --tags --long  c66c71d
v0.7.3-0-gc66c71d
```

5.4.3.1. Fetching Multiple Files from GitHub

The USE_GITHUB framework also supports fetching multiple distribution files from different places in GitHub. It works in a way very similar to Section 5.4.8, "Multiple Distribution or Patches Files from Multiple Locations".

When fetching multiple files from GitHub, sometimes the default distribution file is not fetched from GitHub. To disable fetching the default distribution, set:

```
USE_GITHUB= nodefault
```

Multiple values are added to GH_ACCOUNT, GH_PROJECT , and GH_TAGNAME. Each different value is assigned a group. The main value can either have no group, or the :DEFAULT group. A value can be omitted if it is the same as the default as listed in Table 5.5, "USE_GITHUB Description".

GH_TUPLE can also be used when there are a lot of distribution files. It helps keep the account, project, tagname, and group information at the same place.

For each group, a ${WRKSRC_*group*} helper variable is created, containing the directory into which the file has been extracted. The ${WRKSRC_*group*} variables can be used to move directories around during post-extract , or add to CONFIGURE_ARGS, or whatever is needed so that the software builds correctly.

Caution

The :*group* part *must* be used for *only one* distribution file. It is used as a unique key and using it more than once will overwrite the previous values.

Note

As this is only syntastic sugar above DISTFILES and MASTER_SITES , the group names must adhere to the restrictions on group names outlined in Section 5.4.8, "Multiple Distribution or Patches Files from Multiple Locations"

Example 5.15. Use of USE_GITHUB with Multiple Distribution Files

From time to time, there is a need to fetch more than one distribution file. For example, when the upstream git repository uses submodules. This can be done easily using groups in the GH_* variables:

```
PORTNAME= foo
DISTVERSION= 1.0.2

USE_GITHUB= yes
GH_ACCOUNT= bar:icons,contrib
GH_PROJECT= foo-icons:icons foo-contrib:contrib
GH_TAGNAME= 1.0:icons fa579bc:contrib
GH_SUBDIR= ext/icons:icons

CONFIGURE_ARGS= --with-contrib=${WRKSRC_contrib}
```

This will fetch three distribution files from github. The default one comes from foo/foo and is version 1.0.2. The second one, with the icons group, comes from bar/foo-icons and is in version 1.0. The third one comes from bar/foo-contrib and uses the Git commit fa579bc. The distribution files are named foo-foo-1.0.2_GH0.tar.gz , bar-foo-icons-1.0_GH0.tar.gz , and bar-foo-contrib-fa579bc_GH0.tar.gz .

All the distribution files are extracted in ${WRKDIR} in their respective subdirectories. The default file is still extracted in ${WRKSRC} , in this case, ${WRKDIR}/foo-1.0.2 . Each additional distribution file is extracted in ${WRKSRC_*group*}. Here, for the icons group, it is called ${WRKSRC_icons} and it contains ${WRKDIR}/foo-icons-1.0 . The file with the contrib group is called ${WRKSRC_contrib} and contains ${WRKDIR}/foo-contrib-fa579bc .

The software's build system expects to find the icons in a ext/icons subdirectory in its sources, so GH_SUBDIR is used. GH_SUBDIR makes sure that ext exists, but that ext/icons does not already exist. Then it does this:

```
post-extract:
    @${MV} ${WRKSRC_icons} ${WRKSRC}/ext/icons
```

Example 5.16. Use of USE_GITHUB with Multiple Distribution Files Using GH_TUPLE

This is functionally equivalent to Example 5.15, "Use of USE_GITHUB with Multiple Distribution Files", but using GH_TUPLE:

```
PORTNAME= foo
DISTVERSION= 1.0.2

USE_GITHUB= yes
GH_TUPLE= bar:foo-icons:1.0:icons/ext/icons \
  bar:foo-contrib:fa579bc:contrib

CONFIGURE_ARGS= --with-contrib=${WRKSRC_contrib}
```

Grouping was used in the previous example with bar:icons,contrib. Some redundant information is present with GH_TUPLE because grouping is not possible.

Example 5.17. How to Use USE_GITHUB with Git Submodules?

Ports with GitHub as an upstream repository sometimes use submodules. See git-submodule(1) for more information.

The problem with submodules is that each is a separate repository. As such, they each must be fetched separately.

Using finance/moneymanagerex as an example, its GitHub repository is https://github.com/moneymanagerex/moneymanagerex. It has a .gitmodules file at the root. This file describes all the submodules used in this repository, and lists additional repositories needed. This file will tell what additional repositories are needed:

```
[submodule "lib/wxsqlite3"]
 path = lib/wxsqlite3
 url = https://github.com/utelle/wxsqlite3.git
[submodule "3rd/mongoose"]
 path = 3rd/mongoose
 url = https://github.com/cesanta/mongoose.git
[submodule "3rd/LuaGlue"]
 path = 3rd/LuaGlue
 url = https://github.com/moneymanagerex/LuaGlue.git
[submodule "3rd/cgitemplate"]
 path = 3rd/cgitemplate
 url = https://github.com/moneymanagerex/html-template.git
[...-]
```

The only information missing from that file is the commit hash or tag to use as a version. This information is found after cloning the repository:

```
% git clone --recurse-submodules https://github.com/moneymanagerex/moneymanagerex.↺
git
Cloning into 'moneymanagerex'...
remote: Counting objects: 32387, done.
[...-]
Submodule '3rd/LuaGlue' (https://github.com/moneymanagerex/LuaGlue.git) ↺
registered for path '3rd/LuaGlue'
Submodule '3rd/cgitemplate' (https://github.com/moneymanagerex/html-template.git) ↺
registered for path '3rd/cgitemplate'
Submodule '3rd/mongoose' (https://github.com/cesanta/mongoose.git) registered for ↺
path '3rd/mongoose'
Submodule 'lib/wxsqlite3' (https://github.com/utelle/wxsqlite3.git) registered ↺
for path 'lib/wxsqlite3'
[...-]
Cloning into '/home/mat/work/freebsd/ports/finance/moneymanagerex/
moneymanagerex/3rd/LuaGlue'...
Cloning into '/home/mat/work/freebsd/ports/finance/moneymanagerex/
moneymanagerex/3rd/cgitemplate'...
Cloning into '/home/mat/work/freebsd/ports/finance/moneymanagerex/
moneymanagerex/3rd/mongoose'...
Cloning into '/home/mat/work/freebsd/ports/finance/moneymanagerex/moneymanagerex/
lib/wxsqlite3'...
[...-]
Submodule path '3rd/LuaGlue': checked out
 'c51d11a247ee4d1e9817dfa2a8da8d9e2f97ae3b'
Submodule path '3rd/cgitemplate': checked out
 'cd434eeeb35904ebcd3d718ba29c281a649b192c'
Submodule path '3rd/mongoose': checked out
 '2140e5992ab9a3a9a34ce9a281abf57f00f95cda'
Submodule path 'lib/wxsqlite3': checked out
 'fb66eb230d8aed21dec273b38c7c054dcb7d6b51'
[...-]
```

```
% cd moneymanagerex
% git submodule status
  c51d11a247ee4d1e9817dfa2a8da8d9e2f97ae3b 3rd/LuaGlue (heads/master)
  cd434eeeb35904ebcd3d718ba29c281a649b192c 3rd/cgitemplate (cd434ee)
  2140e5992ab9a3a9a34ce9a281abf57f00f95cda 3rd/mongoose (6.2-138-g2140e59)
  fb66eb230d8aed21dec273b38c7c054dcb7d6b51 lib/wxsqlite3 (v3.4.0)
  [...-]
```

It can also be found on GitHub. Each subdirectory that is a submodule is shown as *directory* @ *hash*, for example, mongoose @ 2140e59 .

Note

While getting the information from GitHub seems more straightforward, the information found using git submodule status will provide more meaningful information. For example, here, lib/wxsqlite3 's commit hash fb66eb2 correspond to v3.4.0. Both can be used interchangeably, but when a tag is available, use it.

Now that all the required information has been gathered, the Makefile can be written (only GitHub-related lines are shown):

```
PORTNAME= moneymanagerex
DISTVERSIONPREFIX= v
DISTVERSION= 1.3.0

USE_GITHUB= yes
GH_TUPLE= utelle:wxsqlite3:v3.4.0:wxsqlite3/lib/wxsqlite3 \
  moneymanagerex:LuaGlue:c51d11a:lua_glue/3rd/LuaGlue \
  moneymanagerex:html-template:cd434ee:html_template/3rd/cgitemplate \
  cesanta:mongoose:2140e59:mongoose/3rd/mongoose \
  [...-]
```

5.4.4. EXTRACT_SUFX

If there is one distribution file, and it uses an odd suffix to indicate the compression mechanism, set EXTRACT_SUFX.

For example, if the distribution file was named foo.tar.gzip instead of the more normal foo.tar.gz , write:

```
DISTNAME= foo
EXTRACT_SUFX= .tar.gzip
```

The USES=tar[: *xxx*], USES=lha or USES=zip automatically set EXTRACT_SUFX to the most common archives extensions as necessary, see Chapter 17, *Using USES Macros* for more details. If neither of these are set then EXTRACT_SUFX defaults to .tar.gz .

Note

As EXTRACT_SUFX is only used in DISTFILES, only set one of them..

5.4.5. DISTFILES

Sometimes the names of the files to be downloaded have no resemblance to the name of the port. For example, it might be called source.tar.gz or similar. In other cases the application's source code might be in several different archives, all of which must be downloaded.

If this is the case, set `DISTFILES` to be a space separated list of all the files that must be downloaded.

```
DISTFILES= source1.tar.gz source2.tar.gz
```

If not explicitly set, `DISTFILES` defaults to `${DISTNAME}${EXTRACT_SUFX}`.

5.4.6. EXTRACT_ONLY

If only some of the `DISTFILES` must be extracted—for example, one of them is the source code, while another is an uncompressed document—list the filenames that must be extracted in `EXTRACT_ONLY`.

```
DISTFILES= source.tar.gz manual.html
EXTRACT_ONLY= source.tar.gz
```

When none of the `DISTFILES` need to be uncompressed, set `EXTRACT_ONLY` to the empty string.

```
EXTRACT_ONLY=
```

5.4.7. PATCHFILES

If the port requires some additional patches that are available by FTP or HTTP, set `PATCHFILES` to the names of the files and `PATCH_SITES` to the URL of the directory that contains them (the format is the same as `MASTER_SITES`).

If the patch is not relative to the top of the source tree (that is, `WRKSRC`) because it contains some extra pathnames, set `PATCH_DIST_STRIP` accordingly. For instance, if all the pathnames in the patch have an extra `foozolix-1.0/` in front of the filenames, then set `PATCH_DIST_STRIP=-p1` .

Do not worry if the patches are compressed; they will be decompressed automatically if the filenames end with `.Z`, `.gz`, `.bz2` or `.xz`.

If the patch is distributed with some other files, such as documentation, in a compressed tarball, using `PATCH-FILES` is not possible. If that is the case, add the name and the location of the patch tarball to `DISTFILES` and `MASTER_SITES` . Then, use `EXTRA_PATCHES` to point to those files and `bsd.port.mk` will automatically apply them. In particular, do *not* copy patch files into `${PATCHDIR}` . That directory may not be writable.

> ### Tip
>
> If there are multiple patches and they need mixed values for the strip parameter, it can be added alongside the patch name in `PATCHFILES`, e.g:
>
> ```
> PATCHFILES= patch1 patch2:-p1
> ```
>
> This does not conflict with the master site grouping feature, adding a group also works:
>
> ```
> PATCHFILES= patch2:-p1:source2
> ```

> ### Note
>
> The tarball will have been extracted alongside the regular source by then, so there is no need to explicitly extract it if it is a regular compressed tarball. Take extra care not to overwrite something that already exists in that directory if extracting it manually. Also, do not forget to add a command to remove the copied patch in the `pre-clean` target.

5.4.8. Multiple Distribution or Patches Files from Multiple Locations

(Consider this to be a somewhat "advanced topic"; those new to this document may wish to skip this section at first).

This section has information on the fetching mechanism known as both MASTER_SITES:n and MASTER_SITES_NN. We will refer to this mechanism as MASTER_SITES:n.

A little background first. OpenBSD has a neat feature inside DISTFILES and PATCHFILES which allows files and patches to be postfixed with :n identifiers. Here, n can be any word containing [0-9a-zA-Z_] and denote a group designation. For example:

```
DISTFILES= alpha:0 beta:1
```

In OpenBSD, distribution file alpha will be associated with variable MASTER_SITES0 instead of our common MASTER_SITES and beta with MASTER_SITES1.

This is a very interesting feature which can decrease that endless search for the correct download site.

Just picture 2 files in DISTFILES and 20 sites in MASTER_SITES, the sites slow as hell where beta is carried by all sites in MASTER_SITES, and alpha can only be found in the 20th site. It would be such a waste to check all of them if the maintainer knew this beforehand, would it not? Not a good start for that lovely weekend!

Now that you have the idea, just imagine more DISTFILES and more MASTER_SITES. Surely our "distfiles survey meister" would appreciate the relief to network strain that this would bring.

In the next sections, information will follow on the FreeBSD implementation of this idea. We improved a bit on OpenBSD's concept.

Important

The group names cannot have dashes in them (-), in fact, they cannot have any characters out of the [a-zA-Z0-9_] range. This is because, while make(1) is ok with variable names containing dashes, sh(1) is not.

5.4.8.1. Simplified Information

This section explains how to quickly prepare fine grained fetching of multiple distribution files and patches from different sites and subdirectories. We describe here a case of simplified MASTER_SITES:n usage. This will be sufficient for most scenarios. More detailed information are available in Section 5.4.8.2, "Detailed Information".

Some applications consist of multiple distribution files that must be downloaded from a number of different sites. For example, Ghostscript consists of the core of the program, and then a large number of driver files that are used depending on the user's printer. Some of these driver files are supplied with the core, but many others must be downloaded from a variety of different sites.

To support this, each entry in DISTFILES may be followed by a colon and a "group name". Each site listed in MASTER_SITES is then followed by a colon, and the group that indicates which distribution files are downloaded from this site.

For example, consider an application with the source split in two parts, source1.tar.gz and source2.tar.gz, which must be downloaded from two different sites. The port's Makefile would include lines like Example 5.18, "Simplified Use of MASTER_SITES:n with One File Per Site".

Example 5.18. Simplified Use of MASTER_SITES:n with One File Per Site

```
MASTER_SITES= ftp://ftp1.example.com/:source1 \
```

```
    http://www.example.com/:source2
DISTFILES= source1.tar.gz:source1 \
    source2.tar.gz:source2
```

Multiple distribution files can have the same group. Continuing the previous example, suppose that there was a third distfile, source3.tar.gz , that is downloaded from ftp.example2.com. The Makefile would then be written like Example 5.19, "Simplified Use of MASTER_SITES:n with More Than One File Per Site".

Example 5.19. Simplified Use of MASTER_SITES:n with More Than One File Per Site

```
MASTER_SITES= ftp://ftp.example.com/:source1 \
    http://www.example.com/:source2
DISTFILES= source1.tar.gz:source1 \
    source2.tar.gz:source2 \
    source3.tar.gz:source2
```

5.4.8.2. Detailed Information

Okay, so the previous example did not reflect the new port's needs? In this section we will explain in detail how the fine grained fetching mechanism MASTER_SITES:n works and how it can be used.

1. Elements can be postfixed with :n where n is [^:,]+, that is, n could conceptually be any alphanumeric string but we will limit it to [a-zA-Z_][0-9a-zA-Z_]+   for now.

   Moreover, string matching is case sensitive; that is, n is different from N.

   However, these words cannot be used for postfixing purposes since they yield special meaning: default, all and ALL (they are used internally in item ii). Furthermore, DEFAULT is a special purpose word (check item 3).

2. Elements postfixed with :n belong to the group n, :m belong to group m and so forth.

3. Elements without a postfix are groupless, they all belong to the special group DEFAULT. Any elements postfixed with DEFAULT, is just being redundant unless an element belongs to both DEFAULT and other groups at the same time (check item 5).

   These examples are equivalent but the first one is preferred:

   ```
   MASTER_SITES= alpha
   ```

   ```
   MASTER_SITES= alpha:DEFAULT
   ```

4. Groups are not exclusive, an element may belong to several different groups at the same time and a group can either have either several different elements or none at all.

5. When an element belongs to several groups at the same time, use the comma operator (,).

   Instead of repeating it several times, each time with a different postfix, we can list several groups at once in a single postfix. For instance, :m,n,o marks an element that belongs to group m, n and o.

   All these examples are equivalent but the last one is preferred:

   ```
   MASTER_SITES= alpha alpha:SOME_SITE
   ```

   ```
   MASTER_SITES= alpha:DEFAULT alpha:SOME_SITE
   ```

```
MASTER_SITES= alpha:SOME_SITE,DEFAULT
```

```
MASTER_SITES= alpha:DEFAULT,SOME_SITE
```

6. All sites within a given group are sorted according to MASTER_SORT_AWK . All groups within MASTER_SITES and PATCH_SITES are sorted as well.

7. Group semantics can be used in any of the variables MASTER_SITES , PATCH_SITES , MASTER_SITE_SUBDIR, PATCH_SITE_SUBDIR, DISTFILES, and PATCHFILES according to this syntax:

a. All MASTER_SITES , PATCH_SITES , MASTER_SITE_SUBDIR and PATCH_SITE_SUBDIR elements must be terminated with the forward slash / character. If any elements belong to any groups, the group postfix :*n* must come right after the terminator /. The MASTER_SITES:n mechanism relies on the existence of the terminator / to avoid confusing elements where a :n is a valid part of the element with occurrences where :n denotes group n. For compatibility purposes, since the / terminator was not required before in both MASTER_SITE_SUBDIR and PATCH_SITE_SUBDIR elements, if the postfix immediate preceding character is not a / then :n will be considered a valid part of the element instead of a group postfix even if an element is postfixed with :n. See both Example 5.20, "Detailed Use of MASTER_SITES:n in MASTER_SITE_SUBDIR" and Example 5.21, "Detailed Use of MASTER_SITES:n with Comma Operator, Multiple Files, Multiple Sites and Multiple Subdirectories".

Example 5.20. Detailed Use of MASTER_SITES:n in MASTER_SITE_SUBDIR

```
MASTER_SITE_SUBDIR= old:n new/:NEW
```

- Directories within group DEFAULT -> old:n

- Directories within group NEW -> new

Example 5.21. Detailed Use of MASTER_SITES:n with Comma Operator, Multiple Files, Multiple Sites and Multiple Subdirectories

```
MASTER_SITES= http://site1/%SUBDIR%/ http://site2/:DEFAULT \
  http://site3/:group3 http://site4/:group4 \
  http://site5/:group5 http://site6/:group6 \
  http://site7/:DEFAULT,group6 \
  http://site8/%SUBDIR%/:group6,group7 \
  http://site9/:group8
DISTFILES= file1 file2:DEFAULT file3:group3 \
  file4:group4,group5,group6 file5:grouping \
  file6:group7
MASTER_SITE_SUBDIR= directory-trial:1 directory-n/:groupn \
  directory-one/:group6,DEFAULT \
  directory
```

The previous example results in this fine grained fetching. Sites are listed in the exact order they will be used.

- file1 will be fetched from

  - MASTER_SITE_OVERRIDE

  - http://site1/directory-trial:1/

  - http://site1/directory-one/

- http://site1/directory/

- http://site2/

- http://site7/

- MASTER_SITE_BACKUP

- file2 will be fetched exactly as file1 since they both belong to the same group

  - MASTER_SITE_OVERRIDE

  - http://site1/directory-trial:1/

  - http://site1/directory-one/

  - http://site1/directory/

  - http://site2/

  - http://site7/

  - MASTER_SITE_BACKUP

- file3 will be fetched from

  - MASTER_SITE_OVERRIDE

  - http://site3/

  - MASTER_SITE_BACKUP

- file4 will be fetched from

  - MASTER_SITE_OVERRIDE

  - http://site4/

  - http://site5/

  - http://site6/

  - http://site7/

  - http://site8/directory-one/

  - MASTER_SITE_BACKUP

- file5 will be fetched from

  - MASTER_SITE_OVERRIDE

  - MASTER_SITE_BACKUP

- file6 will be fetched from

  - MASTER_SITE_OVERRIDE

  - http://site8/

> • MASTER_SITE_BACKUP

8. How do I group one of the special macros from bsd.sites.mk, for example, SourceForge (SF)?

   This has been simplified as much as possible. See Example 5.22, "Detailed Use of MASTER_SITES:n with Source-Forge (SF)".

Example 5.22. Detailed Use of MASTER_SITES:n with SourceForge (SF)

```
MASTER_SITES= http://site1/ SF/something/1.0:sourceforge,TEST
DISTFILES= something.tar.gz:sourceforge
```

something.tar.gz will be fetched from all sites within SourceForge.

---

9. How do I use this with PATCH*?

   All examples were done with MASTER* but they work exactly the same for PATCH* ones as can be seen in Example 5.23, "Simplified Use of MASTER_SITES:n with PATCH_SITES".

Example 5.23. Simplified Use of MASTER_SITES:n with PATCH_SITES

```
PATCH_SITES= http://site1/ http://site2/:test
PATCHFILES= patch1:test
```

5.4.8.3. What Does Change for Ports? What Does Not?

i. All current ports remain the same. The MASTER_SITES:n feature code is only activated if there are elements postfixed with :n like elements according to the aforementioned syntax rules, especially as shown in item 7.

ii. The port targets remain the same: checksum, makesum, patch, configure, build, etc. With the obvious exceptions of do-fetch, fetch-list, master-sites and patch-sites.

   • do-fetch: deploys the new grouping postfixed DISTFILES and PATCHFILES with their matching group elements within both MASTER_SITES and PATCH_SITES which use matching group elements within both MASTER_SITE_SUBDIR and PATCH_SITE_SUBDIR. Check Example 5.21, "Detailed Use of MASTER_SITES:n with Comma Operator, Multiple Files, Multiple Sites and Multiple Subdirectories".

   • fetch-list: works like old fetch-list with the exception that it groups just like do-fetch.

   • master-sites and patch-sites: (incompatible with older versions) only return the elements of group DEFAULT; in fact, they execute targets master-sites-default and patch-sites-default respectively.

   Furthermore, using target either master-sites-all or patch-sites-all is preferred to directly checking either MASTER_SITES or PATCH_SITES. Also, directly checking is not guaranteed to work in any future versions. Check item B for more information on these new port targets.

iii. New port targets

A. There are `master-sites-`*n* and `patch-sites-` *n* targets which will list the elements of the respective group *n* within `MASTER_SITES` and `PATCH_SITES` respectively. For instance, both `master-sites-DEFAULT` and `patch-sites-DEFAULT` will return the elements of group `DEFAULT`, `master-sites-test` and `patch-sites-test` of group `test`, and thereon.

B. There are new targets `master-sites-all` and `patch-sites-all` which do the work of the old `master-sites` and `patch-sites` ones. They return the elements of all groups as if they all belonged to the same group with the caveat that it lists as many `MASTER_SITE_BACKUP` and `MASTER_SITE_OVERRIDE` as there are groups defined within either `DISTFILES` or `PATCHFILES`; respectively for `master-sites-all` and `patch-sites-all` .

5.4.9. DIST_SUBDIR

Do not let the port clutter `/usr/ports/distfiles` . If the port requires a lot of files to be fetched, or contains a file that has a name that might conflict with other ports (for example, `Makefile`), set `DIST_SUBDIR` to the name of the port (`${PORTNAME}` or `${PKGNAMEPREFIX}${PORTNAME}` are fine). This will change `DISTDIR` from the default `/usr/ports/distfiles` to `/usr/ports/distfiles/${DIST_SUBDIR}` , and in effect puts everything that is required for the port into that subdirectory.

It will also look at the subdirectory with the same name on the backup master site at http://distcache.FreeBSD.org (Setting `DISTDIR` explicitly in `Makefile` will not accomplish this, so please use `DIST_SUBDIR`.)

Note

This does not affect `MASTER_SITES` defined in the `Makefile`.

5.5. MAINTAINER

Set your mail-address here. Please. *:-)*

Only a single address without the comment part is allowed as a `MAINTAINER` value. The format used is `user@host-name.domain`. Please do not include any descriptive text such as a real name in this entry. That merely confuses the Ports infrastructure and most tools using it.

The maintainer is responsible for keeping the port up to date and making sure that it works correctly. For a detailed description of the responsibilities of a port maintainer, refer to The challenge for port maintainers.

Note

A maintainer volunteers to keep a port in good working order. Maintainers have the primary responsibility for their ports, but not exclusive ownership. Ports exist for the benefit of the community and, in reality, belong to the community. What this means is that people other than the maintainer can make changes to a port. Large changes to the Ports Collection might require changes to many ports. The FreeBSD Ports Management Team or members of other teams might modify ports to fix dependency issues or other problems, like a version bump for a shared library update.

Some types of fixes have "blanket approval" from the Ports Management Team <portmgr@FreeBSD.org>, allowing any committer to fix those categories of problems on any port. These fixes do not need approval from the maintainer. Blanket approval does not apply to ports that are maintained by teams like <autotools@FreeBSD.org>, <x11@FreeBSD.org>, <gnome@FreeBSD.org>, or <kde@FreeBSD.org>. These teams use external repositories and

> can have work that would conflict with changes that would normally fall under blanket approval.
>
> Blanket approval for most ports applies to these types of fixes:
>
> - Most infrastructure changes to a port (that is, modernizing, but not changing the functionality). For example, converting to staging, USE_GMAKE to USES=gmake, the new LIB_DE-PENDS format...
>
> - Trivial and *tested* build and runtime fixes.

Other changes to the port will be sent to the maintainer for review and approval before being committed. If the maintainer does not respond to an update request after two weeks (excluding major public holidays), then that is considered a maintainer timeout, and the update may be made without explicit maintainer approval. If the maintainer does not respond within three months, or if there have been three consecutive timeouts, then that maintainer is considered absent without leave, and can be replaced as the maintainer of the particular port in question. Exceptions to this are anything maintained by the Ports Management Team <portmgr@FreeBSD.org>, or the Security Officer Team <security-officer@FreeBSD.org>. No unauthorized commits may ever be made to ports maintained by those groups.

We reserve the right to modify the maintainer's submission to better match existing policies and style of the Ports Collection without explicit blessing from the submitter or the maintainer. Also, large infrastructural changes can result in a port being modified without the maintainer's consent. These kinds of changes will never affect the port's functionality.

The Ports Management Team <portmgr@FreeBSD.org> reserves the right to revoke or override anyone's maintainership for any reason, and the Security Officer Team <security-officer@FreeBSD.org> reserves the right to revoke or override maintainership for security reasons.

5.6. COMMENT

The comment is a one-line description of a port shown by pkg info. Please follow these rules when composing it:

1. The COMMENT string should be 70 characters or less.

2. Do *not* include the package name or version number of software.

3. The comment must begin with a capital and end without a period.

4. Do not start with an indefinite article (that is, A or An).

5. Capitalize names such as Apache, JavaScript, or Perl.

6. Use a serial comma for lists of words: "green, red, and blue."

7. Check for spelling errors.

Here is an example:

```
COMMENT= Cat chasing a mouse all over the screen
```

The COMMENT variable immediately follows the MAINTAINER variable in the Makefile.

5.7. Licenses

Each port must document the license under which it is available. If it is not an OSI approved license it must also document any restrictions on redistribution.

5.7.1. LICENSE

A short name for the license or licenses if more than one license apply.

If it is one of the licenses listed in Table 5.6, "Predefined License List", only LICENSE_FILE and LICENSE_DISTFILES variables can be set.

If this is a license that has not been defined in the ports framework (see Table 5.6, "Predefined License List"), the LICENSE_PERMS and LICENSE_NAME must be set, along with either LICENSE_FILE or LICENSE_TEXT. LICENSE_DIST-FILES and LICENSE_GROUPS can also be set, but are not required.

The predefined licenses are shown in Table 5.6, "Predefined License List". The current list is always available in Mk/bsd.licenses.db.mk.

Example 5.24. Simplest Usage, Predefined Licenses

When the README of some software says "This software is under the terms of the GNU Lesser General Public License as published by the Free Software Foundation; either version 2.1 of the License, or (at your option) any later version." but does not provide the license file, use this:

```
LICENSE= LGPL21+
```

When the software provides the license file, use this:

```
LICENSE= LGPL21+
LICENSE_FILE= ${WRKSRC}/COPYING
```

For the predefined licenses, the default permissions are dist-mirror dist-sell pkg-mirror pkg-sell auto-accept.

Table 5.6. Predefined License List

Short Name	Name	Group	Permissions
AGPLv3	GNU Affero General Public License version 3	FSF GPL OSI	(default)
AGPLv3+	GNU Affero General Public License version 3 (or later)	FSF GPL OSI	(default)
APACHE10	Apache License 1.0	FSF	(default)
APACHE11	Apache License 1.1	FSF OSI	(default)
APACHE20	Apache License 2.0	FSF OSI	(default)
ART10	Artistic License version 1.0	OSI	(default)
ART20	Artistic License version 2.0	FSF GPL OSI	(default)
ARTPERL10	Artistic License (perl) version 1.0	OSI	(default)
BSD	BSD license Generic Version (deprecated)	FSF OSI COPYFREE	(default)
BSD2CLAUSE	BSD 2-clause "Simplified" License	FSF OSI COPYFREE	(default)
BSD3CLAUSE	BSD 3-clause "New" or "Revised" License	FSF OSI COPYFREE	(default)

Short Name	Name	Group	Permissions
BSD4CLAUSE	BSD 4-clause "Original" or "Old" License	FSF	(default)
BSL	Boost Software License	FSF OSI COPYFREE	(default)
CC-BY-1.0	Creative Commons Attribution 1.0		(default)
CC-BY-2.0	Creative Commons Attribution 2.0		(default)
CC-BY-2.5	Creative Commons Attribution 2.5		(default)
CC-BY-3.0	Creative Commons Attribution 3.0		(default)
CC-BY-4.0	Creative Commons Attribution 4.0		(default)
CC-BY-NC-1.0	Creative Commons Attribution Non Commercial 1.0		dist-mirror pkg-mirror auto-accept
CC-BY-NC-2.0	Creative Commons Attribution Non Commercial 2.0		dist-mirror pkg-mirror auto-accept
CC-BY-NC-2.5	Creative Commons Attribution Non Commercial 2.5		dist-mirror pkg-mirror auto-accept
CC-BY-NC-3.0	Creative Commons Attribution Non Commercial 3.0		dist-mirror pkg-mirror auto-accept
CC-BY-NC-4.0	Creative Commons Attribution Non Commercial 4.0		dist-mirror pkg-mirror auto-accept
CC-BY-NC-ND-1.0	Creative Commons Attribution Non Commercial No Derivatives 1.0		dist-mirror pkg-mirror auto-accept
CC-BY-NC-ND-2.0	Creative Commons Attribution Non Commercial No Derivatives 2.0		dist-mirror pkg-mirror auto-accept
CC-BY-NC-ND-2.5	Creative Commons Attribution Non Commercial No Derivatives 2.5		dist-mirror pkg-mirror auto-accept
CC-BY-NC-ND-3.0	Creative Commons Attribution Non Commercial No Derivatives 3.0		dist-mirror pkg-mirror auto-accept
CC-BY-NC-ND-4.0	Creative Commons Attribution Non Commercial No Derivatives 4.0		dist-mirror pkg-mirror auto-accept
CC-BY-NC-SA-1.0	Creative Commons Attribution Non Commercial Share Alike 1.0		dist-mirror pkg-mirror auto-accept
CC-BY-NC-SA-2.0	Creative Commons Attribution Non Commercial Share Alike 2.0		dist-mirror pkg-mirror auto-accept

Short Name	Name	Group	Permissions
`CC-BY-NC-SA-2.5`	Creative Commons Attribution Non Commercial Share Alike 2.5		`dist-mirror` `pkg-mirror` `auto-accept`
`CC-BY-NC-SA-3.0`	Creative Commons Attribution Non Commercial Share Alike 3.0		`dist-mirror` `pkg-mirror` `auto-accept`
`CC-BY-NC-SA-4.0`	Creative Commons Attribution Non Commercial Share Alike 4.0		`dist-mirror` `pkg-mirror` `auto-accept`
`CC-BY-ND-1.0`	Creative Commons Attribution No Derivatives 1.0		(default)
`CC-BY-ND-2.0`	Creative Commons Attribution No Derivatives 2.0		(default)
`CC-BY-ND-2.5`	Creative Commons Attribution No Derivatives 2.5		(default)
`CC-BY-ND-3.0`	Creative Commons Attribution No Derivatives 3.0		(default)
`CC-BY-ND-4.0`	Creative Commons Attribution No Derivatives 4.0		(default)
`CC-BY-SA-1.0`	Creative Commons Attribution Share Alike 1.0		(default)
`CC-BY-SA-2.0`	Creative Commons Attribution Share Alike 2.0		(default)
`CC-BY-SA-2.5`	Creative Commons Attribution Share Alike 2.5		(default)
`CC-BY-SA-3.0`	Creative Commons Attribution Share Alike 3.0		(default)
`CC-BY-SA-4.0`	Creative Commons Attribution Share Alike 4.0		(default)
`CC0-1.0`	Creative Commons Zero v1.0 Universal	`FSF GPL COPYFREE`	(default)
`CDDL`	Common Development and Distribution License	`FSF OSI`	(default)
`CPAL-1.0`	Common Public Attribution License	`FSF OSI`	(default)
`ClArtistic`	Clarified Artistic License	`FSF GPL OSI`	(default)
`EPL`	Eclipse Public License	`FSF OSI`	(default)
`GFDL`	GNU Free Documentation License	`FSF`	(default)
`GMGPL`	GNAT Modified General Public License	`FSF GPL OSI`	(default)
`GPLv1`	GNU General Public License version 1	`FSF GPL OSI`	(default)
`GPLv1+`	GNU General Public License version 1 (or later)	`FSF GPL OSI`	(default)

Short Name	Name	Group	Permissions
GPLv2	GNU General Public License version 2	FSF GPL OSI	(default)
GPLv2+	GNU General Public License version 2 (or later)	FSF GPL OSI	(default)
GPLv3	GNU General Public License version 3	FSF GPL OSI	(default)
GPLv3+	GNU General Public License version 3 (or later)	FSF GPL OSI	(default)
GPLv3RLE	GNU GPL version 3 Runtime Library Exception	FSF GPL OSI	(default)
GPLv3RLE+	GNU GPL version 3 Runtime Library Exception (or later)	FSF GPL OSI	(default)
ISCL	Internet Systems Consortium License	FSF GPL OSI COPYFREE	(default)
LGPL20	GNU Library General Public License version 2.0	FSF GPL OSI	(default)
LGPL20+	GNU Library General Public License version 2.0 (or later)	FSF GPL OSI	(default)
LGPL21	GNU Lesser General Public License version 2.1	FSF GPL OSI	(default)
LGPL21+	GNU Lesser General Public License version 2.1 (or later)	FSF GPL OSI	(default)
LGPL3	GNU Lesser General Public License version 3	FSF GPL OSI	(default)
LGPL3+	GNU Lesser General Public License version 3 (or later)	FSF GPL OSI	(default)
LPPL10	LaTeX Project Public License version 1.0	FSF OSI	dist-mirror dist-sell
LPPL11	LaTeX Project Public License version 1.1	FSF OSI	dist-mirror dist-sell
LPPL12	LaTeX Project Public License version 1.2	FSF OSI	dist-mirror dist-sell
LPPL13	LaTeX Project Public License version 1.3	FSF OSI	dist-mirror dist-sell
LPPL13a	LaTeX Project Public License version 1.3a	FSF OSI	dist-mirror dist-sell
LPPL13b	LaTeX Project Public License version 1.3b	FSF OSI	dist-mirror dist-sell
LPPL13c	LaTeX Project Public License version 1.3c	FSF OSI	dist-mirror dist-sell
MIT	MIT license / X11 license	COPYFREE FSF GPL OSI	(default)
MPL10	Mozilla Public License version 1.0	FSF OSI	(default)

Short Name	Name	Group	Permissions
MPL11	Mozilla Public License version 1.1	FSF OSI	(default)
MPL20	Mozilla Public License version 2.0	FSF OSI	(default)
NCSA	University of Illinois/NCSA Open Source License	COPYFREE FSF GPL OSI	(default)
NONE	No license specified		none
OFL10	SIL Open Font License version 1.0 (http://scripts.sil.org/OFL)	FONTS	(default)
OFL11	SIL Open Font License version 1.1 (http://scripts.sil.org/OFL)	FONTS	(default)
OWL	Open Works License (owl.apotheon.org)	COPYFREE	(default)
OpenSSL	OpenSSL License	FSF	(default)
PD	Public Domain	GPL COPYFREE	(default)
PHP202	PHP License version 2.02	FSF OSI	(default)
PHP30	PHP License version 3.0	FSF OSI	(default)
PHP301	PHP License version 3.01	FSF OSI	(default)
PSFL	Python Software Foundation License	FSF GPL OSI	(default)
PostgreSQL	PostgreSQL Licence	FSF GPL OSI COPYFREE	(default)
RUBY	Ruby License	FSF	(default)
UNLICENSE	The Unlicense	COPYFREE FSF GPL	(default)
WTFPL	Do What the Fuck You Want To Public License version 2	GPL FSF COPYFREE	(default)
WTFPL1	Do What the Fuck You Want To Public License version 1	GPL FSF COPYFREE	(default)
ZLIB	zlib License	GPL FSF OSI	(default)
ZPL21	Zope Public License version 2.1	GPL OSI	(default)

5.7.2. LICENSE_PERMS and LICENSE_PERMS_*NAME*

Permissions. use none if empty.

dist-mirror
:   Redistribution of the distribution files is permitted. The distribution files will be added to the FreeBSD MASTER_SITE_BACKUP CDN.

no-dist-mirror
:   Redistribution of the distribution files is prohibited. This is equivalent to setting RESTRICTED. The distribution files will *not* be added to the FreeBSD MASTER_SITE_BACKUP CDN.

dist-sell
:   Selling of distribution files is permitted. The distribution files will be present on the installer images.

`no-dist-sell`

Selling of distribution files is prohibited. This is equivalent to setting `NO_CDROM`.

`pkg-mirror`

Free redistribution of package is permitted. The package will be distributed on the FreeBSD package CDN https://pkg.freebsd.org/.

`no-pkg-mirror`

Free redistribution of package is prohibited. Equivalent to setting `NO_PACKAGE`. The package will *not* be distributed from the FreeBSD package CDN https://pkg.freebsd.org/.

`pkg-sell`

Selling of package is permitted. The package will be present on the installer images.

`no-pkg-sell`

Selling of package is prohibited. This is equivalent to setting `NO_CDROM`. The package will *not* be present on the installer images.

`auto-accept`

License is accepted by default. Prompts to accept a license are not displayed unless the user has defined `LICENSES_ASK`. Use this unless the license states the user must accept the terms of the license.

`no-auto-accept`

License is not accepted by default. The user will always be asked to confirm the acceptance of this license. This must be used if the license states that the user must accept its terms.

When both *permission* and no-*permission* is present the no-*permission* will cancel *permission*.

When *permission* is not present, it is considered to be a no-*permission*.

Example 5.25. Nonstandard License

Read the terms of the license and translate those using the available permissions.

```
LICENSE=        UNKNOWN
LICENSE_NAME=   unknown
LICENSE_TEXT=   This program is NOT in public domain.\
                It can be freely distributed for non-commercial purposes only.
LICENSE_PERMS=  dist-mirror no-dist-sell pkg-mirror no-pkg-sell auto-accept
```

Example 5.26. Standard and Nonstandard Licenses

Read the terms of the license and express those using the available permissions. In case of doubt, please ask for guidance on the FreeBSD ports mailing list.

```
LICENSE=        WARSOW GPLv2
LICENSE_COMB=   multi
LICENSE_NAME_WARSOW=    Warsow Content License
LICENSE_FILE_WARSOW=    ${WRKSRC}/docs/license.txt
LICENSE_PERMS_WARSOW=   dist-mirror pkg-mirror auto-accept
```

When the permissions of the GPLv2 and the UNKNOWN licenses are mixed, the port ends up with dist-mirror dist-sell pkg-mirror pkg-sell auto-accept dist-mirror no-dist-sell pkg-mirror no-pkg-sell auto-accept . The no-*permissions* cancel the *permissions*. The resulting list of permissions are *dist-mirror pkg-mirror auto-accept* . The distribution files and the packages will not be available on the installer images.

5.7.3. LICENSE_GROUPS and LICENSE_GROUPS_*NAME*

Groups the license belongs.

FSF
>   Free Software Foundation Approved, see the FSF Licensing & Compliance Team.

GPL
>   GPL Compatible

OSI
>   OSI Approved, see the Open Source Initiative Open Source Licenses page.

COPYFREE
>   Comply with Copyfree Standard Definition, see the Copyfree Licenses page.

FONTS
>   Font licenses

5.7.4. LICENSE_NAME and LICENSE_NAME_*NAME*

Full name of the license.

Example 5.27. LICENSE_NAME

```
LICENSE=        UNRAR
LICENSE_NAME=   UnRAR License
LICENSE_FILE=   ${WRKSRC}/license.txt
LICENSE_PERMS=  dist-mirror dist-sell pkg-mirror pkg-sell auto-accept
```

5.7.5. LICENSE_FILE and LICENSE_FILE_*NAME*

Full path to the file containing the license text, usually ${WRKSRC}/some/file . If the file is not in the distfile, and its content is too long to be put in LICENSE_TEXT, put it in a new file in ${FILESDIR} .

Example 5.28. LICENSE_FILE

```
LICENSE= GPLv3+
LICENSE_FILE= ${WRKSRC}/COPYING
```

5.7.6. LICENSE_TEXT and LICENSE_TEXT_*NAME*

Text to use as a license. Useful when the license is not in the distribution files and its text is short.

Example 5.29. LICENSE_TEXT

```
LICENSE=        UNKNOWN
```

```
LICENSE_NAME=    unknown
LICENSE_TEXT=    This program is NOT in public domain.\
                 It can be freely distributed for non-commercial purposes only,\
                 and THERE IS NO WARRANTY FOR THIS PROGRAM.
LICENSE_PERMS=   dist-mirror no-dist-sell pkg-mirror no-pkg-sell auto-accept
```

5.7.7. LICENSE_DISTFILES and LICENSE_DISTFILES_*NAME*

The distribution files to which the licenses apply. Defaults to all the distribution files.

Example 5.30. LICENSE_DISTFILES

Used when the distribution files do not all have the same license. For example, one has a code license, and another has some artwork that cannot be redistributed:

```
MASTER_SITES=    SF/some-game
DISTFILES=       ${DISTNAME}${EXTRACT_SUFX} artwork.zip

LICENSE=         BSD3CLAUSE ARTWORK
LICENSE_COMB=    dual
LICENSE_NAME_ARTWORK=     The game artwork license
LICENSE_TEXT_ARTWORK=     The README says that the files cannot be redistributed
LICENSE_PERMS_ARTWORK=    pkg-mirror pkg-sell auto-accept
LICENSE_DISTFILES_BSD3CLAUSE=   ${DISTNAME}${EXTRACT_SUFX}
LICENSE_DISTFILES_ARTWORK= artwork.zip
```

5.7.8. LICENSE_COMB

Set to multi if all licenses apply. Set to dual if any license applies. Defaults to single.

Example 5.31. Dual Licenses

When a port says "This software may be distributed under the GNU General Public License or the Artistic License", it means that either license can be used. Use this:

```
LICENSE= ART10 GPLv1
LICENSE_COMB=    dual
```

If license files are provided, use this:

```
LICENSE= ART10 GPLv1
LICENSE_COMB=    dual
LICENSE_FILE_ART10=      ${WRKSRC}/Artistic
LICENSE_FILE_GPLv1=      ${WRKSRC}/Copying
```

Example 5.32. Multiple Licenses

When part of a port has one license, and another part has a different license, use multi:

```
LICENSE= GPLv2 LGPL21+
```

```
LICENSE_COMB= multi
```

5.8. PORTSCOUT

Portscout is an automated distfile check utility for the FreeBSD Ports Collection, described in detail in Section 16.5, "Portscout: the FreeBSD Ports Distfile Scanner".

PORTSCOUT defines special conditions within which the Portscout distfile scanner is restricted.

Situations where PORTSCOUT is set include:

- When distfiles have to be ignored, whether for specific versions, or specific minor revisions. For example, to exclude version *8.2* from distfile version checks because it is known to be broken, add:

```
PORTSCOUT= ignore:8.2
```

- When specific versions or specific major and minor revisions of a distfile must be checked. For example, if only version *0.6.4* must be monitored because newer versions have compatibility issues with FreeBSD, add:

```
PORTSCOUT= limit:^0\.6\.4
```

- When URLs listing the available versions differ from the download URLs. For example, to limit distfile version checks to the download page for the databases/pgtune port, add:

```
PORTSCOUT= site:http://pgfoundry.org/frs/?group_id=1000416
```

5.9. Dependencies

Many ports depend on other ports. This is a very convenient feature of most Unix-like operating systems, including FreeBSD. Multiple ports can share a common dependency, rather than bundling that dependency with every port or package that needs it. There are seven variables that can be used to ensure that all the required bits will be on the user's machine. There are also some pre-supported dependency variables for common cases, plus a few more to control the behavior of dependencies.

5.9.1. LIB_DEPENDS

This variable specifies the shared libraries this port depends on. It is a list of *lib:dir* tuples where *lib* is the name of the shared library, *dir* is the directory in which to find it in case it is not available. For example,

```
LIB_DEPENDS=    libjpeg.so:graphics/jpeg
```

will check for a shared jpeg library with any version, and descend into the graphics/jpeg subdirectory of the ports tree to build and install it if it is not found.

The dependency is checked twice, once from within the build target and then from within the install target. Also, the name of the dependency is put into the package so that pkg install (see pkg-install(8)) will automatically install it if it is not on the user's system.

5.9.2. RUN_DEPENDS

This variable specifies executables or files this port depends on during run-time. It is a list of *path:dir*[*:target*] tuples where *path* is the name of the executable or file, *dir* is the directory in which to find it in case it is not available, and *target* is the target to call in that directory. If *path* starts with a slash (/), it is treated as a file and its existence is tested with test -e; otherwise, it is assumed to be an executable, and which -s is used to determine if the program exists in the search path.

For example,

```
RUN_DEPENDS= ${LOCALBASE}/news/bin/innd:news/inn \
  xmlcatmgr:textproc/xmlcatmgr
```

will check if the file or directory /usr/local/news/bin/innd exists, and build and install it from the news/inn subdirectory of the ports tree if it is not found. It will also see if an executable called xmlcatmgr is in the search path, and descend into textproc/xmlcatmgr to build and install it if it is not found.

Note

In this case, innd is actually an executable; if an executable is in a place that is not expected to be in the search path, use the full pathname.

Note

The official search PATH used on the ports build cluster is

```
/sbin:/bin:/usr/sbin:/usr/bin:/usr/local/sbin:/usr/local/bin
```

The dependency is checked from within the install target. Also, the name of the dependency is put into the package so that pkg install (see pkg-install(8)) will automatically install it if it is not on the user's system. The *target* part can be omitted if it is the same as DEPENDS_TARGET.

A quite common situation is when RUN_DEPENDS is literally the same as BUILD_DEPENDS, especially if ported software is written in a scripted language or if it requires the same build and run-time environment. In this case, it is both tempting and intuitive to directly assign one to the other:

```
RUN_DEPENDS= ${BUILD_DEPENDS}
```

However, such assignment can pollute run-time dependencies with entries not defined in the port's original BUILD_DEPENDS. This happens because of make(1)'s lazy evaluation of variable assignment. Consider a Makefile with USE_*, which are processed by ports/Mk/bsd.*.mk to augment initial build dependencies. For example, USES= gmake adds devel/gmake to BUILD_DEPENDS. To prevent such additional dependencies from polluting RUN_DEPENDS, create another variable with the current content of BUILD_DEPENDS and assign it to both BUILD_DE-PENDS and RUN_DEPENDS:

```
MY_DEPENDS= some:devel/some \
  other:lang/other
BUILD_DEPENDS= ${MY_DEPENDS}
RUN_DEPENDS= ${MY_DEPENDS}
```

Important

Do not use := to assign BUILD_DEPENDS to RUN_DEPENDS or vice-versa. All variables are expand-ed immediately, which is exactly the wrong thing to do and almost always a failure.

5.9.3. BUILD_DEPENDS

This variable specifies executables or files this port requires to build. Like RUN_DEPENDS, it is a list of *path:dir[:tar-get]* tuples. For example,

```
BUILD_DEPENDS= unzip:archivers/unzip
```

will check for an executable called unzip, and descend into the archivers/unzip subdirectory of the ports tree to build and install it if it is not found.

> **Note**
>
> "build" here means everything from extraction to compilation. The dependency is checked from within the extract target. The *target* part can be omitted if it is the same as DE-PENDS_TARGET

5.9.4. FETCH_DEPENDS

This variable specifies executables or files this port requires to fetch. Like the previous two, it is a list of *path*:*dir*[:*target*] tuples. For example,

```
FETCH_DEPENDS= ncftp2:net/ncftp2
```

will check for an executable called ncftp2, and descend into the net/ncftp2 subdirectory of the ports tree to build and install it if it is not found.

The dependency is checked from within the fetch target. The *target* part can be omitted if it is the same as DEPENDS_TARGET.

5.9.5. EXTRACT_DEPENDS

This variable specifies executables or files this port requires for extraction. Like the previous, it is a list of *path*:*dir*[:*target*] tuples. For example,

```
EXTRACT_DEPENDS= unzip:archivers/unzip
```

will check for an executable called unzip, and descend into the archivers/unzip subdirectory of the ports tree to build and install it if it is not found.

The dependency is checked from within the extract target. The *target* part can be omitted if it is the same as DEPENDS_TARGET.

> **Note**
>
> Use this variable only if the extraction does not already work (the default assumes tar) and cannot be made to work using USES=tar , USES=lha or USES=zip described in Chapter 17, *Using USES Macros*.

5.9.6. PATCH_DEPENDS

This variable specifies executables or files this port requires to patch. Like the previous, it is a list of *path*:*dir*[:*target*] tuples. For example,

```
PATCH_DEPENDS= ${NONEXISTENT}:java/jfc:extract
```

will descend into the java/jfc subdirectory of the ports tree to extract it.

The dependency is checked from within the patch target. The *target* part can be omitted if it is the same as DEPENDS_TARGET.

5.9.7. USES

Parameters can be added to define different features and dependencies used by the port. They are specified by adding this line to the Makefile:

```
USES= feature[:arguments]
```

For the complete list of values, please see Chapter 17, *Using USES Macros*.

Warning

USES cannot be assigned after inclusion of bsd.port.pre.mk.

5.9.8. USE_*

Several variables exist to define common dependencies shared by many ports. Their use is optional, but helps to reduce the verbosity of the port Makefiles. Each of them is styled as USE_*. These variables may be used only in the port Makefiles and ports/Mk/bsd.*.mk . They are not meant for user-settable options — use PORT_OPTIONS for that purpose.

Note

It is *always* incorrect to set any USE_* in /etc/make.conf . For instance, setting

```
USE_GCC=X.Y
```

(where X.Y is version number) would add a dependency on gccXY for every port, including lang/gccXY itself!

Table 5.7. USE_*

Variable	Means
USE_GCC	The port requires GCC (gcc or g++) to build. Some ports need any GCC version, some require modern, recent versions. It is typically set to any (in this case, GCC from base would be used on versions of FreeBSD that still have it, or lang/gcc port would be installed when default C/C++ compiler is Clang); or yes (means always use stable, modern GCC from lang/gcc port). The exact version can also be specified, with a value such as 4.7. The minimal required version can be specified as 4.6+. The GCC from the base system is used when it satisfies the requested version, otherwise an appropriate compiler is built from the port, and CC and CXX are adjusted accordingly.

Variables related to gmake and configure are described in Section 6.5, "Building Mechanisms", while autoconf, automake and libtool are described in Section 6.6, "Using GNU Autotools". Perl related variables are described in Section 6.8, "Using Perl". X11 variables are listed in Section 6.9, "Using X11". Section 6.10, "Using GNOME" deals with GNOME and Section 6.13, "Using KDE" with KDE related variables. Section 6.15, "Using Java" documents Java variables, while Section 6.16, "Web Applications, Apache and PHP" contains information on Apache, PHP and PEAR modules. Python is discussed in Section 6.17, "Using Python", while Ruby in Section 6.19, "Using Ruby". Section 6.20, "Using SDL" provides variables used for SDL applications and finally, Section 6.24, "Using Xfce" contains information on Xfce.

5.9.9. Minimal Version of a Dependency

A minimal version of a dependency can be specified in any *_DEPENDS except LIB_DEPENDS using this syntax:

```
p5-Spiffy>=0.26:devel/p5-Spiffy
```

The first field contains a dependent package name, which must match the entry in the package database, a comparison sign, and a package version. The dependency is satisfied if p5-Spiffy-0.26 or newer is installed on the machine.

5.9.10. Notes on Dependencies

As mentioned above, the default target to call when a dependency is required is DEPENDS_TARGET. It defaults to install. This is a user variable; it is never defined in a port's Makefile. If the port needs a special way to handle a dependency, use the :target part of *_DEPENDS instead of redefining DEPENDS_TARGET.

When running make clean, the port dependencies are automatically cleaned too. If this is not desirable, define NOCLEANDEPENDS in the environment. This may be particularly desirable if the port has something that takes a long time to rebuild in its dependency list, such as KDE, GNOME or Mozilla.

To depend on another port unconditionally, use the variable ${NONEXISTENT} as the first field of BUILD_DEPENDS or RUN_DEPENDS. Use this only when the source of the other port is needed. Compilation time can be saved by specifying the target too. For instance

```
BUILD_DEPENDS= ${NONEXISTENT}:graphics/jpeg:extract
```

will always descend to the jpeg port and extract it.

5.9.11. Circular Dependencies Are Fatal

> **Important**
>
> Do not introduce any circular dependencies into the ports tree!

The ports building technology does not tolerate circular dependencies. If one is introduced, someone, somewhere in the world, will have their FreeBSD installation broken almost immediately, with many others quickly to follow. These can really be hard to detect. If in doubt, before making that change, make sure to run: cd /usr/ports; make index. That process can be quite slow on older machines, but it may be able to save a large number of people, including yourself, a lot of grief in the process.

5.9.12. Problems Caused by Automatic Dependencies

Dependencies must be declared either explicitly or by using the OPTIONS framework. Using other methods like automatic detection complicates indexing, which causes problems for port and package management.

Example 5.33. Wrong Declaration of an Optional Dependency

```
.include <bsd.port.pre.mk>

.if exists(${LOCALBASE}/bin/foo)
LIB_DEPENDS= libbar.so:foo/bar
```

```
.endif
```

The problem with trying to automatically add dependencies is that files and settings outside an individual port can change at any time. For example: an index is built, then a batch of ports are installed. But one of the ports installs the tested file. The index is now incorrect, because an installed port unexpectedly has a new dependency. The index may still be wrong even after rebuilding if other ports also determine their need for dependencies based on the existence of other files.

Example 5.34. Correct Declaration of an Optional Dependency

```
OPTIONS_DEFINE= BAR
BAR_DESC= Calling cellphones via bar

BAR_LIB_DEPENDS= libbar.so:foo/bar
```

Testing option variables is the correct method. It will not cause inconsistencies in the index of a batch of ports, provided the options were defined prior to the index build. Simple scripts can then be used to automate the building, installation, and updating of these ports and their packages.

5.9.13. USE_* and WANT_*

USE_* are set by the port maintainer to define software on which this port depends. A port that needs Firefox would set

```
USE_FIREFOX= yes
```

Some USE_* can accept version numbers or other parameters. For example, a port that requires Apache 2.2 would set

```
USE_APACHE= 22
```

For more control over dependencies in some cases, WANT_* are available to more precisely specify what is needed. For example, consider the mail/squirrelmail port. This port needs some PHP modules, which are listed in USE_PHP:

```
USE_PHP= session mhash gettext mbstring pcre openssl xml
```

Those modules may be available in CLI or web versions, so the web version is selected with WANT_*:

```
WANT_PHP_WEB= yes
```

Available USE_* and WANT_* are defined in the files in /usr/ports/Mk .

5.10. Slave Ports and MASTERDIR

If the port needs to build slightly different versions of packages by having a variable (for instance, resolution, or paper size) take different values, create one subdirectory per package to make it easier for users to see what to do, but try to share as many files as possible between ports. Typically, by using variables cleverly, only a very short Makefile is needed in all but one of the directories. In the sole Makefile, use MASTERDIR to specify the directory where the rest of the files are. Also, use a variable as part of PKGNAMESUFFIX so the packages will have different names.

This will be best demonstrated by an example. This is part of print/pkfonts300/Makefile ;

```
PORTNAME= pkfonts${RESOLUTION}
PORTVERSION= 1.0
DISTFILES= pk${RESOLUTION}.tar.gz

PLIST=  ${PKGDIR}/pkg-plist.${RESOLUTION}

.if !defined(RESOLUTION)
RESOLUTION= 300
.else
.if ${RESOLUTION} != 118 && ${RESOLUTION} != 240 && \
  ${RESOLUTION} != 300 && ${RESOLUTION} != 360 && \
  ${RESOLUTION} != 400 && ${RESOLUTION} != 600
.BEGIN:
@${ECHO_MSG} "Error: invalid value for RESOLUTION: \"${RESOLUTION}\""
@${ECHO_MSG} "Possible values are: 118, 240, 300, 360, 400 and 600."
@${FALSE}
.endif
.endif
```

print/pkfonts300 also has all the regular patches, package files, etc. Running make there, it will take the default value for the resolution (300) and build the port normally.

As for other resolutions, this is the *entire* print/pkfonts360/Makefile :

```
RESOLUTION= 360
MASTERDIR= ${.CURDIR}/../pkfonts300

.include "${MASTERDIR}/Makefile"
```

(print/pkfonts118/Makefile , print/pkfonts600/Makefile , and all the other are similar). MASTERDIR definition tells bsd.port.mk that the regular set of subdirectories like FILESDIR and SCRIPTDIR are to be found under pkfonts300. The RESOLUTION=360 line will override the RESOLUTION=300 line in pkfonts300/Makefile and the port will be built with resolution set to 360.

5.11. Man Pages

If the port anchors its man tree somewhere other than PREFIX, use MANDIRS to specify those directories. Note that the files corresponding to manual pages must be placed in pkg-plist along with the rest of the files. The purpose of MANDIRS is to enable automatic compression of manual pages, therefore the file names are suffixed with .gz.

5.12. Info Files

If the package needs to install GNU info files, list them in INFO (without the trailing .info), one entry per document. These files are assumed to be installed to PREFIX/INFO_PATH. Change INFO_PATH if the package uses a different location. However, this is not recommended. These entries contain just the path relative to PREFIX/INFO_PATH. For example, lang/gcc34 installs info files to PREFIX/INFO_PATH/gcc34 , and INFO will be something like this:

```
INFO= gcc34/cpp gcc34/cppinternals gcc34/g77 ...
```

Appropriate installation/de-installation code will be automatically added to the temporary pkg-plist before package registration.

5.13. Makefile Options

Many applications can be built with optional or differing configurations. Examples include choice of natural (human) language, GUI versus command-line, or type of database to support. Users may need a different configuration than the default, so the ports system provides hooks the port author can use to control which variant will be built. Supporting these options properly will make users happy, and effectively provide two or more ports for the price of one.

5.13.1. OPTIONS

5.13.1.1. Background

OPTIONS_* give the user installing the port a dialog showing the available options, and then saves those options to ${PORT_DBDIR}/${OPTIONS_NAME}/options. The next time the port is built, the options are reused. PORT_DBDIR defaults to /var/db/ports . OPTIONS_NAME is to the port origin with an underscore as the space separator, for example, for dns/bind99 it will be dns_bind99 .

When the user runs make config (or runs make build for the first time), the framework checks for ${PORT_DB-DIR}/${OPTIONS_NAME}/options. If that file does not exist, the values of OPTIONS_* are used, and a dialog box is displayed where the options can be enabled or disabled. Then options is saved and the configured variables are used when building the port.

If a new version of the port adds new OPTIONS, the dialog will be presented to the user with the saved values of old OPTIONS prefilled.

make showconfig shows the saved configuration. Use make rmconfig to remove the saved configuration.

5.13.1.2. Syntax

OPTIONS_DEFINE contains a list of OPTIONS to be used. These are independent of each other and are not grouped:

```
OPTIONS_DEFINE= OPT1 OPT2
```

Once defined, OPTIONS are described (optional, but strongly recommended):

```
OPT1_DESC= Describe OPT1
OPT2_DESC= Describe OPT2
OPT3_DESC= Describe OPT3
OPT4_DESC= Describe OPT4
OPT5_DESC= Describe OPT5
OPT6_DESC= Describe OPT6
```

ports/Mk/bsd.options.desc.mk has descriptions for many common OPTIONS. While often useful, override them if the description is insufficient for the port.

Tip

When describing options, view it from the perspective of the user: "What functionality does it change?" and "Why would I want to enable this?" Do not just repeat the name. For example, describing the NLS option as "include NLS support" does not help the user, who can already see the option name but may not know what it means. Describing it as "Native Language Support via gettext utilities" is much more helpful.

Important

Option names are always in all uppercase. They cannot use mixed case or lowercase.

OPTIONS can be grouped as radio choices, where only one choice from each group is allowed:

```
OPTIONS_SINGLE=  SG1
```

```
OPTIONS_SINGLE_SG1= OPT3 OPT4
```

Warning

There *must* be one of each `OPTIONS_SINGLE` group selected at all times for the options to be valid. One option of each group *must* be added to `OPTIONS_DEFAULT`.

`OPTIONS` can be grouped as radio choices, where none or only one choice from each group is allowed:

```
OPTIONS_RADIO=  RG1
OPTIONS_RADIO_RG1= OPT7 OPT8
```

`OPTIONS` can also be grouped as "multiple-choice" lists, where *at least one* option must be enabled:

```
OPTIONS_MULTI=  MG1
OPTIONS_MULTI_MG1= OPT5 OPT6
```

`OPTIONS` can also be grouped as "multiple-choice" lists, where none or any option can be enabled:

```
OPTIONS_GROUP=  GG1
OPTIONS_GROUP_GG1= OPT9 OPT10
```

`OPTIONS` are unset by default, unless they are listed in `OPTIONS_DEFAULT`:

```
OPTIONS_DEFAULT= OPT1 OPT3 OPT6
```

`OPTIONS` definitions must appear before the inclusion of `bsd.port.options.mk`. `PORT_OPTIONS` values can only be tested after the inclusion of `bsd.port.options.mk`. Inclusion of `bsd.port.pre.mk` can be used instead, too, and is still widely used in ports written before the introduction of `bsd.port.options.mk`. But be aware that some variables will not work as expected after the inclusion of `bsd.port.pre.mk`, typically some `USE_*` flags.

Example 5.35. Simple Use of OPTIONS

```
OPTIONS_DEFINE= FOO BAR
FOO_DESC= Option foo support
BAR_DESC= Feature bar support

OPTIONS_DEFAULT=FOO

# Will add --with-foo / --without-foo
FOO_CONFIGURE_WITH= foo
BAR_RUN_DEPENDS= bar:bar/bar

.include <bsd.port.mk>
```

Example 5.36. Check for Unset Port OPTIONS

```
.if ! ${PORT_OPTIONS:MEXAMPLES}
CONFIGURE_ARGS+=--without-examples
.endif
```

The form shown above is discouraged. The preferred method is using a configure knob to really enable and disable the feature to match the option:

```
# Will add --with-examples / --without-examples
EXAMPLES_CONFIGURE_WITH= examples
```

Example 5.37. Practical Use of OPTIONS

```
OPTIONS_DEFINE=  EXAMPLES

OPTIONS_SINGLE=  BACKEND
OPTIONS_SINGLE_BACKEND= MYSQL PGSQL BDB

OPTIONS_MULTI=  AUTH
OPTIONS_MULTI_AUTH= LDAP PAM SSL

EXAMPLES_DESC=  Install extra examples
MYSQL_DESC=  Use MySQL as backend
PGSQL_DESC=  Use PostgreSQL as backend
BDB_DESC=  Use Berkeley DB as backend
LDAP_DESC=  Build with LDAP authentication support
PAM_DESC=  Build with PAM support
SSL_DESC=  Build with OpenSSL support

OPTIONS_DEFAULT= PGSQL LDAP SSL

# Will add USE_PGSQL=yes
PGSQL_USE= pgsql=yes
# Will add --enable-postgres / --disable-postgres
PGSQL_CONFIGURE_ENABLE= postgres

ICU_LIB_DEPENDS= libicuuc.so:devel/icu

# Will add --with-examples / --without-examples
EXAMPLES_CONFIGURE_WITH= examples

# Check other OPTIONS

.include <bsd.port.mk>
```

5.13.1.3. Default Options

These options are always on by default.

- DOCS — build and install documentation.

- NLS — Native Language Support.

- EXAMPLES — build and install examples.

- IPV6 — IPv6 protocol support.

Note

There is no need to add these to OPTIONS_DEFAULT. To have them active, and show up in the options selection dialog, however, they must be added to OPTIONS_DEFINE.

5.13.2. Feature Auto-Activation

When using a GNU configure script, keep an eye on which optional features are activated by auto-detection. Explicitly disable optional features that are not needed by adding --without-xxx or --disable-xxx in CONFIGURE_ARGS.

Example 5.38. Wrong Handling of an Option

```
.if ${PORT_OPTIONS:MFOO}
LIB_DEPENDS+=  libfoo.so:devel/foo
CONFIGURE_ARGS+= --enable-foo
.endif
```

In the example above, imagine a library libfoo is installed on the system. The user does not want this application to use libfoo, so he toggled the option off in the make config dialog. But the application's configure script detects the library present in the system and includes its support in the resulting executable. Now when the user decides to remove libfoo from the system, the ports system does not protest (no dependency on libfoo was recorded) but the application breaks.

Example 5.39. Correct Handling of an Option

```
FOO_LIB_DEPENDS=  libfoo.so:devel/foo
# Will add --enable-foo / --disable-foo
FOO_CONFIGURE_ENABLE= foo
```

Note

Under some circumstances, the shorthand conditional syntax can cause problems with complex constructs. The errors are usually Malformed conditional, an alternative syntax can be used.

```
.if !empty(VARIABLE:MVALUE)
```

as an alternative to

```
.if ${VARIABLE:MVALUE}
```

5.13.3. Options Helpers

There are some macros to help simplify conditional values which differ based on the options set. For easier access, a comprehensive list is provided:

PLIST_SUB , SUB_LIST
   For automatic %%OPT%% and %%NO_OPT%% generation, see Section 5.13.3.1, "OPTIONS_SUB".

   For more complex usage, see Section 5.13.3.11, "Generic Variables Replacement, *OPT_VARIABLE* and *OPT_VARIABLE*_OFF".

CONFIGURE_ARGS
   For --enable-*x* and --disable-*x*, see Section 5.13.3.3.1, "*OPT*_CONFIGURE_ENABLE".

For --with-*x* and --without-*x*, see Section 5.13.3.3.2, "*OPT*_CONFIGURE_WITH".

For all other cases, see Section 5.13.3.3.3, "*OPT*_CONFIGURE_ON and *OPT*_CONFIGURE_OFF".

CMAKE_ARGS

For arguments that are booleans (on, off, true, false, 0, 1) see Section 5.13.3.4.2, "*OPT*_CMAKE_BOOL and *OP-T*_CMAKE_BOOL_OFF".

For all other cases, see Section 5.13.3.4.1, "*OPT*_CMAKE_ON and *OPT*_CMAKE_OFF".

MESON_ARGS

For arguments that take true or false, see Section 5.13.3.5.2, "*OPT*_MESON_TRUE and *OPT*_MESON_FALSE".

For arguments that take yes or no, use Section 5.13.3.5.3, "*OPT*_MESON_YES and *OPT*_MESON_NO".

For all other cases, use Section 5.13.3.5.1, "*OPT*_MESON_ON and *OPT*_MESON_OFF".

QMAKE_ARGS

See Section 5.13.3.6, "*OPT*_QMAKE_ON and *OPT*_QMAKE_OFF".

USE_*

See Section 5.13.3.2, "*OPT*_USE and *OPT*_USE_OFF".

*_DEPENDS

See Section 5.13.3.10, "Dependencies, *OPT*_DEPTYPE and *OPT*_DEPTYPE_OFF".

* (Any variable)

The most used variables have direct helpers, see Section 5.13.3.11, "Generic Variables Replacement, *OP-T*_VARIABLE and *OPT*_VARIABLE_OFF".

For any variable without a specific helper, see Section 5.13.3.9, "*OPT*_VARS and *OPT*_VARS_OFF".

Options dependencies

When an option need another option to work, see Section 5.13.3.7, "*OPT*_IMPLIES".

Options conflicts

When an option cannot work if another is also enabled, see Section 5.13.3.8, "*OPT*_PREVENTS and *OPT*_PREVENTS_MSG".

Build targets

When an option need some extra processing, see Section 5.13.3.12, "Additional Build Targets, *target-OPT*-on and *target-OPT*-off".

5.13.3.1. OPTIONS_SUB

If OPTIONS_SUB is set to yes then each of the options added to OPTIONS_DEFINE will be added to PLIST_SUB and SUB_LIST, for example:

```
OPTIONS_DEFINE= OPT1
OPTIONS_SUB= yes
```

is equivalent to:

```
OPTIONS_DEFINE= OPT1

.include <bsd.port.options.mk>

.if ${PORT_OPTIONS:MOPT1}
PLIST_SUB+= OPT1="" NO_OPT1="@comment "
SUB_LIST+= OPT1="" NO_OPT1="@comment "
```

```
.else
PLIST_SUB+= OPT1="@comment " NO_OPT1=""
SUB_LIST+= OPT1="@comment " NO_OPT1=""
.endif
```

 Note

The value of OPTIONS_SUB is ignored. Setting it to any value will add PLIST_SUB and SUB_LIST entries for *all* options.

5.13.3.2. *OPT*_USE and *OPT*_USE_OFF

When option *OPT* is selected, for each *key*=*value* pair in *OPT*_USE, *value* is appended to the corresponding USE_*KEY*. If *value* has spaces in it, replace them with commas and they will be changed back to spaces during processing. *OPT*_USE_OFF works the same way, but when OPT is *not* selected. For example:

```
OPTIONS_DEFINE= OPT1
OPT1_USE= mysql=yes xorg=x11,xextproto,xext,xrandr
OPT1_USE_OFF= openssl=yes
```

is equivalent to:

```
OPTIONS_DEFINE= OPT1

.include <bsd.port.options.mk>

.if ${PORT_OPTIONS:MOPT1}
USE_MYSQL= yes
USE_XORG= x11 xextproto xext xrandr
.else
USE_OPENSSL= yes
.endif
```

5.13.3.3. CONFIGURE_ARGS Helpers

5.13.3.3.1. *OPT*_CONFIGURE_ENABLE

When option *OPT* is selected, for each *entry* in *OPT*_CONFIGURE_ENABLE then --enable-*entry* is appended to CONFIGURE_ARGS. When option *OPT* is *not* selected, --disable-*entry* is appended to CONFIGURE_ARGS. An optional argument can be specified with an = symbol. This argument is only appended to the --enable-*entry* configure option. For example:

```
OPTIONS_DEFINE= OPT1 OPT2
OPT1_CONFIGURE_ENABLE= test1 test2
OPT2_CONFIGURE_ENABLE= test2=exhaustive
```

is equivalent to:

```
OPTIONS_DEFINE= OPT1

.include <bsd.port.options.mk>

.if ${PORT_OPTIONS:MOPT1}
CONFIGURE_ARGS+= --enable-test1 --enable-test2
.else
CONFIGURE_ARGS+= --disable-test1 --disable-test2
.endif

.if ${PORT_OPTIONS:MOPT2}
CONFIGURE_ARGS+= --enable-test2=exhaustive
```

```
.else
CONFIGURE_ARGS+= --disable-test2
.endif
```

5.13.3.3.2. *OPT*_CONFIGURE_WITH

When option *OPT* is selected, for each *entry* in *OPT*_CONFIGURE_WITH then --with-*entry* is appended to CON-FIGURE_ARGS. When option *OPT* is *not* selected, --without-*entry* is appended to CONFIGURE_ARGS. An optional argument can be specified with an = symbol. This argument is only appended to the --with-*entry* configure option. For example:

```
OPTIONS_DEFINE= OPT1 OPT2
OPT1_CONFIGURE_WITH= test1
OPT2_CONFIGURE_WITH= test2=exhaustive
```

is equivalent to:

```
OPTIONS_DEFINE= OPT1 OPT2

.include <bsd.port.options.mk>

.if ${PORT_OPTIONS:MOPT1}
CONFIGURE_ARGS+= --with-test1
.else
CONFIGURE_ARGS+= --without-test1
.endif

.if ${PORT_OPTIONS:MOPT2}
CONFIGURE_ARGS+= --with-test2=exhaustive
.else
CONFIGURE_ARGS+= --without-test2
.endif
```

5.13.3.3.3. *OPT*_CONFIGURE_ON and *OPT*_CONFIGURE_OFF

When option *OPT* is selected, the value of *OPT*_CONFIGURE_ON, if defined, is appended to CONFIGURE_ARGS. *OPT*_CON-FIGURE_OFF works the same way, but when OPT is *not* selected. For example:

```
OPTIONS_DEFINE= OPT1
OPT1_CONFIGURE_ON= --add-test
OPT1_CONFIGURE_OFF= --no-test
```

is equivalent to:

```
OPTIONS_DEFINE= OPT1

.include <bsd.port.options.mk>

.if ${PORT_OPTIONS:MOPT1}
CONFIGURE_ARGS+= --add-test
.else
CONFIGURE_ARGS+= --no-test
.endif
```

> ## Tip
>
> Most of the time, the helpers in Section 5.13.3.3.1, "*OPT*_CONFIGURE_ENABLE" and Section 5.13.3.3.2, "*OPT*_CONFIGURE_WITH" provide a shorter and more comprehensive functionality.

5.13.3.4. CMAKE_ARGS **Helpers**

5.13.3.4.1. *OPT*_CMAKE_ON **and** *OPT*_CMAKE_OFF

When option *OPT* is selected, the value of *OPT*_CMAKE_ON, if defined, is appended to CMAKE_ARGS . *OPT*_CMAKE_OFF works the same way, but when OPT is *not* selected. For example:

```
OPTIONS_DEFINE= OPT1
OPT1_CMAKE_ON= -DTEST:BOOL=true -DDEBUG:BOOL=true
OPT1_CMAKE_OFF= -DOPTIMIZE:BOOL=true
```

is equivalent to:

```
OPTIONS_DEFINE= OPT1

.include <bsd.port.options.mk>

.if ${PORT_OPTIONS:MOPT1}
CMAKE_ARGS+= -DTEST:BOOL=true -DDEBUG:BOOL=true
.else
CMAKE_ARGS+= -DOPTIMIZE:BOOL=true
.endif
```

> **Tip**
>
> See Section 5.13.3.4.2, "*OPT*_CMAKE_BOOL and *OPT*_CMAKE_BOOL_OFF" for a shorter helper when the value is boolean.

5.13.3.4.2. *OPT*_CMAKE_BOOL **and** *OPT*_CMAKE_BOOL_OFF

When option *OPT* is selected, for each *entry* in *OPT*_CMAKE_BOOL then -D*entry*:BOOL=true is appended to CMAKE_ARGS . When option *OPT* is *not* selected, -D*entry*:BOOL=false is appended to CONFIGURE_ARGS. *OPT*_C-MAKE_BOOL_OFF is the oposite, -D*entry*:BOOL=false is appended to CMAKE_ARGS when the option is selected, and -D*entry*:BOOL=true when the option is *not* selected. For example:

```
OPTIONS_DEFINE= OPT1
OPT1_CMAKE_BOOL= TEST DEBUG
OPT1_CMAKE_BOOL_OFF= OPTIMIZE
```

is equivalent to:

```
OPTIONS_DEFINE= OPT1

.include <bsd.port.options.mk>

.if ${PORT_OPTIONS:MOPT1}
CMAKE_ARGS+= -DTEST:BOOL=true -DDEBUG:BOOL=true \
  -DOPTIMIZE:BOOL=false
.else
CMAKE_ARGS+= -DTEST:BOOL=false -DDEBUG:BOOL=false \
  -DOPTIMIZE:BOOL=true
.endif
```

5.13.3.5. MESON_ARGS **Helpers**

5.13.3.5.1. *OPT*_MESON_ON **and** *OPT*_MESON_OFF

When option *OPT* is selected, the value of *OPT*_MESON_ON , if defined, is appended to MESON_ARGS . *OPT*_MESON_OFF works the same way, but when OPT is *not* selected. For example:

```
OPTIONS_DEFINE= OPT1
OPT1_MESON_ON= -Dopt=1
OPT1_MESON_OFF= -Dopt=2
```

is equivalent to:

```
OPTIONS_DEFINE= OPT1

.include <bsd.port.options.mk>

.if ${PORT_OPTIONS:MOPT1}
MESON_ARGS+= -Dopt=1
.else
MESON_ARGS+= -Dopt=2
.endif
```

5.13.3.5.2. *OPT*_MESON_TRUE and *OPT*_MESON_FALSE

When option *OPT* is selected, for each *entry* in *OPT*_MESON_TRUE then -D*entry*=true is appended to CMAKE_ARGS. When option *OPT* is *not* selected, -D*entry*=false is appended to CONFIGURE_ARGS. *OPT*_MESON_FALSE is the oposite, -D*entry*=false is appended to CMAKE_ARGS when the option is selected, and -D*entry*=true when the option is *not* selected. For example:

```
OPTIONS_DEFINE= OPT1
OPT1_MESON_TRUE= test debug
OPT1_MESON_FALSE= optimize
```

is equivalent to:

```
OPTIONS_DEFINE= OPT1

.include <bsd.port.options.mk>

.if ${PORT_OPTIONS:MOPT1}
CMAKE_ARGS+= -Dtest=true -Ddebug=true \
  -Doptimize=false
.else
CMAKE_ARGS+= -Dtest=false -Ddebug=false \
  -Doptimize=true
.endif
```

5.13.3.5.3. *OPT*_MESON_YES and *OPT*_MESON_NO

When option *OPT* is selected, for each *entry* in *OPT*_MESON_YES then -D*entry*=yes is appended to CMAKE_ARGS. When option *OPT* is *not* selected, -D*entry*=no is appended to CONFIGURE_ARGS. *OPT*_MESON_NO is the oposite, -D*entry*=no is appended to CMAKE_ARGS when the option is selected, and -D*entry*=yes when the option is *not* selected. For example:

```
OPTIONS_DEFINE= OPT1
OPT1_MESON_YES= test debug
OPT1_MESON_NO= optimize
```

is equivalent to:

```
OPTIONS_DEFINE= OPT1

.include <bsd.port.options.mk>

.if ${PORT_OPTIONS:MOPT1}
CMAKE_ARGS+= -Dtest=yes -Ddebug=yes \
  -Doptimize=no
.else
CMAKE_ARGS+= -Dtest=no -Ddebug=no \
  -Doptimize=yes
```

```
.endif
```

5.13.3.6. *OPT*_QMAKE_ON and *OPT*_QMAKE_OFF

When option *OPT* is selected, the value of *OPT*_QMAKE_ON, if defined, is appended to QMAKE_ARGS . *OPT*_QMAKE_OFF works the same way, but when OPT is *not* selected. For example:

```
OPTIONS_DEFINE= OPT1
OPT1_QMAKE_ON= -DTEST:BOOL=true
OPT1_QMAKE_OFF= -DPRODUCTION:BOOL=true
```

is equivalent to:

```
OPTIONS_DEFINE= OPT1

.include <bsd.port.options.mk>

.if ${PORT_OPTIONS:MOPT1}
QMAKE_ARGS+= -DTEST:BOOL=true
.else
QMAKE_ARGS+= -DPRODUCTION:BOOL=true
.endif
```

5.13.3.7. *OPT*_IMPLIES

Provides a way to add dependencies between options.

When *OPT* is selected, all the options listed in this variable will be selected too. Using the *OPT*_CONFIGURE_ENABLE described earlier to illustrate:

```
OPTIONS_DEFINE= OPT1 OPT2
OPT1_IMPLIES= OPT2

OPT1_CONFIGURE_ENABLE= opt1
OPT2_CONFIGURE_ENABLE= opt2
```

Is equivalent to:

```
OPTIONS_DEFINE= OPT1 OPT2

.include <bsd.port.options.mk>

.if ${PORT_OPTIONS:MOPT1}
CONFIGURE_ARGS+= --enable-opt1
.else
CONFIGURE_ARGS+= --disable-opt1
.endif

.if ${PORT_OPTIONS:MOPT2} || ${PORT_OPTIONS:MOPT1}
CONFIGURE_ARGS+= --enable-opt2
.else
CONFIGURE_ARGS+= --disable-opt2
.endif
```

Example 5.40. Simple Use of *OPT*_IMPLIES

This port has a X11 option, and a GNOME option that needs the X11 option to be selected to build.

```
OPTIONS_DEFINE= X11 GNOME
OPTIONS_DEFAULT= X11

X11_USE= xorg=xi,xextproto
```

```
GNOME_USE= gnome=gtk30
GNOME_IMPLIES= X11
```

5.13.3.8. *OPT*_PREVENTS and *OPT*_PREVENTS_MSG

Provides a way to add conflicts between options.

When *OPT* is selected, all the options listed in this variable must be un-selected. If *OPT*_PREVENTS_MSG is also selected, its content will be shown, explaining why they conflict. For example:

```
OPTIONS_DEFINE= OPT1 OPT2
OPT1_PREVENTS= OPT2
OPT1_PREVENTS_MSG= OPT1 and OPT2 enable conflicting options
```

Is roughly equivalent to:

```
OPTIONS_DEFINE= OPT1 OPT2

.include <bsd.port.options.mk>

.if ${PORT_OPTIONS:MOPT2} && ${PORT_OPTIONS:MOPT1}
BROKEN= Option OPT1 conflicts with OPT2 (select only one)
.endif
```

The only difference is that the first one will write an error after running make config, suggesting changing the selected options.

Example 5.41. Simple Use of *OPT*_PREVENTS

This port has X509 and SCTP options. Both options add patches, but the patches conflict with each other, so they cannot be selected at the same time.

```
OPTIONS_DEFINE= X509 SCTP

SCTP_PATCHFILES= ${PORTNAME}-6.8p1-sctp-2573.patch.gz:-p1
SCTP_CONFIGURE_WITH= sctp

X509_PATCH_SITES= http://www.roumenpetrov.info/openssh/x509/:x509
X509_PATCHFILES= ${PORTNAME}-7.0p1+x509-8.5.diff.gz:-p1:x509
X509_PREVENTS=   SCTP
X509_PREVENTS_MSG= X509 and SCTP patches conflict
```

5.13.3.9. *OPT*_VARS and *OPT*_VARS_OFF

Provides a generic way to set and append to variables.

Warning

Before using *OPT*_VARS and *OPT*_VARS_OFF, see if there is already a more specific helper available in Section 5.13.3.11, "Generic Variables Replacement, *OPT_VARIABLE* and *OPT_VARIABLE*_OFF".

When option *OPT* is selected, and *OPT*_VARS defined, *key=value* and *key+=value* pairs are evaluated from *OPT*_VARS. An = cause the existing value of KEY to be overwritten, an += appends to the value. *OPT*_VARS_OFF works the same way, but when OPT is *not* selected.

```
OPTIONS_DEFINE= OPT1 OPT2 OPT3
OPT1_VARS= also_build+=bin1
OPT2_VARS= also_build+=bin2
OPT3_VARS= bin3_build=yes
OPT3_VARS_OFF= bin3_build=no

MAKE_ARGS= ALSO_BUILD="${ALSO_BUILD}" BIN3_BUILD="${BIN3_BUILD}"
```

is equivalent to:

```
OPTIONS_DEFINE= OPT1 OPT2

MAKE_ARGS= ALSO_BUILD="${ALSO_BUILD}" BIN3_BUILD="${BIN3_BUILD}"

.include <bsd.port.options.mk>

.if ${PORT_OPTIONS:MOPT1}
ALSO_BUILD+= bin1
.endif

.if ${PORT_OPTIONS:MOPT2}
ALSO_BUILD+= bin2
.endif

.if ${PORT_OPTIONS:MOPT2}
BIN3_BUILD= yes
.else
BIN3_BUILD= no
.endif
```

Important

Values containing whitespace must be enclosed in quotes:

```
OPT_VARS= foo="bar baz"
```

This is due to the way make(1) variable expansion deals with whitespace. When OPT_VARS= foo=bar baz is expanded, the variable ends up containing two strings, foo=bar and baz. But the submitter probably intended there to be only one string, foo=bar baz. Quoting the value prevents whitespace from being used as a delimiter.

Also, *do not* add extra spaces after the *var=* sign and before the value, it would also be split into two strings. *This will not work*:

```
OPT_VARS= foo= bar
```

5.13.3.10. Dependencies, *OPT_DEPTYPE* and *OPT_DEPTYPE*_OFF

For any of these dependency types:

- PKG_DEPENDS

- EXTRACT_DEPENDS

- PATCH_DEPENDS

- FETCH_DEPENDS

- BUILD_DEPENDS

- LIB_DEPENDS

- RUN_DEPENDS

When option *OPT* is selected, the value of *OPT_DEPTYPE*, if defined, is appended to *DEPTYPE*. *OPT_DEPTYPE*_OFF works the same, but when OPT is *not* selected. For example:

```
OPTIONS_DEFINE= OPT1
OPT1_LIB_DEPENDS= liba.so:devel/a
OPT1_LIB_DEPENDS_OFF= libb.so:devel/b
```

is equivalent to:

```
OPTIONS_DEFINE= OPT1

.include <bsd.port.options.mk>

.if ${PORT_OPTIONS:MOPT1}
LIB_DEPENDS+= liba.so:devel/a
.else
LIB_DEPENDS+= libb.so:devel/b
.endif
```

5.13.3.11. Generic Variables Replacement, *OPT_VARIABLE* and *OPT_VARIABLE*_OFF

For any of these variables:

- ALL_TARGET

- BROKEN

- CATEGORIES

- CFLAGS

- CONFIGURE_ENV

- CONFLICTS

- CONFLICTS_BUILD

- CONFLICTS_INSTALL

- CPPFLAGS

- CXXFLAGS

- DESKTOP_ENTRIES

- DISTFILES

- EXTRACT_ONLY

- EXTRA_PATCHES

- GH_ACCOUNT

- GH_PROJECT

- GH_SUBDIR

- GH_TAGNAME

- GH_TUPLE

- IGNORE

- INFO

- INSTALL_TARGET

- LDFLAGS

- LIBS

- MAKE_ARGS

- MAKE_ENV

- MASTER_SITES

- PATCHFILES

- PATCH_SITES

- PLIST_DIRS

- PLIST_FILES

- PLIST_SUB

- PORTDOCS

- PORTEXAMPLES

- SUB_FILES

- SUB_LIST

- TEST_TARGET

- USES

When option *OPT* is selected, the value of *OPT_ABOVEVARIABLE*, if defined, is appended to *ABOVEVARIABLE*. *OPT_ABOVEVARIABLE_*OFF works the same way, but when OPT is *not* selected. For example:

```
OPTIONS_DEFINE= OPT1
OPT1_USES= gmake
OPT1_CFLAGS_OFF= -DTEST
```

is equivalent to:

```
OPTIONS_DEFINE= OPT1

.include <bsd.port.options.mk>

.if ${PORT_OPTIONS:MOPT1}
USES+=  gmake
.else
CFLAGS+= -DTEST
.endif
```

> ## Note
>
> Some variables are not in this list, in particular PKGNAMEPREFIX and PKGNAMESUFFIX. This is intentional. A port *must not* change its name when its option set changes.

Warning

Some of these variables, at least `ALL_TARGET`, `DISTFILES` and `INSTALL_TARGET`, have their default values set *after* the options are processed.

With these lines in the `Makefile`:

```
ALL_TARGET= all

DOCS_ALL_TARGET= doc
```

If the `DOCS` option is enabled, `ALL_TARGET` will have a final value of `all  doc`; if the option is disabled, it would have a value of `all`.

With only the options helper line in the `Makefile`:

```
DOCS_ALL_TARGET= doc
```

If the `DOCS` option is enabled, `ALL_TARGET` will have a final value of `doc`; if the option is disabled, it would have a value of `all`.

5.13.3.12. Additional Build Targets, *target-OPT*-on and *target-OPT*-off

These `Makefile` targets can accept optional extra build targets:

* pre-fetch

* do-fetch

* post-fetch

* pre-extract

* do-extract

* post-extract

* pre-patch

* do-patch

* post-patch

* pre-configure

* do-configure

* post-configure

* pre-build

* do-build

* post-build

* pre-install

* do-install

- post-install

- post-stage

- pre-package

- do-package

- post-package

When option *OPT* is selected, the target *TARGET-OPT*-on, if defined, is executed after *TARGET*. *TARGET-OPT*-off works the same way, but when **OPT** is *not* selected. For example:

```
OPTIONS_DEFINE= OPT1

post-patch:
 @${REINPLACE_CMD} -e 's/echo/true/' ${WRKSRC}/Makefile

post-patch-OPT1-on:
 @${REINPLACE_CMD} -e '/opt1/d' ${WRKSRC}/Makefile

post-patch-OPT1-off:
 @${REINPLACE_CMD} -e '/opt1/s|/usr/bin/|${LOCALBASE}/bin/|' ${WRKSRC}/Makefile
```

is equivalent to:

```
OPTIONS_DEFINE= OPT1

.include <bsd.port.options.mk>

post-patch:
 @${REINPLACE_CMD} -e 's/echo/true/' ${WRKSRC}/Makefile
.if ${PORT_OPTIONS:MOPT1}
 @${REINPLACE_CMD} -e '/opt1/d' ${WRKSRC}/Makefile
.else
 @${REINPLACE_CMD} -e '/opt1/s|/usr/bin/|${LOCALBASE}/bin/|' ${WRKSRC}/Makefile
.endif
```

5.14. Specifying the Working Directory

Each port is extracted into a working directory, which must be writable. The ports system defaults to having DIST-FILES unpack in to a directory called ${DISTNAME}. In other words, if the Makefile has:

```
PORTNAME= foo
DISTVERSION= 1.0
```

then the port's distribution files contain a top-level directory, foo-1.0, and the rest of the files are located under that directory.

A number of variables can be overridden if that is not the case.

5.14.1. WRKSRC

The variable lists the name of the directory that is created when the application's distfiles are extracted. If our previous example extracted into a directory called foo (and not foo-1.0) write:

```
WRKSRC= ${WRKDIR}/foo
```

or possibly

```
WRKSRC= ${WRKDIR}/${PORTNAME}
```

5.14.2. `WRKSRC_SUBDIR`

If the source files needed for the port are in a subdirectory of the extracted distribution file, set `WRKSRC_SUBDIR` to that directory.

```
WRKSRC_SUBDIR= src
```

5.14.3. `NO_WRKSUBDIR`

If the port does not extract in to a subdirectory at all, then set `NO_WRKSUBDIR` to indicate that.

```
NO_WRKSUBDIR= yes
```

> ### Note
>
> Because `WRKDIR` is the only directory that is supposed to be writable during the build, and is used to store many files recording the status of the build, the port's extraction will be forced into a subdirectory.

5.15. Conflict Handling

There are three different variables to register a conflict between packages and ports: `CONFLICTS`, `CONFLICTS_INSTALL` and `CONFLICTS_BUILD`.

> ### Note
>
> The conflict variables automatically set the variable `IGNORE`, which is more fully documented in Section 13.14, "Marking a Port Not Installable with `BROKEN`, `FORBIDDEN`, or `IGNORE`".

When removing one of several conflicting ports, it is advisable to retain `CONFLICTS` in those other ports for a few months to cater for users who only update once in a while.

`CONFLICTS_INSTALL`
> If the package cannot coexist with other packages (because of file conflicts, runtime incompatibilities, etc.). `CONFLICTS_INSTALL` check is done after the build stage and prior to the install stage.

`CONFLICTS_BUILD`
> If the port cannot be built when other specific ports are already installed. Build conflicts are not recorded in the resulting package.

`CONFLICTS`
> If the port cannot be built if a certain port is already installed and the resulting package cannot coexist with the other package. `CONFLICTS` check is done prior to the build stage and prior to the install stage.

The most common content of one of these variable is the package base of another port. The package base is the package name without the appended version, it can be obtained by running `make -V PKGBASE`.

Example 5.42. Basic usage of `CONFLICTS` *

dns/bind99 cannot be installed if dns/bind910 is present because they install same files. First gather the package base to use:

```
% make -C dns/bind99 -V PKGBASE
bind99
% make -C dns/bind910 -V PKGBASE
bind910
```

Then add to the Makefile of dns/bind99:

```
CONFLICTS_INSTALL= bind910
```

And add to the Makefile of dns/bind910:

```
CONFLICTS_INSTALL= bind99
```

Sometime, only some version of another port is incompatible, in this case, use the full package name, with the version, and use shell globs, like * and ? to make sure all possible versions are matched.

Example 5.43. Using CONFLICTS * With Globs.

From versions from 2.0 and up-to 2.4.1_2, deskutils/gnotime used to install a bundled version of databases/qof.

To reflect this past, the Makefile of databases/qof contains:

```
CONFLICTS_INSTALL= gnotime-2.[0-3]* \
    gnotime-2.4.0* gnotime-2.4.1 \
    gnotime-2.4.1_[12]
```

The first entry match versions 2.0 through 2.3, the second all the revisions of 2.4.0, the third the exact 2.4.1 version, and the last the first and second revisions of the 2.4.1 version.

deskutils/gnotime does not have any conflicts line because its current version does not conflict with anything else.

5.16. Installing Files

Important

The install phase is very important to the end user because it adds files to their system. All the additional commands run in the port Makefile's *-install targets should be echoed to the screen. *Do not* silence these commands with @ or .SILENT.

5.16.1. INSTALL_* Macros

Use the macros provided in bsd.port.mk to ensure correct modes of files in the port's *-install targets. Set ownership directly in pkg-plist with the corresponding entries, such as @(owner,group,), @owner owner, and @group group. These operators work until overridden, or until the end of pkg-plist, so remember to reset them after they are no longer needed. The default ownership is root:wheel. See Section 8.6.13, "Base Keywords" for more information.

- INSTALL_PROGRAM is a command to install binary executables.

- `INSTALL_SCRIPT` is a command to install executable scripts.

- `INSTALL_LIB` is a command to install shared libraries (but not static libraries).

- `INSTALL_KLD` is a command to install kernel loadable modules. Some architectures do not like having the modules stripped, so use this command instead of `INSTALL_PROGRAM`.

- `INSTALL_DATA` is a command to install sharable data, including static libraries.

- `INSTALL_MAN` is a command to install manpages and other documentation (it does not compress anything).

These variables are set to the install(1) command with the appropriate flags for each situation.

Important

Do not use `INSTALL_LIB` to install static libraries, because stripping them renders them useless. Use `INSTALL_DATA` instead.

5.16.2. Stripping Binaries and Shared Libraries

Installed binaries should be stripped. Do not strip binaries manually unless absolutely required. The `INSTALL_PRO-GRAM` macro installs and strips a binary at the same time. The `INSTALL_LIB` macro does the same thing to shared libraries.

When a file must be stripped, but neither `INSTALL_PROGRAM` nor `INSTALL_LIB` macros are desirable, `${STRIP_CMD}` strips the program or shared library. This is typically done within the post-install target. For example:

```
post-install:
  ${STRIP_CMD} ${STAGEDIR}${PREFIX}/bin/xdl
```

When multiple files need to be stripped:

```
post-install:
.for l in geometry media body track world
  ${STRIP_CMD} ${STAGEDIR}${PREFIX}/lib/lib${PORTNAME}-${l}.so.0
.endfor
```

Use file(1) on a file to determine if it has been stripped. Binaries are reported by file(1) as stripped, or not stripped. Additionally, strip(1) will detect programs that have already been stripped and exit cleanly.

5.16.3. Installing a Whole Tree of Files

Sometimes, a large number of files must be installed while preserving their hierarchical organization. For example, copying over a whole directory tree from `WRKSRC` to a target directory under `PREFIX`. Note that `PREFIX`, `EXAMPLESDIR`, `DATADIR`, and other path variables must always be prepended with `STAGEDIR` to respect staging (see Section 6.1, "Staging").

Two macros exist for this situation. The advantage of using these macros instead of cp is that they guarantee proper file ownership and permissions on target files. The first macro, `COPYTREE_BIN`, will set all the installed files to be executable, thus being suitable for installing into `PREFIX/bin`. The second macro, `COPYTREE_SHARE`, does not set executable permissions on files, and is therefore suitable for installing files under `PREFIX/share` target.

```
post-install:
  ${MKDIR} ${STAGEDIR}${EXAMPLESDIR}
  (cd ${WRKSRC}/examples && ${COPYTREE_SHARE} . ${STAGEDIR}${EXAMPLESDIR})
```

This example will install the contents of the examples directory in the vendor distfile to the proper examples location of the port.

```
post-install:
 ${MKDIR} ${STAGEDIR}${DATADIR}/summer
 (cd ${WRKSRC}/temperatures && ${COPYTREE_SHARE} "June July August" ↺
${STAGEDIR}${DATADIR}/summer)
```

And this example will install the data of summer months to the summer subdirectory of a DATADIR.

Additional find arguments can be passed via the third argument to COPYTREE_* macros. For example, to install all files from the first example except Makefiles, one can use these commands.

```
post-install:
 ${MKDIR} ${STAGEDIR}${EXAMPLESDIR}
 (cd ${WRKSRC}/examples && \
 ${COPYTREE_SHARE} . ${STAGEDIR}${EXAMPLESDIR} "! -name Makefile")
```

These macros do not add the installed files to pkg-plist. They must be added manually. For optional documentation (PORTDOCS, see Section 5.16.4, "Install Additional Documentation") and examples (PORTEXAMPLES), the %%PORT-DOCS%% or %%PORTEXAMPLES%% prefixes must be prepended in pkg-plist.

5.16.4. Install Additional Documentation

If the software has some documentation other than the standard man and info pages that is useful for the user, install it under DOCSDIR This can be done, like the previous item, in the post-install target.

Create a new directory for the port. The directory name is DOCSDIR. This usually equals PORTNAME. However, if the user might want different versions of the port to be installed at the same time, the whole PKGNAME can be used.

Since only the files listed in pkg-plist are installed, it is safe to always install documentation to STAGEDIR (see Section 6.1, "Staging"). Hence .if blocks are only needed when the installed files are large enough to cause significant I/O overhead.

```
post-install:
 ${MKDIR} ${STAGEDIR}${DOCSDIR}
 ${INSTALL_MAN} ${WRKSRC}/docs/xvdocs.ps ${STAGEDIR}${DOCSDIR}
```

On the other hand, if there is a DOCS option in the port, install the documentation in a post-install-DOCS-on target. These targets are described in Section 5.13.3.12, "Additional Build Targets, *target*-OPT-on and *target*-OPT-off".

Here are some handy variables and how they are expanded by default when used in the Makefile:

- DATADIR gets expanded to PREFIX/share/PORTNAME.

- DATADIR_REL gets expanded to share/PORTNAME.

- DOCSDIR gets expanded to PREFIX/share/doc/PORTNAME.

- DOCSDIR_REL gets expanded to share/doc/PORTNAME.

- EXAMPLESDIR gets expanded to PREFIX/share/examples/PORTNAME.

- EXAMPLESDIR_REL gets expanded to share/examples/PORTNAME.

Note

The DOCS option only controls additional documentation installed in DOCSDIR. It does not apply to standard man pages and info pages. Things installed in EXAMPLESDIR are controlled by the EXAMPLES option.

These variables are exported to `PLIST_SUB` . Their values will appear there as pathnames relative to `PREFIX` if possible. That is, `share/doc/PORTNAME` will be substituted for `%%DOCSDIR%%` in the packing list by default, and so on. (See more on `pkg-plist` substitution here.)

All conditionally installed documentation files and directories are included in `pkg-plist` with the `%%PORTDOCS%` `%` prefix, for example:

```
%%PORTDOCS%%%%DOCSDIR%%/AUTHORS
%%PORTDOCS%%%%DOCSDIR%%/CONTACT
```

As an alternative to enumerating the documentation files in `pkg-plist` , a port can set the variable `PORTDOCS` to a list of file names and shell glob patterns to add to the final packing list. The names will be relative to `DOCSDIR`. Therefore, a port that utilizes `PORTDOCS`, and uses a non-default location for its documentation, must set `DOCSDIR` accordingly. If a directory is listed in `PORTDOCS` or matched by a glob pattern from this variable, the entire subtree of contained files and directories will be registered in the final packing list. If the `DOCS` option has been unset then files and directories listed in `PORTDOCS` would not be installed or added to port packing list. Installing the documentation at `PORTDOCS` as shown above remains up to the port itself. A typical example of utilizing `PORTDOCS`:

```
PORTDOCS= README.* ChangeLog docs/*
```

Note

The equivalents of `PORTDOCS` for files installed under `DATADIR` and `EXAMPLESDIR` are `PORTDATA` and `PORTEXAMPLES`, respectively.

The contents of `pkg-message` are displayed upon installation. See the section on using pkg-message for details. `pkg-message` does not need to be added to `pkg-plist` .

5.16.5. Subdirectories Under PREFIX

Try to let the port put things in the right subdirectories of `PREFIX`. Some ports lump everything and put it in the subdirectory with the port's name, which is incorrect. Also, many ports put everything except binaries, header files and manual pages in a subdirectory of `lib`, which does not work well with the BSD paradigm. Many of the files must be moved to one of these directories: `etc` (setup/configuration files), `libexec` (executables started internally), `sbin` (executables for superusers/managers), `info` (documentation for info browser) or `share` (architecture independent files). See hier(7) for details; the rules governing /usr pretty much apply to /usr/local too. The exception are ports dealing with USENET "news". They may use `PREFIX/news` as a destination for their files.

Chapter 6. Special Considerations

This section explains the most common things to consider when creating a port.

6.1. Staging

bsd.port.mk expects ports to work with a "stage directory". This means that a port must not install files directly to the regular destination directories (that is, under PREFIX, for example) but instead into a separate directory from which the package is then built. In many cases, this does not require root privileges, making it possible to build packages as an unprivileged user. With staging, the port is built and installed into the stage directory, STAGEDIR. A package is created from the stage directory and then installed on the system. Automake tools refer to this concept as DESTDIR, but in FreeBSD, DESTDIR has a different meaning (see Section 10.4, "PREFIX and DESTDIR").

> Note
>
> No port *really* needs to be root. It can mostly be avoided by using USES=uidfix. If the port still runs commands like chown(8), chgrp(1), or forces owner or group with install(1) then use USES=fakeroot to fake those calls. Some patching of the port's Makefiles will be needed.

Meta ports, or ports that do not install files themselves but only depend on other ports, must avoid needlessly extracting the mtree(8) to the stage directory. This is the basic directory layout of the package, and these empty directories will be seen as orphans. To prevent mtree(8) extraction, add this line:

```
NO_MTREE= yes
```

> Tip
>
> Metaports should use USES=metaport. It sets up defaults for ports that do not fetch, build, or install anything.

Staging is enabled by prepending STAGEDIR to paths used in the pre-install, do-install, and post-install targets (see the examples through the book). Typically, this includes PREFIX, ETCDIR, DATADIR, EXAMPLESDIR, MAN-PREFIX, DOCSDIR, and so on. Directories should be created as part of the post-install target. Avoid using absolute paths whenever possible.

> Tip
>
> Ports that install kernel modules must prepend STAGEDIR to their destination, by default /boot/modules.

6.1.1. Handling Symbolic Links

When creating a symlink, there are two cases, either the source and target are both within ${PREFIX}. In that case, use ${RLN}. In the other case, if one or both of the paths are outside of ${PREFIX} use ${LN} -s and only prepend ${STAGEDIR} to the target's path.

Example 6.1. Inside **${PREFIX}**, Create Relative Symbolic Links

${RLN} uses install(1)'s relative symbolic feature which frees the porter of computing the relative path.

```
${RLN} ${STAGEDIR}${PREFIX}/lib/libfoo.so.42  ${STAGEDIR}${PREFIX}/lib/libfoo.so
```

Will generate:

```
% ls -lF ${STAGEDIR}${PREFIX}/lib
  lrwxr-xr-x  1 nobody   nobody       181 Aug  3 11:27 libfoo.so@ -> libfoo.so.42
  -rwxr-xr-x  1 nobody   nobody        15 Aug  3 11:24 libfoo.so.42*
```

When used with paths not in the same directory:

```
${RLN} ${STAGEDIR}${PREFIX}/libexec/foo/bar  ${STAGEDIR}${PREFIX}/bin/bar
```

Will automatically generate the relative symbolic links:

```
% ls -lF ${STAGEDIR}${PREFIX}/bin
  lrwxr-xr-x  1 nobody   nobody       181 Aug  3 11:27 bar@ -> ../libexec/foo/bar
```

Example 6.2. Outside **${PREFIX}**, Create Absolute Symbolic Links

When creating a symbolic link outside of ${PREFIX}, the source must not contain ${STAGEDIR}, the target, however, must:

```
${LN} -sf /var/cache/${PORTNAME}  ${STAGEDIR}${PREFIX}/share/${PORTNAME}
```

Will generate:

```
% ls -lF ${STAGEDIRDIR}${PREFIX}/share
  lrwxr-xr-x  1 nobody   nobody       181 Aug  3 11:27 foo@ -> /var/cache/foo
```

6.2. Bundled Libraries

This section explains why bundled dependencies are considered bad and what to do about them.

6.2.1. Why Bundled Libraries Are Bad

Some software requires the porter to locate third-party libraries and add the required dependencies to the port. Other software bundles all necessary libraries into the distribution file. The second approach seems easier at first, but there are some serious drawbacks:

This list is loosely based on the Fedora and Gentoo wikis, both licensed under the CC-BY-SA 3.0 license.

Security
  If vulnerabilities are found in the upstream library and fixed there, they might not be fixed in the library bundled with the port. One reason could be that the author is not aware of the problem. This means that the porter must fix them, or upgrade to a non-vulnerable version, and send a patch to the author. This all takes time, which results in software being vulnerable longer than necessary. This in turn makes it harder to coordinate a fix without unnecessarily leaking information about the vulnerability.

Bugs
> This problem is similar to the problem with security in the last paragraph, but generally less severe.

Forking
> It is easier for the author to fork the upstream library once it is bundled. While convenient on first sight, it means that the code diverges from upstream making it harder to address security or other problems with the software. A reason for this is that patching becomes harder.
>
> Another problem of forking is that because code diverges from upstream, bugs get solved over and over again instead of just once at a central location. This defeats the idea of open source software in the first place.

Symbol collision
> When a library is installed on the system, it might collide with the bundled version. This can cause immediate errors at compile or link time. It can also cause errors when running the program which might be harder to track down. The latter problem could be caused because the versions of the two libraries are incompatible.

Licensing
> When bundling projects from different sources, license issues can arise more easily, especially when licenses are incompatible.

Waste of resources
> Bundled libraries waste resources on several levels. It takes longer to build the actual application, especially if these libraries are already present on the system. At run-time, they can take up unnecessary memory when the system-wide library is already loaded by one program and the bundled library is loaded by another program.

Waste of effort
> When a library needs patches for FreeBSD, these patches have to be duplicated again in the bundled library. This wastes developer time because the patches might not apply cleanly. It can also be hard to notice that these patches are required in the first place.

6.2.2. What to do About Bundled Libraries

Whenever possible, use the unbundled version of the library by adding a LIB_DEPENDS to the port. If such a port does not exist yet, consider creating it.

Only use bundled libraries if the upstream has a good track record on security and using unbundled versions leads to overly complex patches.

Note

In some very special cases, for example emulators, like Wine, a port has to bundle libraries, because they are in a different architecture, or they have been modified to fit the software's use. In that case, those libraries should not be exposed to other ports for linking. Add BUNDLE_LIBS=yes to the port's Makefile. This will tell pkg(8) to not compute provided libraries. Always ask the Ports Management Team <portmgr@FreeBSD.org> before adding this to a port.

6.3. Shared Libraries

If the port installs one or more shared libraries, define a USE_LDCONFIG make variable, which will instruct a bsd.port.mk to run ${LDCONFIG} -m on the directory where the new library is installed (usually PREFIX/lib) during post-install target to register it into the shared library cache. This variable, when defined, will also facilitate addition of an appropriate @exec /sbin/ldconfig -m and @unexec /sbin/ldconfig -R pair into pkg-plist, so that a user who installed the package can start using the shared library immediately and de-installation will not cause the system to still believe the library is there.

```
USE_LDCONFIG= yes
```

The default directory can be overridden by setting USE_LDCONFIG to a list of directories into which shared libraries are to be installed. For example, if the port installs shared libraries into PREFIX/lib/foo and PREFIX/lib/bar use this in Makefile:

```
USE_LDCONFIG= ${PREFIX}/lib/foo ${PREFIX}/lib/bar
```

Please double-check, often this is not necessary at all or can be avoided through -rpath or setting LD_RUN_PATH during linking (see lang/mosml for an example), or through a shell-wrapper which sets LD_LIBRARY_PATH before invoking the binary, like www/seamonkey does.

When installing 32-bit libraries on 64-bit system, use USE_LDCONFIG32 instead.

If the software uses autotools, and specifically libtool, add USES=libtool .

When the major library version number increments in the update to the new port version, all other ports that link to the affected library must have their PORTREVISION incremented, to force recompilation with the new library version.

6.4. Ports with Distribution Restrictions or Legal Concerns

Licenses vary, and some of them place restrictions on how the application can be packaged, whether it can be sold for profit, and so on.

> Important
>
> It is the responsibility of a porter to read the licensing terms of the software and make sure that the FreeBSD project will not be held accountable for violating them by redistributing the source or compiled binaries either via FTP/HTTP or CD-ROM. If in doubt, please contact the FreeBSD ports mailing list.

In situations like this, the variables described in the next sections can be set.

6.4.1. NO_PACKAGE

This variable indicates that we may not generate a binary package of the application. For instance, the license may disallow binary redistribution, or it may prohibit distribution of packages created from patched sources.

However, the port's DISTFILES may be freely mirrored on FTP/HTTP. They may also be distributed on a CD-ROM (or similar media) unless NO_CDROM is set as well.

If the binary package is not generally useful, and the application must always be compiled from the source code, use NO_PACKAGE. For example, if the application has configuration information that is site specific hard coded into it at compile time, set NO_PACKAGE.

Set NO_PACKAGE to a string describing the reason why the package cannot be generated.

6.4.2. NO_CDROM

This variable alone indicates that, although we are allowed to generate binary packages, we may put neither those packages nor the port's DISTFILES onto a CD-ROM (or similar media) for resale. However, the binary packages and the port's DISTFILES will still be available via FTP/HTTP.

If this variable is set along with NO_PACKAGE, then only the port's DISTFILES will be available, and only via FTP/HTTP.

Set `NO_CDROM` to a string describing the reason why the port cannot be redistributed on CD-ROM. For instance, use this if the port's license is for "non-commercial" use only.

6.4.3. NOFETCHFILES

Files defined in `NOFETCHFILES` are not fetchable from any of `MASTER_SITES` . An example of such a file is when the file is supplied on CD-ROM by the vendor.

Tools which check for the availability of these files on `MASTER_SITES` have to ignore these files and not report about them.

6.4.4. RESTRICTED

Set this variable alone if the application's license permits neither mirroring the application's `DISTFILES` nor distributing the binary package in any way.

Do not set `NO_CDROM` or `NO_PACKAGE` along with `RESTRICTED`, since the latter variable implies the former ones.

Set `RESTRICTED` to a string describing the reason why the port cannot be redistributed. Typically, this indicates that the port contains proprietary software and that the user will need to manually download the `DISTFILES`, possibly after registering for the software or agreeing to accept the terms of an EULA.

6.4.5. RESTRICTED_FILES

When `RESTRICTED` or `NO_CDROM` is set, this variable defaults to `${DISTFILES} ${PATCHFILES}`, otherwise it is empty. If only some of the distribution files are restricted, then set this variable to list them.

6.4.6. LEGAL_TEXT

If the port has legal concerns not addressed by the above variables, set `LEGAL_TEXT` to a string explaining the concern. For example, if special permission was obtained for FreeBSD to redistribute the binary, this variable must indicate so.

6.4.7. /usr/ports/LEGAL and LEGAL

A port which sets any of the above variables must also be added to `/usr/ports/LEGAL` . The first column is a glob which matches the restricted distfiles. The second column is the port's origin. The third column is the output of `make -VLEGAL` .

6.4.8. Examples

The preferred way to state "the distfiles for this port must be fetched manually" is as follows:

```
.if !exists(${DISTDIR}/${DISTNAME}${EXTRACT_SUFX})
IGNORE= may not be redistributed because of licensing reasons. Please visit some-
website to accept their license and download ${DISTFILES} into ${DISTDIR}
.endif
```

This both informs the user, and sets the proper metadata on the user's machine for use by automated programs.

Note that this stanza must be preceded by an inclusion of `bsd.port.pre.mk`.

6.5. Building Mechanisms

6.5.1. Building Ports in Parallel

The FreeBSD ports framework supports parallel building using multiple `make` sub-processes, which allows SMP systems to utilize all of their available CPU power, allowing port builds to be faster and more effective.

This is achieved by passing -jX flag to make(1) running on vendor code. This is the default build behavior of ports. Unfortunately, not all ports handle parallel building well and it may be required to explicitly disable this feature by adding the MAKE_JOBS_UNSAFE=yes variable. It is used when a port is known to be broken with -jX.

6.5.2. `make`, `gmake`, `fmake`, and `imake`

Several differing make implementations exist. Ported software often requires a particular implementation, like GNU make, known in FreeBSD as gmake, or fmake, the legacy FreeBSD make.

If the port uses GNU make, add gmake to USES. If the legacy FreeBSD make is needed, add fmake there.

MAKE_CMD can be used to reference the specific command configured by the USES setting in the port's Makefile. In rare cases when more than one make implementation is listed in USES, the variables GMAKE (for the GNU version) or FMAKE (for the legacy FreeBSD version) are available. Only use MAKE_CMD within the application Makefiles in WRKSRC to call the make implementation expected by the ported software.

If the port is an X application that uses imake to create Makefiles from Imakefiles, set USES= imake .. See the USES=imake section of Chapter 17, *Using USES Macros* for more details.

If the port's source Makefile has something other than all as the main build target, set ALL_TARGET accordingly. The same goes for install and INSTALL_TARGET.

6.5.3. `configure` Script

If the port uses the configure script to generate Makefile from Makefile.in, set GNU_CONFIGURE=yes. To give extra arguments to the configure script (the default argument is --prefix=${PREFIX} --infodir=${PREFIX}/${IN-FO_PATH} --mandir=${MANPREFIX}/man --build=${CONFIGURE_TARGET}), set those extra arguments in CON-FIGURE_ARGS. Extra environment variables can be passed using CONFIGURE_ENV.

Table 6.1. Variables for Ports That Use `configure`

Variable	Means
GNU_CONFIGURE	The port uses configure script to prepare build.
HAS_CONFIGURE	Same as GNU_CONFIGURE, except default configure target is not added to CONFIGURE_ARGS.
CONFIGURE_ARGS	Additional arguments passed to configure script.
CONFIGURE_ENV	Additional environment variables to be set for configure script run.
CONFIGURE_TARGET	Override default configure target. Default value is ${MACHINE_ARCH}-portbld-freebsd${OSREL} .

6.5.4. Using `cmake`

For ports that use CMake, define USES= cmake , or USES= cmake:outsource to build in a separate directory (see below).

Table 6.2. Variables for Ports That Use `cmake`

Variable	Means
CMAKE_ARGS	Port specific CMake flags to be passed to the cmake binary.
CMAKE_ON	For each entry in CMAKE_ON , an enabled boolean value is added to CMAKE_ARGS . See Example 6.4, "CMAKE_ON and CMAKE_OFF".

Variable	Means
CMAKE_OFF	For each entry in CMAKE_OFF , a disabled boolean value is added to CMAKE_ARGS . See Example 6.4, "CMAKE_ON and CMAKE_OFF".
CMAKE_BUILD_TYPE	Type of build (CMake predefined build profiles). Default is Release, or Debug if WITH_DEBUG is set.
CMAKE_ENV	Environment variables to be set for the cmake binary. Default is ${CONFIGURE_ENV}.
CMAKE_SOURCE_PATH	Path to the source directory. Default is ${WRKSRC} .

Table 6.3. Variables the Users Can Define for cmake Builds

Variable	Means
CMAKE_VERBOSE	Enable verbose build output. Default not set, unless BATCH or PACKAGE_BUILDING are set.
CMAKE_NOCOLOR	Disables color build output. Default not set, unless BATCH or PACKAGE_BUILDING are set.

CMake supports these build profiles: Debug, Release, RelWithDebInfo and MinSizeRel. Debug and Release profiles respect system *FLAGS, RelWithDebInfo and MinSizeRel will set CFLAGS to -O2 -g and -Os -DNDEBUG correspondingly. The lower-cased value of CMAKE_BUILD_TYPE is exported to PLIST_SUB and must be used if the port installs *.cmake depending on the build type (see deskutils/strigi for an example). Please note that some projects may define their own build profiles and/or force particular build type by setting CMAKE_BUILD_TYPE in CMakeLists.txt. To make a port for such a project respect CFLAGS and WITH_DEBUG, the CMAKE_BUILD_TYPE definitions must be removed from those files.

Most CMake-based projects support an out-of-source method of building. The out-of-source build for a port can be requested by using the :outsource suffix. When enabled, CONFIGURE_WRKSRC, BUILD_WRKSRC and INSTALL_WRKSRC will be set to ${WRKDIR}/.build and this directory will be used to keep all files generated during configuration and build stages, leaving the source directory intact.

Example 6.3. USES= cmake Example

This snippet demonstrates the use of CMake for a port. CMAKE_SOURCE_PATH is not usually required, but can be set when the sources are not located in the top directory, or if only a subset of the project is intended to be built by the port.

```
USES=    cmake:outsource
CMAKE_SOURCE_PATH= ${WRKSRC}/subproject
```

Example 6.4. CMAKE_ON and CMAKE_OFF

When adding boolean values to CMAKE_ARGS , it is easier to use the CMAKE_ON and CMAKE_OFF variables instead. This:

```
CMAKE_ON= VAR1 VAR2
CMAKE_OFF= VAR3
```

Is equivalent to:

```
CMAKE_ARGS= -DVAR1:BOOL=TRUE -DVAR2:BOOL=TRUE -DVAR3:BOOL=FALSE
```

> **Important**
>
>
>
> This is only for the default values off `CMAKE_ARGS` . The helpers described in Section 5.13.3.4.2, "*OPT*_CMAKE_BOOL and *OPT*_CMAKE_BOOL_OFF" use the same semantics, but for optional values.

6.5.5. Using scons

If the port uses SCons, define USES=scons.

To make third party `SConstruct` respect everything that is passed to SCons in the environment (that is, most importantly, `CC/CXX/CFLAGS/CXXFLAGS`), patch `SConstruct` so build `Environment` is constructed like this:

```
env = Environment(**ARGUMENTS)
```

It may be then modified with env.`Append` and env.`Replace`.

6.6. Using GNU Autotools

6.6.1. Introduction

The various GNU autotools provide an abstraction mechanism for building a piece of software over a wide variety of operating systems and machine architectures. Within the Ports Collection, an individual port can make use of these tools via a simple construct:

```
USE_AUTOTOOLS= tool[:env] ...
```

At the time of writing, *tool* can be one of `autoconf`, `autoheader`, `automake`, `aclocal`, `libtoolize` . It can also be one the older legacy of `autoconf213`, `autoheader213`, `automake14`, `aclocal14`.

env is used to specify that the environmental variables are needed. It also adds a build dependency on the tool. The relevant tool is *not* ran as part of the `run-autotools` target.

Multiple tools can be specified at once, either by including them all on a single line, or using the += Makefile construct.

6.6.2. libtool and libtoolize

Ports shipping with their own copy of libtool (search for a file named ltmain.sh) need to have `USES=libtool` . If a port has `USE_AUTOTOOLS=libtoolize` it probably also needs `USES=libtool` . See the USES=libtool section in Chapter 17, *Using USES Macros* for more details.

6.6.3. libltdl.so

Some ports make use of the `libltdl.so` library package, which is part of the `libtool` suite. Use of this library does not automatically necessitate the use of `libtool` itself. If the port needs `libltdl.so`, add a dependency on it:

```
LIB_DEPENDS= libltdl.so:devel/libltdl
```

6.6.4. autoconf and autoheader

Some ports do not contain a configure script, but do contain an autoconf template in `configure.ac`. Use these assignments to let `autoconf` create the configure script, and also have `autoheader` create template headers for use by the configure script.

```
USE_AUTOTOOLS= autoconf[:env]
```

and

```
USE_AUTOTOOLS= autoheader
```

which also implies the use of autoconf.

The additional optional variables AUTOCONF_ARGS and AUTOHEADER_ARGS can be overridden by the port Makefile if specifically requested. Most ports are unlikely to need this. See bsd.autotools.mk for further details.

6.6.5. automake and aclocal

Some packages only contain Makefile.am. These have to be converted into Makefile.in using automake, and the further processed by configure to generate an actual Makefile.

Similarly, packages occasionally do not ship with an included aclocal.m4, again required to build the software. This can be achieved with aclocal, which scans configure.ac or configure.in.

aclocal has a similar relationship to automake as autoheader does to autoconf, described in the previous section. aclocal implies the use of automake, thus we have:

```
USE_AUTOTOOLS= automake[:env]
```

and

```
USE_AUTOTOOLS= aclocal
```

As with autoconf and autoheader, both automake and aclocal have optional argument variables, AUTOMAKE_ARGS and ACLOCAL_ARGS respectively, which may be overridden by the port Makefile if required.

6.7. Using GNU gettext

6.7.1. Basic Usage

If the port requires gettext, set USES= gettext, and the port will inherit a dependency on libintl.so from devel/gettext. Other values for gettext usage are listed in USES=gettext.

A rather common case is a port using gettext and configure. Generally, GNU configure should be able to locate gettext automatically.

```
USES= gettext
GNU_CONFIGURE= yes
```

If it ever fails to, hints at the location of gettext can be passed in CPPFLAGS and LDFLAGS as follows:

```
USES= gettext
CPPFLAGS+= -I${LOCALBASE}/include
LDFLAGS+= -L${LOCALBASE}/lib

GNU_CONFIGURE= yes
```

6.7.2. Optional Usage

Some software products allow for disabling NLS. For example, through passing --disable-nls to configure. In that case, the port must use gettext conditionally, depending on the status of the NLS option. For ports of low to medium complexity, use this idiom:

```
GNU_CONFIGURE= yes

OPTIONS_DEFINE= NLS
```

```
OPTIONS_SUB=  yes

NLS_USES=  gettext
NLS_CONFIGURE_ENABLE= nls

.include <bsd.port.mk>
```

Or using the older way of using options:

```
GNU_CONFIGURE=  yes

OPTIONS_DEFINE=  NLS

.include <bsd.port.options.mk>

.if ${PORT_OPTIONS:MNLS}
USES+=   gettext
PLIST_SUB+=  NLS=""
.else
CONFIGURE_ARGS+= --disable-nls
PLIST_SUB+=  NLS="@comment "
.endif

.include <bsd.port.mk>
```

The next item on the to-do list is to arrange so that the message catalog files are included in the packing list conditionally. The Makefile part of this task is already provided by the idiom. It is explained in the section on advanced pkg-plist practices. In a nutshell, each occurrence of %%NLS%% in pkg-plist will be replaced by "@comment " if NLS is disabled, or by a null string if NLS is enabled. Consequently, the lines prefixed by %%NLS%% will become mere comments in the final packing list if NLS is off; otherwise the prefix will be just left out. Then insert %%NLS%% before each path to a message catalog file in pkg-plist . For example:

```
%%NLS%%share/locale/fr/LC_MESSAGES/foobar.mo
%%NLS%%share/locale/no/LC_MESSAGES/foobar.mo
```

In high complexity cases, more advanced techniques may be needed, such as dynamic packing list generation.

6.7.3. Handling Message Catalog Directories

There is a point to note about installing message catalog files. The target directories for them, which reside under LOCALBASE/share/locale , must not be created and removed by a port. The most popular languages have their respective directories listed in PORTSDIR/Templates/BSD.local.dist . The directories for many other languages are governed by the devel/gettext port. Consult its pkg-plist and see whether the port is going to install a message catalog file for a unique language.

6.8. Using Perl

If MASTER_SITES is set to CPAN, the correct subdirectory is usually selected automatically. If the default subdirectory is wrong, CPAN/Module can be used to change it. MASTER_SITES can also be set to the old MASTER_SITE_PERL_CPAN, then the preferred value of MASTER_SITE_SUBDIR is the top-level hierarchy name. For example, the recommended value for p5-Module-Name is Module. The top-level hierarchy can be examined at cpan.org. This keeps the port working when the author of the module changes.

The exception to this rule is when the relevant directory does not exist or the distfile does not exist in that directory. In such case, using author's id as MASTER_SITE_SUBDIR is allowed. The CPAN:AUTHOR macro can be used, which will be translated to the hashed author directory. For example, CPAN:AUTHOR will be converted to authors/id/A/AU/AUTHOR.

When a port needs Perl support, it must set USES=perl5 with the optional USE_PERL5 described in the perl5 USES description.

Table 6.4. Read-Only Variables for Ports That Use Perl

Read only variables	Means
PERL	The full path of the Perl 5 interpreter, either in the system or installed from a port, but without the version number. Use this when the software needs the path to the Perl interpreter. To replace "#!"lines in scripts, use USES=shebangfix.
PERL_VERSION	The full version of Perl installed (for example, 5.8.9).
PERL_LEVEL	The installed Perl version as an integer of the form MNNNPP (for example, 500809).
PERL_ARCH	Where Perl stores architecture dependent libraries. Defaults to ${ARCH}-freebsd.
PERL_PORT	Name of the Perl port that is installed (for example, perl5).
SITE_PERL	Directory name where site specific Perl packages go. This value is added to PLIST_SUB.

Note

Ports of Perl modules which do not have an official website must link to cpan.org in the WWW line of pkg-descr. The preferred URL form is http://search.cpan.org/dist/Module-Name/ (including the trailing slash).

Note

Do not use ${SITE_PERL} in dependency declarations. Doing so assumes that perl5.mk has been included, which is not always true. Ports depending on this port will have incorrect dependencies if this port's files move later in an upgrade. The right way to declare Perl module dependencies is shown in the example below.

Example 6.5. Perl Dependency Example

```
p5-IO-Tee>=0.64:devel/p5-IO-Tee
```

For Perl ports that install manual pages, the macro PERL5_MAN3 and PERL5_MAN1 can be used inside pkg-plist. For example,

```
lib/perl5/5.14/man/man1/event.1.gz
lib/perl5/5.14/man/man3/AnyEvent::I3.3.gz
```

can be replaced with

```
%%PERL5_MAN1%%/event.1.gz
%%PERL5_MAN3%%/AnyEvent::I3.3.gz
```

> **Note**
>
> There are no PERL5_MANx macros for the other sections (*x* in 2 and 4 to 9) because those get installed in the regular directories.

Example 6.6. A Port Which Only Requires Perl to Build

As the default USE_PERL5 value is build and run, set it to:

```
USES=  perl5
USE_PERL5= build
```

Example 6.7. A Port Which Also Requires Perl to Patch

From time to time, using sed(1) for patching is not enough. When using perl(1) is easier, use:

```
USES=  perl5
USE_PERL5= patch build run
```

Example 6.8. A Perl Module Which Needs `ExtUtils::MakeMaker` to Build

Most Perl modules come with a `Makefile.PL` configure script. In this case, set:

```
USES=  perl5
USE_PERL5= configure
```

Example 6.9. A Perl Module Which Needs `Module::Build` to Build

When a Perl module comes with a `Build.PL` configure script, it can require Module::Build, in which case, set

```
USES=  perl5
USE_PERL5= modbuild
```

If it instead requires Module::Build::Tiny, set

```
USES=  perl5
USE_PERL5= modbuildtiny
```

6.9. Using X11

6.9.1. X.Org Components

The X11 implementation available in The Ports Collection is X.Org. If the application depends on X components, set USE_XORG to the list of required components. Available components, at the time of writing, are:

bigreqsproto compositeproto damageproto dmx dmxproto dri2proto dri3proto evieproto fixesproto fontcacheproto fontenc fontsproto fontutil glproto ice inputproto kbproto libfs oldx pciaccess pixman presentproto printproto randrproto recordproto renderproto resourceproto scrnsaverproto sm trapproto videoproto x11 xau xaw xaw6 xaw7 xbitmaps xcb xcmiscproto xcomposite xcursor xdamage xdmcp xevie xext xextproto xf86bigfontproto xf86dgaproto xf86driproto xf86miscproto xf86rushproto xf86vidmodeproto xfixes xfont xfontcache xft xi xinerama xineramaproto xkbfile xkbui xmu xmuu xorg-macros xorg-server xp xpm xprintapputil xprintutil xproto xproxymngproto xrandr xrender xres xscrnsaver xshmfence xt xtrans xtrap xtst xv xvmc xxf86dga xxf86misc xxf86vm .

Always up-to-date list can be found in /usr/ports/Mk/bsd.xorg.mk .

The Mesa Project is an effort to provide free OpenGL implementation. To specify a dependency on various components of this project, use USE_GL. Valid options are: egl, gl, glesv2, glew, glu, glut, glw and linux. For backwards compatibility, the value of yes maps to glu.

Example 6.10. USE_XORG Example

```
USE_XORG= xrender xft xkbfile xt xaw
USE_GL=  glu
```

Table 6.5. Variables for Ports That Use X

USES= imake	The port uses imake.
XMKMF	Set to the path of xmkmf if not in the PATH. Defaults to xmkmf -a.

Example 6.11. Using X11-Related Variables

```
# Use some X11 libraries
USE_XORG= x11 xpm
```

6.9.2. Ports That Require Motif

If the port requires a Motif library, define USES= motif in the Makefile. Default Motif implementation is x11-toolkits/open-motif. Users can choose x11-toolkits/lesstif instead by setting WANT_LESSTIF in their make.conf .

MOTIFLIB will be set by motif.mk to reference the appropriate Motif library. Please patch the source of the port to use ${MOTIFLIB} wherever the Motif library is referenced in the original Makefile or Imakefile.

There are two common cases:

• If the port refers to the Motif library as -lXm in its Makefile or Imakefile, substitute ${MOTIFLIB} for it.

- If the port uses XmClientLibs in its Imakefile, change it to ${MOTIFLIB} ${XTOOLLIB} ${XLIB} .

Note that MOTIFLIB (usually) expands to -L/usr/local/lib -lXm -lXp or /usr/local/lib/libXm.a , so there is no need to add -L or -l in front.

6.9.3. X11 Fonts

If the port installs fonts for the X Window System, put them in LOCALBASE/lib/X11/fonts/local .

6.9.4. Getting a Fake DISPLAY with Xvfb

Some applications require a working X11 display for compilation to succeed. This poses a problem for machines that operate headless. When this variable is used, the build infrastructure will start the virtual framebuffer X server. The working DISPLAY is then passed to the build. See USES=display for the possible arguments.

```
USES= display
```

6.9.5. Desktop Entries

Desktop entries (a Freedesktop standard) provide a way to automatically adjust desktop features when a new program is installed, without requiring user intervention. For example, newly-installed programs automatically appear in the application menus of compatible desktop environments. Desktop entries originated in the GNOME desktop environment, but are now a standard and also work with KDE and Xfce. This bit of automation provides a real benefit to the user, and desktop entries are encouraged for applications which can be used in a desktop environment.

6.9.5.1. Using Predefined .desktop Files

Ports that include predefined *.desktop must include those files in pkg-plist and install them in the $LOCAL-BASE/share/applications directory. The INSTALL_DATA macro is useful for installing these files.

6.9.5.2. Updating Desktop Database

If a port has a MimeType entry in its *portname*.desktop, the desktop database must be updated after install and deinstall. To do this, define USES= desktop-file-utils.

6.9.5.3. Creating Desktop Entries with DESKTOP_ENTRIES

Desktop entries can be easily created for applications by using DESKTOP_ENTRIES. A file named *name*.desktop will be created, installed, and added to pkg-plist automatically. Syntax is:

```
DESKTOP_ENTRIES= "NAME" "COMMENT" "ICON" "COMMAND" "CATEGORY" StartupNotify
```

The list of possible categories is available on the Freedesktop website. StartupNotify indicates whether the application is compatible with *startup notifications*. These are typically a graphic indicator like a clock that appear at the mouse pointer, menu, or panel to give the user an indication when a program is starting. A program that is compatible with startup notifications clears the indicator after it has started. Programs that are not compatible with startup notifications would never clear the indicator (potentially confusing and infuriating the user), and must have StartupNotify set to false so the indicator is not shown at all.

Example:

```
DESKTOP_ENTRIES= "ToME" "Roguelike game based on JRR Tolkien's work" \
    "${DATADIR}/xtra/graf/tome-128.png" \
    "tome -v -g" "Application;Game;RolePlaying;" \
    false
```

6.10. Using GNOME

6.10.1. Introduction

This chapter explains the GNOME framework as used by ports. The framework can be loosely divided into the base components, GNOME desktop components, and a few special macros that simplify the work of port maintainers.

While developing a port or changing one, please set

```
DEVELOPER=yes
```

in the environment or in /etc/make.conf . This causes the ports framework to enable additional checks.

6.10.2. Using USE_GNOME

Adding this variable to the port allows the use of the macros and components defined in bsd.gnome.mk. The code in bsd.gnome.mk adds the needed build-time, run-time or library dependencies or the handling of special files. GNOME applications under FreeBSD use the USE_GNOME infrastructure. Include all the needed components as a space-separated list. The USE_GNOME components are divided into these virtual lists: basic components, GNOME 3 components and legacy components. If the port needs only GTK3 libraries, this is the shortest way to define it:

```
USE_GNOME= gtk30
```

USE_GNOME components automatically add the dependencies they need. Please see Section 6.11, "GNOME Components" for an exhaustive list of all USE_GNOME components and which other components they imply and their dependencies.

Here is an example Makefile for a GNOME port that uses many of the techniques outlined in this document. Please use it as a guide for creating new ports.

```
# $FreeBSD$

PORTNAME=   regexxer
DISTVERSION=  0.10
CATEGORIES=  devel textproc gnome
MASTER_SITES=  GNOME

MAINTAINER=  kwm@FreeBSD.org
COMMENT=  Interactive tool for performing search and replace operations

USES=   gettext gmake pathfix pkgconfig tar:xz
GNU_CONFIGURE= yes
USE_GNOME=  gnomeprefix intlhack gtksourceviewmm3
CPPFLAGS+=  -I${LOCALBASE}/include
LDFLAGS+=   -L${LOCALBASE}/lib
INSTALLS_ICONS= yes

GLIB_SCHEMAS=  org.regexxer.gschema.xml

.include <bsd.port.mk>
```

> **Note**
>
> The USE_GNOME macro without any arguments does not add any dependencies to the port. USE_GNOME cannot be set after bsd.port.pre.mk.

6.10.3. Variables

This section explains which macros are available and how they are used. Like they are used in the above example. The Section 6.11, "GNOME Components" has a more in-depth explanation. USE_GNOME has to be set for these macros to be of use.

INSTALLS_ICONS
> GTK+ ports which install Freedesktop-style icons to ${LOCALBASE}/share/icons should use this macro to ensure that the icons are cached and will display correctly. The cache file is named icon-theme.cache . Do not include that file in pkg-plist . This macro handles that automatically. This macro is not needed for Qt, which use a internal method.

GLIB_SCHEMAS
> List of all the glib schema files the port installs. The macro will add the files to the port plist and handle the registration of these files on install and deinstall.
>
> The glib schema files are written in XML and end with the gschema.xml extension. They are installed in the share/glib-2.0/schemas/ directory. These schema files contain all application config values with there default settings. The actual database used by the applications is built by glib-compile-schema, which is run by the GLIB_SCHEMAS macro.

```
GLIB_SCHEMAS=foo.gschema.xml
```

> ### Note
>
> Do not add glib schemas to the pkg-plist . If they are listed in pkg-plist , they will not be registered and the applications might not work properly.

GCONF_SCHEMAS
> List all the gconf schema files. The macro will add the schema files to the port plist and will handle their registration on install and deinstall.
>
> GConf is the XML-based database that virtually all GNOME applications use for storing their settings. These files are installed into the etc/gconf/schemas directory. This database is defined by installed schema files that are used to generate %gconf.xml key files. For each schema file installed by the port, there be an entry in the Makefile:

```
GCONF_SCHEMAS=my_app.schemas my_app2.schemas my_app3.schemas
```

> ### Note
>
> Gconf schemas are listed in the GCONF_SCHEMAS macro rather than pkg-plist . If they are listed in pkg-plist , they will not be registered and the applications might not work properly.

INSTALLS_OMF
> Open Source Metadata Framework (OMF) files are commonly used by GNOME 2 applications. These files contain the application help file information, and require special processing by ScrollKeeper/rarian. To properly register OMF files when installing GNOME applications from packages, make sure that omf files are listed in pkg-plist and that the port Makefile has INSTALLS_OMF defined:

```
INSTALLS_OMF=yes
```

When set, `bsd.gnome.mk` automatically scans `pkg-plist` and adds appropriate `@exec` and `@unexec` directives for each `.omf` to track in the OMF registration database.

6.11. GNOME Components

For further help with a GNOME port, look at some of the existing ports for examples. The FreeBSD GNOME page has contact information if more help is needed. The components are divided into GNOME components that are currently in use and legacy components. If the component supports argument, they are listed between parenthesis in the description. The first is the default. "Both" is shown if the component defaults to adding to both build and run dependencies.

Table 6.6. GNOME Components

Component	Associated program	Description
atk	accessibility/atk	Accessibility toolkit (ATK)
atkmm	accessibility/atkmm	c++ bindings for atk
cairo	graphics/cairo	Vector graphics library with cross-device output support
cairomm	graphics/cairomm	c++ bindings for cairo
dconf	devel/dconf	Configuration database system (both, build, run)
evolutiondataserver3	databases/evolution-data-server	Data backends for the Evolution integrated mail/PIM suite
gdkpixbuf2	graphics/gdk-pixbuf2	Graphics library for GTK+
glib20	devel/glib20	GNOME core library glib20
glibmm	devel/glibmm	c++ bindings for glib20
gnomecontrolcenter3	sysutils/gnome-control-center	GNOME 3 Control Center
gnomedesktop3	x11/gnome-desktop	GNOME 3 desktop UI library
gsound	audio/gsound	GObject library for playing system sounds (both, build, run)
gtk-update-icon-cache	graphics/gtk-update-icon-cache	Gtk-update-icon-cache utility from the Gtk+ toolkit
gtk20	x11-toolkits/gtk20	Gtk+ 2 toolkit
gtk30	x11-toolkits/gtk30	Gtk+ 3 toolkit
gtkmm20	x11-toolkits/gtkmm20	c++ bindings 2.0 for the gtk20 toolkit
gtkmm24	x11-toolkits/gtkmm24	c++ bindings 2.4 for the gtk20 toolkit
gtkmm30	x11-toolkits/gtkmm30	c++ bindings 3.0 for the gtk30 toolkit
gtksourceview2	x11-toolkits/gtksourceview2	Widget that adds syntax highlighting to GtkTextView
gtksourceview3	x11-toolkits/gtksourceview3	Text widget that adds syntax highlighting to the GtkTextView widget
gtksourceviewmm3	x11-toolkits/gtksourceviewmm3	c++ bindings for the gtksourceview3 library
gvfs	devel/gvfs	GNOME virtual file system
intltool	textproc/intltool	Tool for internationalization (also see intlhack)

Component	Associated program	Description
introspection	devel/gobject-introspection	Basic introspection bindings and tools to generate introspection bindings. Most of the time :build is enough, :both/:run is only need for applications that use introspection bindings. (both, build, run)
libgda5	databases/libgda5	Provides uniform access to different kinds of data sources
libgda5-ui	databases/libgda5-ui	UI library from the libgda5 library
libgdamm5	databases/libgdamm5	c++ bindings for the libgda5 library
libgsf	devel/libgsf	Extensible I/O abstraction for dealing with structured file formats
librsvg2	graphics/librsvg2	Library for parsing and rendering SVG vector-graphic files
libsigc++20	devel/libsigc++20	Callback Framework for C++
libxml++26	textproc/libxml++26	c++ bindings for the libxml2 library
libxml2	textproc/libxml2	XML parser library (both, build, run)
libxslt	textproc/libxslt	XSLT C library (both, build, run)
metacity	x11-wm/metacity	Window manager from GNOME
nautilus3	x11-fm/nautilus	GNOME file manager
pango	x11-toolkits/pango	Open-source framework for the layout and rendering of i18n text
pangomm	x11-toolkits/pangomm	c++ bindings for the pango library
py3gobject3	devel/py3-gobject3	Python 3, GObject 3.0 bindings
pygobject3	devel/py-gobject3	Python 2, GObject 3.0 bindings
vte3	x11-toolkits/vte3	Terminal widget with improved accessibility and I18N support

Table 6.7. GNOME Macro Components

Component	Description
gnomeprefix	Supply configure with some default locations.
intlhack	Same as intltool, but patches to make sure share/locale/ is used. Please only use when intltool alone is not enough.
referencehack	This macro is there to help splitting of the API or reference documentation into its own port.

Table 6.8. GNOME Legacy Components

Component	Associated program	Description
atspi	accessibility/at-spi	Assistive Technology Service Provider Interface
esound	audio/esound	Enlightenment sound package
gal2	x11-toolkits/gal2	Collection of widgets taken from GNOME 2 gnumeric

Component	Associated program	Description
gconf2	devel/gconf2	Configuration database system for GNOME 2
gconfmm26	devel/gconfmm26	c++ bindings for gconf2
gdkpixbuf	graphics/gdk-pixbuf	Graphics library for GTK+
glib12	devel/glib12	glib 1.2 core library
gnomedocutils	textproc/gnome-doc-utils	GNOME doc utils
gnomemimedata	misc/gnome-mime-data	MIME and Application database for GNOME 2
gnomesharp20	x11-toolkits/gnome-sharp20	GNOME 2 interfaces for the .NET runtime
gnomespeech	accessibility/gnome-speech	GNOME 2 text-to-speech API
gnomevfs2	devel/gnome-vfs	GNOME 2 Virtual File System
gtk12	x11-toolkits/gtk12	Gtk+ 1.2 toolkit
gtkhtml3	www/gtkhtml3	Lightweight HTML rendering/printing/editing engine
gtkhtml4	www/gtkhtml4	Lightweight HTML rendering/printing/editing engine
gtksharp20	x11-toolkits/gtk-sharp20	GTK+ and GNOME 2 interfaces for the .NET runtime
gtksourceview	x11-toolkits/gtksourceview	Widget that adds syntax highlighting to GtkTextView
libartgpl2	graphics/libart_lgpl	Library for high-performance 2D graphics
libbonobo	devel/libbonobo	Component and compound document system for GNOME 2
libbonoboui	x11-toolkits/libbonoboui	GUI frontend to the libbonobo component of GNOME 2
libgda4	databases/libgda4	Provides uniform access to different kinds of data sources
libglade2	devel/libglade2	GNOME 2 glade library
libgnome	x11/libgnome	Libraries for GNOME 2, a GNU desktop environment
libgnomecanvas	graphics/libgnomecanvas	Graphics library for GNOME 2
libgnomekbd	x11/libgnomekbd	GNOME 2 keyboard shared library
libgnomeprint	print/libgnomeprint	Gnome 2 print support library
libgnomeprintui	x11-toolkits/libgnomeprintui	Gnome 2 print support library
libgnomeui	x11-toolkits/libgnomeui	Libraries for the GNOME 2 GUI, a GNU desktop environment
libgtkhtml	www/libgtkhtml	Lightweight HTML rendering/printing/editing engine
libgtksourceviewmm	x11-toolkits/libgtksourceviewmm	c++ binding of GtkSourceView
libidl	devel/libIDL	Library for creating trees of CORBA IDL file

Component	Associated program	Description
libsigc++12	devel/libsigc++12	Callback Framework for C++
libwnck	x11-toolkits/libwnck	Library used for writing pagers and taskslists
libwnck3	x11-toolkits/libwnck3	Library used for writing pagers and taskslists
orbit2	devel/ORBit2	High-performance CORBA ORB with support for the C language
pygnome2	x11-toolkits/py-gnome2	Python bindings for GNOME 2
pygobject	devel/py-gobject	Python 2, GObject 2.0 bindings
pygtk2	x11-toolkits/py-gtk2	Set of Python bindings for GTK+
pygtksourceview	x11-toolkits/py-gtksourceview	Python bindings for GtkSourceView 2
vte	x11-toolkits/vte	Terminal widget with improved accessibility and I18N support

Table 6.9. Deprecated Components: Do Not Use

Component	Description
HAVE_GNOME	Deprecated, do not use. Was used to check if a component was installed. This was used for ports that did not have --enable/--disable switches for their configure script. But the building of parts of a port without a implicit request is discouraged.
WANT_GNOME	Deprecated, do not use. Was used by ports that needed USE_GNOME for optional dependencies, which where defined after bsd.port.pre.mk. Since USE_GNOME can be used after the inclusion of bsd.port.options.mk, there is little need for this macro any more.
pangox-compat	pangox-compat has been deprecated and split off from the pango package.

6.12. Using Qt

6.12.1. Ports That Require Qt

The Ports Collection provides support for Qt 4 and Qt 5 frameworks with USE_QTx, where x is 4 or 5. Set USE_QTx to the list of required Qt components (libraries, tools, plugins). The Qt 4 and Qt 5 frameworks are quite similar. The main difference is the set of supported components.

The Qt framework exports a number of variables which can be used by ports, some of them listed below:

Table 6.10. Variables Provided to Ports That Use Qt

QT_PREFIX	Set to the path where Qt was installed (${LOCALBASE}).
QMAKE	Full path to qmake binary.
LRELEASE	Full path to lrelease utility.
MOC	Full path to moc.
RCC	Full path to rcc.

UIC	Full path to uic.
QT_INCDIR	Qt include directory.
QT_LIBDIR	Qt libraries path.
QT_PLUGINDIR	Qt plugins path.

When using the Qt framework, these settings are deployed:

```
CONFIGURE_ARGS+= --with-qt-includes=${QT_INCDIR} \
    --with-qt-libraries=${QT_LIBDIR} \
    --with-extra-libs=${LOCALBASE}/lib \
    --with-extra-includes=${LOCALBASE}/include

CONFIGURE_ENV+= QTDIR="${QT_PREFIX}" QMAKE="${QMAKE}" \
    MOC="${MOC}" RCC="${RCC}" UIC="${UIC}" \
    QMAKESPEC="${QMAKESPEC}"

PLIST_SUB+= QT_INCDIR=${QT_INCDIR_REL} \
    QT_LIBDIR=${QT_LIBDIR_REL} \
    QT_PLUGINDIR=${QT_PLUGINDIR_REL}
```

Some configure scripts do not support the arguments above. To suppress modification of CONFIGURE_ENV and CONFIGURE_ARGS, set QT_NONSTANDARD.

6.12.2. Component Selection

Individual Qt tool and library dependencies must be specified in USE_QT*x*. Every component can be suffixed with _build or _run, the suffix indicating whether the dependency on the component is at buildtime or runtime. If unsuffixed, the component will be depended on at both build- and runtime. Usually, library components are specified unsuffixed, tool components are mostly specified with the _build suffix and plugin components are specified with the _run suffix. The most commonly used components are listed below (all available components are listed in _USE_QT_ALL , _USE_QT4_ONLY, and _USE_QT5_ONLY in /usr/ports/Mk/bsd.qt.mk):

Table 6.11. Available Qt Library Components

Name	Description
core	core library (Qt 5 only)
corelib	core library (Qt 4 only)
dbus	Qt DBus library
gui	graphical user interface library
network	network library
opengl	Qt OpenGL library
script	script library
sql	SQL library
testlib	unit testing library
webkit	Qt WebKit library
xml	Qt XML library

To determine the libraries an application depends on, run ldd on the main executable after a successful compilation.

Table 6.12. Available Qt Tool Components

Name	Description
qmake	Makefile generator/build utility

Name	Description
buildtools	build tools (moc, rcc), needed for almost every Qt application (Qt 5 only)
linguisttools	localization tools: lrelease, lupdate (Qt 5 only)
linguist	localization tools: lrelease, lupdate (Qt 4 only)
moc	meta object compiler, needed for almost every Qt application at buildtime (Qt 4 only)
rcc	resource compiler, needed if the application comes with *.rc or *.qrc files (Qt 4 only)
uic	user interface compiler, needed if the application comes with *.ui files, in practice, every Qt application with a GUI (Qt 4 only)

Table 6.13. Available Qt Plugin Components

Name	Description
iconengines	SVG icon engine plugin, needed if the application ships SVG icons (Qt 4 only)
imageformats	plugins for TGA, TIFF, and MNG image formats

Example 6.12. Selecting Qt 4 Components

In this example, the ported application uses the Qt 4 graphical user interface library, the Qt 4 core library, all of the Qt 4 code generation tools and Qt 4's Makefile generator. Since the gui library implies a dependency on the core library, corelib does not need to be specified. The Qt 4 code generation tools moc, uic and rcc, as well as the Makefile generator qmake are only needed at buildtime, thus they are specified with the _build suffix:

```
USE_QT4= gui moc_build qmake_build rcc_build uic_build
```

6.12.3. Using qmake

If the application provides a qmake project file (*.pro), define USES= qmake along with USE_QT x. Note that USES= qmake already implies a build dependency on qmake, therefore the qmake component can be omitted from USE_QT x. Similar to CMake, qmake supports out-of-source builds, which can be enabled by specifying the outsource argument (see USES= qmake example).

Table 6.14. Variables for Ports That Use qmake

Variable	Means
QMAKE_ARGS	Port specific qmake flags to be passed to the qmake binary.
QMAKE_ENV	Environment variables to be set for the qmake binary. The default is ${CONFIGURE_ENV}.
QMAKE_SOURCE_PATH	Path to qmake project files (.pro). The default is ${WRKSRC} if an out-of-source build is requested, empty otherwise.

Example 6.13. `USES= qmake` Example

This snippet demonstrates the use of qmake for a Qt 4 port:

```
USES=  qmake:outsource
USE_QT4= moc_build
```

For a Qt 5 port:

```
USES=  qmake:outsource
USE_QT5= buildtools_build
```

Qt applications are often written to be cross-platform and often X11/Unix is not the platform they are developed on, which in turn leads to certain loose ends, like:

- *Missing additional include paths.* Many applications come with system tray icon support, but neglect to look for includes and/or libraries in the X11 directories. To add directories to qmake's include and library search paths via the command line, use:

```
QMAKE_ARGS+= INCLUDEPATH+=${LOCALBASE}/include \
   LIBS+=-L${LOCALBASE}/lib
```

- *Bogus installation paths.* Sometimes data such as icons or .desktop files are by default installed into directories which are not scanned by XDG-compatible applications. editors/texmaker is an example for this - look at patch-texmaker.pro in the `files` directory of that port for a template on how to remedy this directly in the qmake project file.

6.13. Using KDE

6.13.1. KDE 4 Variable Definitions

If the application depends on KDE 4, set `USES+=kde:4` and `USE_KDE` to the list of required components. `_build` and `_run` suffixes can be used to force components dependency type (for example, `baseapps_run`). If no suffix is set, a default dependency type will be used. To force both types, add the component twice with both suffixes (for example, `automoc4_build automoc4_run`). The most commonly used components are listed below (up-to-date components are documented at the top of `/usr/ports/Mk/bsd.kde4.mk`):

Table 6.15. Available KDE 4 Components

Name	Description
kdehier	Hierarchy of common KDE directories
kdelibs	KDE core libraries
kdeprefix	If set, port will be installed into ${KDE_PREFIX}
automoc4	Build tool to automatically generate moc files
akonadi	Storage server for KDE PIM data
soprano	Library for Resource Description Framework (RDF)
strigi	Strigi desktop search library
libkcddb	KDE CDDB (compact disc database) library
libkcompactdisc	KDE library for interfacing with audio CDs
libkdeedu	Libraries used by educational applications

Name	Description
libkdcraw	KDE LibRaw library
libkexiv2	KDE Exiv2 library
libkipi	KDE Image Plugin Interface
libkonq	Konqueror core library
libksane	KDE SANE ("Scanner Access Now Easy") library
pimlibs	Personal information management libraries
kate	Advanced text editor framework
marble	Virtual globe and world atlas
okular	Universal document viewer
korundum	KDE Ruby bindings
perlkde	KDE Perl bindings
pykde4	KDE Python bindings
pykdeuic4	PyKDE user interface compiler
smokekde	KDE SMOKE libraries

KDE 4 ports are installed into KDE_PREFIX. This is achieved by specifying the kdeprefix component, which overrides the default PREFIX. The ports, however, respect any PREFIX set via the MAKEFLAGS environment variable and/or make arguments. Currently KDE_PREFIX is identical to the default PREFIX, ${LOCALBASE}.

Example 6.14. USE_KDE Example

This is a simple example for a KDE 4 port. USES= cmake:outsource instructs the port to utilize CMake, a configuration tool widely used by KDE 4 projects (see Section 6.5.4, "Using cmake" for detailed usage). USE_KDE brings dependency on KDE libraries and makes port using automoc4 at build stage. Required KDE components and other dependencies can be determined through configure log. USE_KDE does not imply USE_QT4. If a port requires some Qt 4 components, specify them in USE_QT4.

```
USES=   cmake:outsource kde:4
USE_KDE= kdelibs kdeprefix automoc4
USE_QT4= moc_build qmake_build rcc_build uic_build
```

6.14. Using LXQt

Applications depending on LXQt should set USES+= lxqt and set USE_LXQT to the list of required components from the table below

Table 6.16. Available LXQt Components

Name	Description
buildtools	Helpers for additional CMake modules
libfmqt	Libfm Qt bindings
lxqt	LXQt core library
qtxdg	Qt implementation of freedesktop.org XDG specifications

---

> ## Example 6.15. USE_LXQT Example
>
> This is a simple example, USE_LXQT adds a dependency on LXQt libraries. Required LXQt components and other dependencies can be determined from the configure log.
>
> ```
> USES=    cmake:outsource lxqt tar:xz
> USE_QT5=           buildtools_build qmake_build core dbus widgets
> USE_LXQT=          buildtools libfmqt
> ```

6.15. Using Java

6.15.1. Variable Definitions

If the port needs a Java™ Development Kit (JDK™) to either build, run or even extract the distfile, then define USE_JAVA.

There are several JDKs in the ports collection, from various vendors, and in several versions. If the port must use a particular version, specify it using the JAVA_VERSION variable. The most current version is java/openjdk8, with java/openjdk6 and java/openjdk7 also available.

Table 6.17. Variables Which May be Set by Ports That Use Java

Variable	Means
USE_JAVA	Define for the remaining variables to have any effect.
JAVA_VERSION	List of space-separated suitable Java versions for the port. An optional "+" allows specifying a range of versions (allowed values: 1.5[+] 1.6[+] 1.7[+]).
JAVA_OS	List of space-separated suitable JDK port operating systems for the port (allowed values: native linux).
JAVA_VENDOR	List of space-separated suitable JDK port vendors for the port (allowed values: freebsd bsdjava sun openjdk).
JAVA_BUILD	When set, add the selected JDK port to the build dependencies.
JAVA_RUN	When set, add the selected JDK port to the run dependencies.
JAVA_EXTRACT	When set, add the selected JDK port to the extract dependencies.

Below is the list of all settings a port will receive after setting USE_JAVA:

Table 6.18. Variables Provided to Ports That Use Java

Variable	Value
JAVA_PORT	The name of the JDK port (for example, java/openjdk6).
JAVA_PORT_VERSION	The full version of the JDK port (for example, 1.6.0). Only the first two digits of this version number are needed, use ${JAVA_PORT_VERSION:C/^([0-9])\.([0-9])(.*)$/\1.\2/} .

Variable	Value
JAVA_PORT_OS	The operating system used by the JDK port (for example, 'native').
JAVA_PORT_VENDOR	The vendor of the JDK port (for example, 'openjdk').
JAVA_PORT_OS_DESCRIPTION	Description of the operating system used by the JDK port (for example, 'Native').
JAVA_PORT_VENDOR_DESCRIPTION	Description of the vendor of the JDK port (for example, 'OpenJDK BSD Porting Team').
JAVA_HOME	Path to the installation directory of the JDK (for example, '/usr/local/openjdk6').
JAVAC	Path to the Java compiler to use (for example, '/usr/local/openjdk6/bin/javac').
JAR	Path to the jar tool to use (for example, '/usr/local/openjdk6/bin/jar' or '/usr/local/bin/fastjar').
APPLETVIEWER	Path to the appletviewer utility (for example, '/usr/local/openjdk6/bin/appletviewer').
JAVA	Path to the java executable. Use this for executing Java programs (for example, '/usr/local/openjdk6/bin/java').
JAVADOC	Path to the javadoc utility program.
JAVAH	Path to the javah program.
JAVAP	Path to the javap program.
JAVA_KEYTOOL	Path to the keytool utility program.
JAVA_N2A	Path to the native2ascii tool.
JAVA_POLICYTOOL	Path to the policytool program.
JAVA_SERIALVER	Path to the serialver utility program.
RMIC	Path to the RMI stub/skeleton generator, rmic.
RMIREGISTRY	Path to the RMI registry program, rmiregistry.
RMID	Path to the RMI daemon program rmid.
JAVA_CLASSES	Path to the archive that contains the JDK class files, ${JAVA_HOME}/jre/lib/rt.jar .

Use the java-debug make target to get information for debugging the port. It will display the value of many of the previously listed variables.

Additionally, these constants are defined so all Java ports may be installed in a consistent way:

Table 6.19. Constants Defined for Ports That Use Java

Constant	Value
JAVASHAREDIR	The base directory for everything related to Java. Default: ${PREFIX}/share/java .
JAVAJARDIR	The directory where JAR files is installed. Default: ${JAVASHAREDIR}/classes .
JAVALIBDIR	The directory where JAR files installed by other ports are located. Default: ${LOCALBASE}/share/java/classes .

The related entries are defined in both PLIST_SUB (documented in Section 8.1, "Changing pkg-plist Based on Make Variables") and SUB_LIST.

6.15.2. Building with Ant

When the port is to be built using Apache Ant, it has to define USE_ANT. Ant is thus considered to be the sub-make command. When no do-build target is defined by the port, a default one will be set that runs Ant according to MAKE_ENV, MAKE_ARGS and ALL_TARGET. This is similar to the USES= gmake mechanism, which is documented in Section 6.5, "Building Mechanisms".

6.15.3. Best Practices

When porting a Java library, the port has to install the JAR file(s) in ${JAVAJARDIR}, and everything else under ${JAVASHAREDIR}/${PORTNAME} (except for the documentation, see below). To reduce the packing file size, reference the JAR file(s) directly in the Makefile. Use this statement (where myport.jar is the name of the JAR file installed as part of the port):

```
PLIST_FILES+= ${JAVAJARDIR}/myport.jar
```

When porting a Java application, the port usually installs everything under a single directory (including its JAR dependencies). The use of ${JAVASHAREDIR}/${PORTNAME} is strongly encouraged in this regard. It is up the porter to decide whether the port installs the additional JAR dependencies under this directory or uses the already installed ones (from ${JAVAJARDIR}).

When porting a Java™ application that requires an application server such as www/tomcat7 to run the service, it is quite common for a vendor to distribute a .war. A .war is a Web application ARchive and is extracted when called by the application. Avoid adding a .war to pkg-plist. It is not considered best practice. An application server will expand war archive, but not clean it up properly if the port is removed. A more desirable way of working with this file is to extract the archive, then install the files, and lastly add these files to pkg-plist.

```
TOMCATDIR= ${LOCALBASE}/apache-tomcat-7.0
WEBAPPDIR= myapplication

post-extract:
 @${MKDIR} ${WRKDIR}/${PORTDIRNAME}
 @${TAR} xf ${WRKDIR}/myapplication.war -C ${WRKDIR}/${PORTDIRNAME}

do-install:
 cd ${WRKDIR} && \
 ${INSTALL} -d -o ${WWWOWN} -g ${WWWGRP} ${TOMCATDIR}/webapps/${PORTDIRNAME}
 cd ${WRKDIR}/${PORTDIRNAME} && ${COPYTREE_SHARE} \* ${WEBAPPDIR}/${PORTDIRNAME}
```

Regardless of the type of port (library or application), the additional documentation is installed in the same location as for any other port. The Javadoc tool is known to produce a different set of files depending on the version of the JDK that is used. For ports that do not enforce the use of a particular JDK, it is therefore a complex task to specify the packing list (pkg-plist). This is one reason why porters are strongly encouraged to use PORTDOCS. Moreover, even if the set of files that will be generated by javadoc can be predicted, the size of the resulting pkg-plist advocates for the use of PORTDOCS.

The default value for DATADIR is ${PREFIX}/share/${PORTNAME}. It is a good idea to override DATADIR to ${JAVASHAREDIR}/${PORTNAME} for Java ports. Indeed, DATADIR is automatically added to PLIST_SUB (documented in Section 8.1, "Changing pkg-plist Based on Make Variables") so use %%DATADIR%% directly in pkg-plist.

As for the choice of building Java ports from source or directly installing them from a binary distribution, there is no defined policy at the time of writing. However, people from the FreeBSD Java Project encourage porters to have their ports built from source whenever it is a trivial task.

All the features that have been presented in this section are implemented in bsd.java.mk. If the port needs more sophisticated Java support, please first have a look at the bsd.java.mk Subversion log as it usually takes some time to document the latest features. Then, if the needed support that is lacking would be beneficial to many other Java ports, feel free to discuss it on the FreeBSD Java Language mailing list.

Although there is a java category for PRs, it refers to the JDK porting effort from the FreeBSD Java project. Therefore, submit the Java port in the ports category as for any other port, unless the issue is related to either a JDK implementation or bsd.java.mk.

Similarly, there is a defined policy regarding the CATEGORIES of a Java port, which is detailed in Section 5.3, "Categorization".

6.16. Web Applications, Apache and PHP

6.16.1. Apache

Table 6.20. Variables for Ports That Use Apache

USE_APACHE	The port requires Apache. Possible values: yes (gets any version), 22, 24, 22-24, 22+, etc. The default APACHE version is 22. More details are available in ports/Mk/bsd.apache.mk and at wiki.freebsd.org/Apache/.
APXS	Full path to the apxs binary. Can be overridden in the port.
HTTPD	Full path to the httpd binary. Can be overridden in the port.
APACHE_VERSION	The version of present Apache installation (read-only variable). This variable is only available after inclusion of bsd.port.pre.mk. Possible values: 22, 24.
APACHEMODDIR	Directory for Apache modules. This variable is automatically expanded in pkg-plist.
APACHEINCLUDEDIR	Directory for Apache headers. This variable is automatically expanded in pkg-plist.
APACHEETCDIR	Directory for Apache configuration files. This variable is automatically expanded in pkg-plist.

Table 6.21. Useful Variables for Porting Apache Modules

MODULENAME	Name of the module. Default value is PORTNAME. Example: mod_hello
SHORTMODNAME	Short name of the module. Automatically derived from MODULENAME, but can be overridden. Example: hello
AP_FAST_BUILD	Use apxs to compile and install the module.
AP_GENPLIST	Also automatically creates a pkg-plist.
AP_INC	Adds a directory to a header search path during compilation.
AP_LIB	Adds a directory to a library search path during compilation.
AP_EXTRAS	Additional flags to pass to apxs.

6.16.2. Web Applications

Web applications must be installed into PREFIX/www/appname. This path is available both in Makefile and in pkg-plist as WWWDIR, and the path relative to PREFIX is available in Makefile as WWWDIR_REL.

The user and group of web server process are available as WWWOWN and WWWGRP, in case the ownership of some files needs to be changed. The default values of both are www. Use WWWOWN?= myuser and WWWGRP?= mygroup if the port needs different values. This allows the user to override them easily.

Important

Use WWWOWN and WWWGRP sparingly. Remember that every file the web server can write to is a security risk waiting to happen.

Do not depend on Apache unless the web app explicitly needs Apache. Respect that users may wish to run a web application on a web server other than Apache.

6.16.3. PHP

PHP web applications declare their dependency on it with USES=php . See Section 17.66, "php" for more information.

6.16.4. PEAR Modules

Porting PEAR modules is a very simple process.

Add USES=pear to the port's Makefile. The framework will install the relevant files in the right places and automatically generate the plist at install time.

Example 6.16. Example Makefile for PEAR Class

```
PORTNAME=       Date
DISTVERSION= 1.4.3
CATEGORIES= devel www pear

MAINTAINER= example@domain.com
COMMENT= PEAR Date and Time Zone Classes

USES= pear

.include <bsd.port.mk>
```

6.16.4.1. Horde Modules

In the same way, porting Horde modules is a simple process.

Add USES=horde to the port's Makefile. The framework will install the relevant files in the right places and automatically generate the plist at install time.

The USE_HORDE_BUILD and USE_HORDE_RUN variables can be used to add buildtime and runtime dependencies on other Horde modules. See Mk/Uses/horde.mk for a complete list of available modules.

Example 6.17. Example Makefile for Horde Module

```
PORTNAME= Horde_Core
DISTVERSION= 2.14.0
CATEGORIES= devel www pear
```

```
MAINTAINER= horde@FreeBSD.org
COMMENT= Horde Core Framework libraries

OPTIONS_DEFINE= KOLAB SOCKETS
KOLAB_DESC= Enable Kolab server support
SOCKETS_DESC= Depend on sockets PHP extension

USES= horde
USE_PHP= session

USE_HORDE_BUILD= Horde_Role
USE_HORDE_RUN= Horde_Role Horde_History Horde_Pack \
  Horde_Text_Filter Horde_View

KOLAB_USE= HORDE_RUN=Horde_Kolab_Server,Horde_Kolab_Session
SOCKETS_USE= PHP=sockets

.include <bsd.port.mk>
```

6.17. Using Python

The Ports Collection supports parallel installation of multiple Python versions. Ports must use a correct python interpreter, according to the user-settable PYTHON_VERSION . Most prominently, this means replacing the path to python executable in scripts with the value of PYTHON_CMD .

Ports that install files under PYTHON_SITELIBDIR must use the pyXY- package name prefix, so their package name embeds the version of Python they are installed into.

```
PKGNAMEPREFIX= ${PYTHON_PKGNAMEPREFIX}
```

Table 6.22. Most Useful Variables for Ports That Use Python

USES=python	The port needs Python. The minimal required version can be specified with values such as 2.7+. Version ranges can also be specified by separating two version numbers with a dash: USES=python:3.2-3.3
USE_PYTHON=distutils	Use Python distutils for configuring, compiling, and installing. This is required when the port comes with setup.py. This overrides the do-build and do-install targets and may also override do-configure if GNU_CONFIGURE is not defined. Additionally, it implies USE_PYTHON=flavors.
USE_PYTHON=autoplist	Create the packaging list automatically. This also requires USE_PYTHON=distutils to be set.
USE_PYTHON=concurrent	The port will use an unique prefix, typically PYTHON_P-KGNAMEPREFIX for certain directories, such as EXAMPLESDIR and DOCSDIR and also will append a suffix, the python version from PYTHON_VER , to binaries and scripts to be installed. This allows ports to be installed for different Python versions at the same time, which otherwise would install conflicting files.
USE_PYTHON=flavors	The port does not use distutils but still supports multiple Python versions. FLAVORS will be set to the supported Python versions. See Section 7.3.1, "USES=python and Flavors" for more information.

USE_PYTHON=optsuffix	If the current Python version is not the default version, the port will gain PKGNAMESUFFIX=${PYTHON_PKG-NAMESUFFIX}. Only useful with flavors.
PYTHON_PKGNAMEPREFIX	Used as a PKGNAMEPREFIX to distinguish packages for different Python versions. Example: py27-
PYTHON_SITELIBDIR	Location of the site-packages tree, that contains installation path of Python (usually LOCALBASE). PYTHON_SITELIBDIR can be very useful when installing Python modules.
PYTHONPREFIX_SITELIBDIR	The PREFIX-clean variant of PYTHON_SITELIBDIR. Always use %%PYTHON_SITELIBDIR%% in pkg-plist when possible. The default value of %%PYTHON_SITELIBDIR%% is lib/python%%PYTHON_VERSION%%/site-packages
PYTHON_CMD	Python interpreter command line, including version number.

Table 6.23. Python Module Dependency Helpers

PYNUMERIC	Dependency line for numeric extension.
PYNUMPY	Dependency line for the new numeric extension, numpy. (PYNUMERIC is deprecated by upstream vendor).
PYXML	Dependency line for XML extension (not needed for Python 2.0 and higher as it is also in base distribution).
PY_ENUM34	Conditionnal dependency on devel/py-enum34 depending on the Python version.
PY_ENUM_COMPAT	Conditionnal dependency on devel/py-enum-compat depending on the Python version.
PY_PATHLIB	Conditionnal dependency on devel/py-pathlib depending on the Python version.
PY_IPADDRESS	Conditionnal dependency on net/py-ipaddress depending on the Python version.
PY_FUTURES	Conditionnal dependency on devel/py-futures depending on the Python version.

A complete list of available variables can be found in /usr/ports/Mk/Uses/python.mk .

Important

All dependencies to Python ports using Python flavors (either with USE_PYTHON=distutils or USE_PYTHON=flavors) must have the Python flavor appended to their origin using @${PY_FLAVOR}. See Example 6.18, "Makefile for a Simple Python Module".

If the port in question is also using Python flavors, it can simply use @${FLAVOR} as its content will be the same.

Example 6.18. Makefile for a Simple Python Module

```
PORTNAME= sample
```

```
DISTVERSION= 1.2.3
CATEGORIES= devel

MAINTAINER= john@doe.tld
COMMENT= Python sample module

RUN_DEPENDS= ${PYTHON_PKGNAMEPREFIX}six>0:devel/py-six@${PY_FLAVOR}

USES=   python
USE_PYTHON= autoplist distutils

.include <bsd.port.mk>
```

Some Python applications claim to have DESTDIR support (which would be required for staging) but it is broken (Mailman up to 2.1.16, for instance). This can be worked around by recompiling the scripts. This can be done, for example, in the post-build target. Assuming the Python scripts are supposed to reside in PYTHONPREFIX_SITELIB-DIR after installation, this solution can be applied:

```
(cd ${STAGEDIR}${PREFIX} \
  && ${PYTHON_CMD} ${PYTHON_LIBDIR}/compileall.py \
  -d ${PREFIX} -f ${PYTHONPREFIX_SITELIBDIR:S;${PREFIX}/;;})
```

This recompiles the sources with a path relative to the stage directory, and prepends the value of PREFIX to the file name recorded in the byte-compiled output file by -d. -f is required to force recompilation, and the :S;${PRE-FIX}/;; strips prefixes from the value of PYTHONPREFIX_SITELIBDIR to make it relative to PREFIX.

6.18. Using Tcl/Tk

The Ports Collection supports parallel installation of multiple Tcl/Tk versions. Ports should try to support at least the default Tcl/Tk version and higher with USES=tcl. It is possible to specify the desired version of tcl by appending :xx, for example, USES=tcl:85.

Table 6.24. The Most Useful Read-Only Variables for Ports That Use Tcl/Tk

TCL_VER	chosen major.minor version of Tcl
TCLSH	full path of the Tcl interpreter
TCL_LIBDIR	path of the Tcl libraries
TCL_INCLUDEDIR	path of the Tcl C header files
TK_VER	chosen major.minor version of Tk
WISH	full path of the Tk interpreter
TK_LIBDIR	path of the Tk libraries
TK_INCLUDEDIR	path of the Tk C header files

See the USES=tcl and USES=tk of Chapter 17, *Using USES Macros* for a full description of those variables. A complete list of those variables is available in /usr/ports/Mk/Uses/tcl.mk .

6.19. Using Ruby

Table 6.25. Useful Variables for Ports That Use Ruby

Variable	Description
USE_RUBY	Adds build and run dependencies on Ruby.
USE_RUBY_EXTCONF	The port uses extconf.rb to configure.

Variable	Description
USE_RUBY_SETUP	The port uses setup.rb to configure.
RUBY_SETUP	Override the name of the setup script from setup.rb. Another common value is install.rb.

This table shows the selected variables available to port authors via the ports infrastructure. These variables are used to install files into their proper locations. Use them in pkg-plist as much as possible. Do not redefine these variables in the port.

Table 6.26. Selected Read-Only Variables for Ports That Use Ruby

Variable	Description	Example value
RUBY_PKGNAMEPREFIX	Used as a PKGNAMEPREFIX to distinguish packages for different Ruby versions.	ruby19-
RUBY_VERSION	Full version of Ruby in the form of x.y.z[.p].	1.9.3.484
RUBY_SITELIBDIR	Architecture independent libraries installation path.	/usr/local/lib/ ruby/site_ruby/1.9
RUBY_SITEARCHLIBDIR	Architecture dependent libraries installation path.	/usr/local/lib/ ruby/site_ruby/1.9/amd64- freebsd10
RUBY_MODDOCDIR	Module documentation installation path.	/usr/local/share/doc/ ruby19/patsy
RUBY_MODEXAMPLESDIR	Module examples installation path.	/usr/local/share/ examples/ruby19/patsy

A complete list of available variables can be found in /usr/ports/Mk/bsd.ruby.mk .

6.20. Using SDL

USE_SDL is used to autoconfigure the dependencies for ports which use an SDL based library like devel/sdl12 and graphics/sdl_image.

These SDL libraries for version 1.2 are recognized:

- sdl: devel/sdl12

- console: devel/sdl_console

- gfx: graphics/sdl_gfx

- image: graphics/sdl_image

- mixer: audio/sdl_mixer

- mm: devel/sdlmm

- net: net/sdl_net

- pango: x11-toolkits/sdl_pango

- sound: audio/sdl_sound

- ttf: graphics/sdl_ttf

These SDL libraries for version 2.0 are recognized:

- **sdl:** devel/sdl20

- **gfx:** graphics/sdl2_gfx

- **image:** graphics/sdl2_image

- **mixer:** audio/sdl2_mixer

- **net:** net/sdl2_net

- **ttf:** graphics/sdl2_ttf

Therefore, if a port has a dependency on net/sdl_net and audio/sdl_mixer, the syntax will be:

```
USE_SDL= net mixer
```

The dependency devel/sdl12, which is required by net/sdl_net and audio/sdl_mixer, is automatically added as well.

Using `USE_SDL` with entries for SDL 1.2, it will automatically:

- Add a dependency on sdl12-config to `BUILD_DEPENDS`

- Add the variable `SDL_CONFIG` to `CONFIGURE_ENV`

- Add the dependencies of the selected libraries to `LIB_DEPENDS`

Using `USE_SDL` with entries for SDL 2.0, it will automatically:

- Add a dependency on sdl2-config to `BUILD_DEPENDS`

- Add the variable `SDL2_CONFIG` to `CONFIGURE_ENV`

- Add the dependencies of the selected libraries to `LIB_DEPENDS`

6.21. Using wxWidgets

This section describes the status of the wxWidgets libraries in the ports tree and its integration with the ports system.

6.21.1. Introduction

There are many versions of the wxWidgets libraries which conflict between them (install files under the same name). In the ports tree this problem has been solved by installing each version under a different name using version number suffixes.

The obvious disadvantage of this is that each application has to be modified to find the expected version. Fortunately, most of the applications call the wx-config script to determine the necessary compiler and linker flags. The script is named differently for every available version. Majority of applications respect an environment variable, or accept a configure argument, to specify which wx-config script to call. Otherwise they have to be patched.

6.21.2. Version Selection

To make the port use a specific version of wxWidgets there are two variables available for defining (if only one is defined the other will be set to a default value):

Table 6.27. Variables to Select wxWidgets Versions

Variable	Description	Default value
USE_WX	List of versions the port can use	All available versions

Variable	Description	Default value
USE_WX_NOT	List of versions the port cannot use	None

The available wxWidgets versions and the corresponding ports in the tree are:

Table 6.28. Available wxWidgets Versions

Version	Port
2.8	x11-toolkits/wxgtk28
3.0	x11-toolkits/wxgtk30

The variables in Table 6.27, "Variables to Select wxWidgets Versions" can be set to one or more of these combinations separated by spaces:

Table 6.29. wxWidgets Version Specifications

Description	Example
Single version	2.8
Ascending range	2.8+
Descending range	3.0-
Full range (must be ascending)	2.8-3.0

There are also some variables to select the preferred versions from the available ones. They can be set to a list of versions, the first ones will have higher priority.

Table 6.30. Variables to Select Preferred wxWidgets Versions

Name	Designed for
WANT_WX_VER	the port
WITH_WX_VER	the user

6.21.3. Component Selection

There are other applications that, while not being wxWidgets libraries, are related to them. These applications can be specified in WX_COMPS. These components are available:

Table 6.31. Available wxWidgets Components

Name	Description	Version restriction
wx	main library	none
contrib	contributed libraries	none
python	wxPython (Python bindings)	2.8-3.0

The dependency type can be selected for each component by adding a suffix separated by a semicolon. If not present then a default type will be used (see Table 6.33, "Default wxWidgets Dependency Types"). These types are available:

Table 6.32. Available wxWidgets Dependency Types

Name	Description
build	Component is required for building, equivalent to BUILD_DEPENDS
run	Component is required for running, equivalent to RUN_DEPENDS

Name	Description
lib	Component is required for building and running, equivalent to LIB_DEPENDS

The default values for the components are detailed in this table:

Table 6.33. Default wxWidgets Dependency Types

Component	Dependency type
wx	lib
contrib	lib
python	run
mozilla	lib
svg	lib

Example 6.19. Selecting wxWidgets Components

This fragment corresponds to a port which uses wxWidgets version 2.4 and its contributed libraries.

```
USE_WX=   2.8
WX_COMPS= wx contrib
```

6.21.4. Detecting Installed Versions

To detect an installed version, define WANT_WX. If it is not set to a specific version then the components will have a version suffix. HAVE_WX will be filled after detection.

Example 6.20. Detecting Installed wxWidgets Versions and Components

This fragment can be used in a port that uses wxWidgets if it is installed, or an option is selected.

```
WANT_WX= yes

.include <bsd.port.pre.mk>

.if defined(WITH_WX) || !empty(PORT_OPTIONS:MWX) || !empty(HAVE_WX:Mwx-2.8)
USE_WX=   2.8
CONFIGURE_ARGS+= --enable-wx
.endif
```

This fragment can be used in a port that enables wxPython support if it is installed or if an option is selected, in addition to wxWidgets, both version 2.8.

```
USE_WX=   2.8
WX_COMPS= wx
WANT_WX= 2.8

.include <bsd.port.pre.mk>

.if defined(WITH_WXPYTHON) || !empty(PORT_OPTIONS:MWXPYTHON) || !empty⏎
(HAVE_WX:Mpython)
WX_COMPS+=  python
CONFIGURE_ARGS+= --enable-wxpython
```

```
.endif
```

6.21.5. Defined Variables

These variables are available in the port (after defining one from Table 6.27, "Variables to Select wxWidgets Versions").

Table 6.34. Variables Defined for Ports That Use wxWidgets

Name	Description
WX_CONFIG	The path to the wxWidgets wx-config script (with different name)
WXRC_CMD	The path to the wxWidgets wxrc program (with different name)
WX_VERSION	The wxWidgets version that is going to be used (for example, 2.6)

6.21.6. Processing in bsd.port.pre.mk

Define WX_PREMK to be able to use the variables right after including bsd.port.pre.mk.

Important

When defining WX_PREMK, then the version, dependencies, components and defined variables will not change if modifying the wxWidgets port variables *after* including bsd.port.pre.mk.

Example 6.21. Using wxWidgets Variables in Commands

This fragment illustrates the use of WX_PREMK by running the wx-config script to obtain the full version string, assign it to a variable and pass it to the program.

```
USE_WX=  2.8
WX_PREMK= yes

.include <bsd.port.pre.mk>

.if exists(${WX_CONFIG})
VER_STR!= ${WX_CONFIG} --release

PLIST_SUB+= VERSION="${VER_STR}"
.endif
```

Note

The wxWidgets variables can be safely used in commands when they are inside targets without the need of WX_PREMK.

6.21.7. Additional configure Arguments

Some GNU configure scripts cannot find wxWidgets with just the WX_CONFIG environment variable set, requiring additional arguments. WX_CONF_ARGS can be used for provide them.

Table 6.35. Legal Values for WX_CONF_ARGS

Possible value	Resulting argument
absolute	--with-wx-config=${WX_CONFIG}
relative	--with-wx=${LOCALBASE} --with-wx-config=${WX_CONFIG:T}

6.22. Using Lua

This section describes the status of the Lua libraries in the ports tree and its integration with the ports system.

6.22.1. Introduction

There are many versions of the Lua libraries and corresponding interpreters, which conflict between them (install files under the same name). In the ports tree this problem has been solved by installing each version under a different name using version number suffixes.

The obvious disadvantage of this is that each application has to be modified to find the expected version. But it can be solved by adding some additional flags to the compiler and linker.

6.22.2. Version Selection

A port using Lua only needs to have this line:

```
USES= lua
```

If a specific version of Lua is needed, instructions on how to select it are given in the USES=lua part of Chapter 17, *Using USES Macros*.

6.22.3. Defined Variables

These variables are available in the port.

Table 6.36. Variables Defined for Ports That Use Lua

Name	Description
LUA_VER	The Lua version that is going to be used (for example, 5.1)
LUA_VER_STR	The Lua version without the dots (for example, 51)
LUA_PREFIX	The prefix where Lua (and components) is installed
LUA_SUBDIR	The directory under ${PREFIX}/bin, ${PREFIX}/share and ${PREFIX}/lib where Lua is installed
LUA_INCDIR	The directory where Lua and tolua header files are installed
LUA_LIBDIR	The directory where Lua and tolua libraries are installed
LUA_MODLIBDIR	The directory where Lua module libraries (.so) are installed
LUA_MODSHAREDIR	The directory where Lua modules (.lua) are installed
LUA_PKGNAMEPREFIX	The package name prefix used by Lua modules

Name	Description
LUA_CMD	The path to the Lua interpreter
LUAC_CMD	The path to the Lua compiler

6.23. Using `iconv`

After 2013-10-08 (254273), FreeBSD 10-CURRENT and newer versions have a native iconv in the operating system. On earlier versions, converters/libiconv was used as a dependency.

For software that needs iconv, define USES=iconv. FreeBSD versions before 10-CURRENT on 2013-08-13 (254273) do not have a native iconv. On these earlier versions, a dependency on converters/libiconv will be added automatically.

When a port defines USES=iconv, these variables will be available:

Variable name	Purpose	Value before Free-BSD 10-CURRENT 254273 (2013-08-13)	Value after Free-BSD 10-CURRENT 254273 (2013-08-13)
ICONV_CMD	Directory where the iconv binary resides	${LOCALBASE}/bin/iconv	/usr/bin/iconv
ICONV_LIB	ld argument to link to libiconv (if needed)	-liconv	(empty)
ICONV_PREFIX	Directory where the iconv implementation resides (useful for configure scripts)	${LOCALBASE}	/usr
ICONV_CONFIGURE_ARG	Preconstructed configure argument for configure scripts	--with-libiconv-prefix=${LOCALBASE}	(empty)
ICONV_CONFIGURE_BASE	Preconstructed configure argument for configure scripts	--with-libiconv=${LOCALBASE}	(empty)

These two examples automatically populate the variables with the correct value for systems using converters/libiconv or the native iconv respectively:

Example 6.22. Simple `iconv` Usage

```
USES=   iconv
LDFLAGS+= -L${LOCALBASE}/lib ${ICONV_LIB}
```

Example 6.23. `iconv` Usage with `configure`

```
USES=   iconv
CONFIGURE_ARGS+=${ICONV_CONFIGURE_ARG}
```

As shown above, `ICONV_LIB` is empty when a native `iconv` is present. This can be used to detect the native `iconv` and respond appropriately.

Sometimes a program has an `ld` argument or search path hardcoded in a `Makefile` or configure script. This approach can be used to solve that problem:

Example 6.24. Fixing Hardcoded `-liconv`

```
USES=  iconv

post-patch:
 @${REINPLACE_CMD} -e 's/-liconv/${ICONV_LIB}/' ${WRKSRC}/Makefile
```

In some cases it is necessary to set alternate values or perform operations depending on whether there is a native `iconv`. `bsd.port.pre.mk` must be included before testing the value of `ICONV_LIB`:

Example 6.25. Checking for Native `iconv` Availability

```
USES=  iconv

.include <bsd.port.pre.mk>

post-patch:
.if empty(ICONV_LIB)
 # native iconv detected
 @${REINPLACE_CMD} -e 's|iconv||' ${WRKSRC}/Config.sh
.endif

.include <bsd.port.post.mk>
```

6.24. Using Xfce

Ports that need Xfce libraries or applications set `USES=xfce`.

Specific Xfce library and application dependencies are set with values assigned to `USE_XFCE`. They are defined in `/usr/ports/Mk/Uses/xfce.mk`. The possible values are:

garcon
> sysutils/garcon

libexo
> x11/libexo

libgui
> x11-toolkits/libxfce4gui

libmenu
> x11/libxfce4menu

libutil
> x11/libxfce4util

panel
> x11-wm/xfce4-panel

thunar
> x11-fm/thunar

xfconf
> x11/xfce4-conf

Example 6.26. `USES=xfce` Example

```
USES=  xfce
USE_XFCE= libmenu
```

Example 6.27. Using Xfce's Own GTK3 Widgets

In this example, the ported application uses the GTK3-specific widgets x11/libxfce4menu and x11/xfce4-conf.

```
USES=  xfce:gtk3
USE_XFCE= libmenu xfconf
```

Tip

Xfce components included this way will automatically include any dependencies they need. It is no longer necessary to specify the entire list. If the port only needs x11-wm/xfce4-panel, use:

```
USES=  xfce
USE_XFCE= panel
```

There is no need to list the components x11-wm/xfce4-panel needs itself like this:

```
USES=  xfce
USE_XFCE= libexo libmenu libutil panel
```

However, Xfce components and non-Xfce dependencies of the port must be included explicitly. Do not count on an Xfce component to provide a sub-dependency other than itself for the main port.

6.25. Using Mozilla

Table 6.37. Variables for Ports That Use Mozilla

USE_GECKO	Gecko backend the port can handle. Possible values: libxul (libxul.so), seamonkey (libgtkembedmoz.so, deprecated, must not be used any more).

127

USE_FIREFOX	The port requires Firefox as a runtime dependency. Possible values: yes (get default version), 40, 36, 35. Default dependency is on version 40.
USE_FIREFOX_BUILD	The port requires Firefox as a buildtime dependency. Possible values: see USE_FIREFOX. This automatically sets USE_FIREFOX and assigns the same value.
USE_SEAMONKEY	The port requires SeaMonkey as a runtime dependency. Possible values: yes (get default version), 20, 11 (deprecated, must not be used any more). Default dependency is on version 20.
USE_SEAMONKEY_BUILD	The port requires SeaMonkey as a buildtime dependency. Possible values: see USE_SEAMONKEY. This automatically sets USE_SEAMONKEY and assigns the same value.
USE_THUNDERBIRD	The port requires Thunderbird as a runtime dependency. Possible values: yes (get default version), 31, 30 (deprecated, must not be used any more). Default dependency is on version 31.
USE_THUNDERBIRD_BUILD	The port requires Thunderbird as a buildtime dependency. Possible values: see USE_THUNDERBIRD. This automatically sets USE_THUNDERBIRD and assigns the same value.

A complete list of available variables can be found in /usr/ports/Mk/bsd.gecko.mk .

6.26. Using Databases

Table 6.38. Variables for Ports Using Databases

Variable	Means
USE_BDB	Obsolete. Replaced by USES=bdb
USE_MYSQL	Obsolete. Replaced by USES=mysql
USE_PGSQL	Obsolete. Replaced by USES=pgsql .
USE_SQLITE	Obsolete. Replaced by USES=sqlite

6.27. Starting and Stopping Services (rc Scripts)

rc.d scripts are used to start services on system startup, and to give administrators a standard way of stopping, starting and restarting the service. Ports integrate into the system rc.d framework. Details on its usage can be found in the rc.d Handbook chapter. Detailed explanation of the available commands is provided in rc(8) and rc.subr(8). Finally, there is an article on practical aspects of rc.d scripting.

With a mythical port called *doorman*, which needs to start a *doormand* daemon. Add the following to the Makefile:

```
USE_RC_SUBR= doormand
```

Multiple scripts may be listed and will be installed. Scripts must be placed in the files subdirectory and a .in suffix must be added to their filename. Standard SUB_LIST expansions will be ran against this file. Use of the %%PREFIX%% and %%LOCALBASE%% expansions is strongly encouraged as well. More on SUB_LIST in the relevant section.

As of FreeBSD 6.1-RELEASE, local rc.d scripts (including those installed by ports) are included in the overall rcorder(8) of the base system.

An example simple `rc.d` script to start the doormand daemon:

```
#!/bin/sh

# $FreeBSD$
#
# PROVIDE: doormand
# REQUIRE: LOGIN
# KEYWORD: shutdown
#
# Add these lines to /etc/rc.conf.local or /etc/rc.conf
# to enable this service:
#
# doormand_enable (bool): Set to NO by default.
#     Set it to YES to enable doormand .
# doormand_config (path): Set to %%PREFIX%%/etc/doormand/doormand.cf
#     by default.

. /etc/rc.subr

name=doormand
rcvar=doormand_enable

load_rc_config $name

: ${doormand_enable:="NO"}
: ${doormand_config="%%PREFIX%%/etc/doormand/doormand.cf "}

command=%%PREFIX%%/sbin/${name}
pidfile=/var/run/${name}.pid

command_args="-p $pidfile -f $doormand_config "

run_rc_command "$1"
```

Unless there is a very good reason to start the service earlier, or it runs as a particular user (other than root), all ports scripts must use:

```
REQUIRE: LOGIN
```

If the startup script launches a daemon that must be shutdown, the following will trigger a stop of the service on system shutdown:

```
KEYWORD: shutdown
```

If the script is not starting a persistent service this is not necessary.

For optional configuration elements the "=" style of default variable assignment is preferable to the ":=" style here, since the former sets a default value only if the variable is unset, and the latter sets one if the variable is unset *or* null. A user might very well include something like:

```
doormand_flags=""
```

in their `rc.conf.local`, and a variable substitution using ":=" would inappropriately override the user's intention. The _enable variable is not optional, and must use the ":" for the default.

6.27.1. Pre-Commit Checklist

Before contributing a port with an `rc.d` script, and more importantly, before committing one, please consult this checklist to be sure that it is ready.

The devel/rclint port can check for most of these, but it is not a substitute for proper review.

1. If this is a new file, does it have a `.sh` extension? If so, that must be changed to just *file*.in since `rc.d` files may not end with that extension.

2. Does the file have a $FreeBSD$ tag?

3. Do the name of the file (minus .in), the PROVIDE line, and $name all match? The file name matching PROVIDE makes debugging easier, especially for rcorder(8) issues. Matching the file name and $name makes it easier to figure out which variables are relevant in rc.conf[.local]. It is also a policy for all new scripts, including those in the base system.

4. Is the REQUIRE line set to LOGIN? This is mandatory for scripts that run as a non-root user. If it runs as root, is there a good reason for it to run prior to LOGIN? If not, it must run after so that local scrips can be loosely grouped to a point in rcorder(8) after most everything in the base is already running.

5. Does the script start a persistent service? If so, it must have KEYWORD: shutdown.

6. Make sure there is no KEYWORD: FreeBSD present. This has not been necessary nor desirable for years. It is also an indication that the new script was copy/pasted from an old script, so extra caution must be given to the review.

7. If the script uses an interpreted language like perl, python, or ruby, make certain that command_interpreter is set appropriately, for example, for Perl, by adding PERL=${PERL} to SUB_LIST and using %%PERL%%. Otherwise,

```
# service name stop
```

will probably not work properly. See service(8) for more information.

8. Have all occurrences of /usr/local been replaced with %%PREFIX%%?

9. Do the default variable assignments come after load_rc_config?

10. Are there default assignments to empty strings? They should be removed, but double-check that the option is documented in the comments at the top of the file.

11. Are things that are set in variables actually used in the script?

12. Are options listed in the default name_flags things that are actually mandatory? If so, they must be in command_args. -d is a red flag (pardon the pun) here, since it is usually the option to "daemonize" the process, and therefore is actually mandatory.

13. name_flags must never be included in command_args (and vice versa, although that error is less common).

14. Does the script execute any code unconditionally? This is frowned on. Usually these things must be dealt with through a start_precmd.

15. All boolean tests must use the checkyesno function. No hand-rolled tests for [Yy][Ee][Ss], etc.

16. If there is a loop (for example, waiting for something to start) does it have a counter to terminate the loop? We do not want the boot to be stuck forever if there is an error.

17. Does the script create files or directories that need specific permissions, for example, a pid that needs to be owned by the user that runs the process? Rather than the traditional touch(1)/chown(8)/chmod(1) routine, consider using install(1) with the proper command line arguments to do the whole procedure with one step.

6.28. Adding Users and Groups

Some ports require a particular user account to be present, usually for daemons that run as that user. For these ports, choose a *unique* UID from 50 to 999 and register it in ports/UIDs (for users) and ports/GIDs (for groups). The unique identification should be the same for users and groups.

Please include a patch against these two files when requiring a new user or group to be created for the port.

Then use `USERS` and `GROUPS` in `Makefile`, and the user will be automatically created when installing the port.

```
USERS= pulse
GROUPS= pulse pulse-access pulse-rt
```

The current list of reserved UIDs and GIDs can be found in `ports/UIDs` and `ports/GIDs`.

6.29. Ports That Rely on Kernel Sources

Some ports (such as kernel loadable modules) need the kernel source files so that the port can compile. Here is the correct way to determine if the user has them installed:

```
USES= kmod
```

Apart from this check, the `kmod` feature takes care of most items that these ports need to take into account.

6.30. Go Libraries

Ports must not package or install Go libs or source code. Only `lang/go*` should install into `GO_SRCDIR` and `GO_LIB-DIR`. Go ports must fetch the required deps at the normal fetch time and should only install the programs and things users need, not the things Go developers would need.

Ports should (in order of preference):

- Use vendored dependencies included with the package source.

- Fetch the versions of deps specified by upstream (in the case of vendor.json or similar).

- As a last resort (deps are not included nor versions specified exactly) fetch versions of dependencies available at the time of upstream development/release.

6.31. Shell Completion Files

Many modern shells (including bash, tcsh, and zsh) support parameter and/or option tab-completion. This support usually comes from completion files, which contain the definitions for how tab completion will work for a certain command. Ports sometimes ship with their own completion files, or porters may have created them themselves.

When available, completion files should always be installed. It is not necessary to make an option for it. If an option is used, though, always enable it in `OPTIONS_DEFAULT`.

Table 6.39. Shell completion file paths

bash	${PREFIX}/etc/bash_completion.d
zsh	${PREFIX}/share/zsh/site-functions

Do not register any dependencies on the shells themselves.

Chapter 7. Flavors

7.1. An Introduction to Flavors

Flavors are a way to have multiple variations of a port. The port is built multiple times, with variations. For example, a port can have a normal version with many features and quite a few dependencies, and a light "lite" version with only basic features and minimal dependencies.

7.2. Using FLAVORS

To declare a port having multiple flavors, add FLAVORS to its Makefile. The first flavor in FLAVORS is the default flavor.

Tip

It can help simplify the logic of the Makefile to also define FLAVOR as:

```
FLAVOR?= ${FLAVORS:[1]}
```

Important

To distinguish flavors from options, which are always uppercase letters, flavor names can *only* contain lowercase letters, numbers, and the underscore _.

Example 7.1. Basic Flavors Usage

If a port has a "lite" slave port, the slave port can be removed, and the port can be converted to flavors with:

```
FLAVORS= default lite
lite_PKGNAMESUFFIX= -lite
[...-]
.if ${FLAVOR:U} != lite
[enable non lite features]
.endif
```

Note

The first flavor is the default one, and is called, here, default. It is not an obligation, and if possible, use a more specific flavor name, like in Example 7.2, "Another Basic Flavors Usage".

Example 7.2. Another Basic Flavors Usage

If a port has a -nox11 slave port, the slave port can be removed, and the port can be converted to flavors
with:

```
FLAVORS= x11 nox11
FLAVOR?= ${FLAVORS:[1]}
nox11_PKGNAMESUFFIX= -nox11
[...-]
.if ${FLAVOR} = x11
[enable x11 features]
.endif
```

Example 7.3. More Complex Flavors Usage

Here is a slightly edited excerpt of what is present in devel/libpeas, a port that uses the Python flavors.
With the default Python 2 and 3 versions being 2.7 and 3.6, it will automatically get FLAVORS=py27 py36

```
USES=  gnome python
USE_PYTHON= flavors ❶

.if ${FLAVOR:Upy27:Mpy2*} ❷
USE_GNOME= pygobject3 ❸

CONFIGURE_ARGS+= --enable-python2 --disable-python3

BUILD_WRKSRC= ${WRKSRC}/loaders/python ❹
INSTALL_WRKSRC= ${WRKSRC}/loaders/python ❺
.else # py3*
USE_GNOME+= py3gobject3 ❻

CONFIGURE_ARGS+= --disable-python2 --enable-python3 \
    ac_cv_path_PYTHON3_CONFIG=${LOCALBASE}/bin/python${PYTHON_VER}-config ❼

BUILD_WRKSRC= ${WRKSRC}/loaders/python3 ❽
INSTALL_WRKSRC= ${WRKSRC}/loaders/python3 ❾
.endif

py34_PLIST= ${.CURDIR}/pkg-plist-py3 ❿
py35_PLIST= ${.CURDIR}/pkg-plist-py3 ⓫
py36_PLIST= ${.CURDIR}/pkg-plist-py3 ⓬
```

❶   This port does not use USE_PYTHON=distutils but needs Python flavors anyway.
❷   To guard against FLAVOR being empty, which would cause a make(1) error, use ${FLAVOR:U} in string
    comparisons instead of ${FLAVOR}.
❸❻   The Gnome Python gobject3 bindings have two different names, one for Python 2, pygobject3 and
    one for Python 3, py3gobject3.
❹❺❽❾The configure script has to run in ${WRKSRC} , but we are only interested in building and installing the
    Python 2 or Python 3 parts of the software, so set the build and install base directories appropriately.
❼   Hint about the correct Python 3 config script path name.
❿⓫⓬The packing list is different when the built with Python 3. As there are three possible Python 3 ver-
    sions, set PLIST for all three using the helper.

7.2.1. Flavors Helpers

To make the Makefile easier to write, a few flavors helpers exist.

This list of helpers will set their variable:

- *flavor*_PKGNAMEPREFIX

- *flavor*_PKGNAMESUFFIX

- *flavor*_PLIST

- *flavor*_DESCR

This list of helpers will append to their variable:

- *flavor*_CONFLICTS

- *flavor*_CONFLICTS_BUILD

- *flavor*_CONFLICTS_INSTALL

- *flavor*_PKG_DEPENDS

- *flavor*_EXTRACT_DEPENDS

- *flavor*_PATCH_DEPENDS

- *flavor*_FETCH_DEPENDS

- *flavor*_BUILD_DEPENDS

- *flavor*_LIB_DEPENDS

- *flavor*_RUN_DEPENDS

- *flavor*_TEST_DEPENDS

Example 7.4. Flavor Specific PKGNAME

As all packages must have a different package name, flavors must change theirs, using *flavor*_PKGNAMEPRE-
FIX and *flavor*_PKGNAMESUFFIX makes this easy:

```
FLAVORS= normal lite
lite_PKGNAMESUFFIX= -lite
```

7.3. Flavors Auto-Activation

7.3.1. USES=python and Flavors

When using USES=python and USE_PYTHON=distutils, the port will automatically have FLAVORS filled in with the
Python versions it supports.

Example 7.5. Simple USES=python

Supposing the current Python supported versions are 2.7, 3.4, 3.5, and 3.6, and the default Python 2 and
3 versions are 2.7 and 3.6, a port with:

```
USES= python
USE_PYTHON= distutils
```

Will get these flavors: py27, and py36.

```
USES= python
USE_PYTHON= distutils allflavors
```

Will get these flavors: py27, py34, py35 and py36.

Example 7.6. USES=python with Version Requirements

Supposing the current Python supported versions are 2.7, 3.4, 3.5, and 3.6, and the default Python 2 and 3 versions are 2.7 and 3.6, a port with:

```
USES= python:-3.5
USE_PYTHON= distutils
```

Will get this flavor: py27.

```
USES= python:-3.5
USE_PYTHON= distutils allflavors
```

Will get these flavors: py27, py34, and py35.

```
USES= python:3.4+
USE_PYTHON= distutils
```

Will get this flavor: py36.

```
USES= python:3.4+
USE_PYTHON= distutils allflavors
```

Will get these flavors: py34, py35, and py36.

PY_FLAVOR will be available to depend on the correct version of Python modules. This is most useful for ports that are not Python modules and do not have Python flavors but do use python for some part of their operations.

Example 7.7. For a Port Not Using distutils

If the default Python 3 version is 3.6, the following will set PY_FLAVOR to py36:

```
RUN_DEPENDS= ${PYTHON_PKGNAMEPREFIX}mutagen>0:audio/py-mutagen@${PY_FLAVOR}

USES= python:3.5+
```

Chapter 8. Advanced pkg-plist Practices

8.1. Changing pkg-plist Based on Make Variables

Some ports, particularly the p5- ports, need to change their pkg-plist depending on what options they are configured with (or version of perl, in the case of p5- ports). To make this easy, any instances in pkg-plist of %%OSREL%%, %%PERL_VER%%, and %%PERL_VERSION%% will be substituted appropriately. The value of %%OSREL%% is the numeric revision of the operating system (for example, 4.9). %%PERL_VERSION%% and %%PERL_VER%% is the full version number of perl (for example, 5.8.9). Several other %%VARS%% related to port's documentation files are described in the relevant section.

To make other substitutions, set PLIST_SUB with a list of *VAR=VALUE* pairs and instances of %%*VAR*%% will be substituted with *VALUE* in pkg-plist.

For instance, if a port installs many files in a version-specific subdirectory, use a placeholder for the version so that pkg-plist does not have to be regenerated every time the port is updated. For example:

```
OCTAVE_VERSION= ${PORTREVISION}
PLIST_SUB= OCTAVE_VERSION=${OCTAVE_VERSION}
```

in the Makefile and use %%OCTAVE_VERSION%% wherever the version shows up in pkg-plist. When the port is upgraded, it will not be necessary to edit dozens (or in some cases, hundreds) of lines in pkg-plist.

If files are installed conditionally on the options set in the port, the usual way of handling it is prefixing pkg-plist lines with a %%OPT%% for lines needed when the option is enabled, or %%NO_OPT%% when the option is disabled, and adding OPTIONS_SUB=yes to the Makefile. See Section 5.13.3.1, "OPTIONS_SUB" for more information.

For instance, if there are files that are only installed when the X11 option is enabled, and Makefile has:

```
OPTIONS_DEFINE= X11
OPTIONS_SUB= yes
```

In pkg-plist, put %%X11%% in front of the lines only being installed when the option is enabled, like this:

```
%%X11%%bin/foo-gui
```

This substitution will be done between the pre-install and do-install targets, by reading from PLIST and writing to TMPPLIST (default: WRKDIR/.PLIST.mktmp). So if the port builds PLIST on the fly, do so in or before pre-install. Also, if the port needs to edit the resulting file, do so in post-install to a file named TMPPLIST.

Another way of modifying a port's packing list is based on setting the variables PLIST_FILES and PLIST_DIRS. The value of each variable is regarded as a list of pathnames to write to TMPPLIST along with PLIST contents. While names listed in PLIST_FILES and PLIST_DIRS are subject to %%*VAR*%% substitution as described above, it is better to use the ${*VAR*} directly. Except for that, names from PLIST_FILES will appear in the final packing list unchanged, while @dir will be prepended to names from PLIST_DIRS. To take effect, PLIST_FILES and PLIST_DIRS must be set before TMPPLIST is written, that is, in pre-install or earlier.

From time to time, using OPTIONS_SUB is not enough. In those cases, adding a specific *TAG* to PLIST_SUB inside the Makefile with a special value of @comment, makes package tools to ignore the line. For instance, if some files are only installed when the X11 option is on and the architecture is i386:

```
.include <bsd.port.pre.mk>

.if ${PORT_OPTIONS:MX11} && ${ARCH} == "i386"
PLIST_SUB+= X11I386=""
.else
```

```
PLIST_SUB+= X11I386="@comment "
.endif
```

8.2. Empty Directories

8.2.1. Cleaning Up Empty Directories

When being de-installed, a port has to remove empty directories it created. Most of these directories are removed automatically by pkg(8), but for directories created outside of ${PREFIX}, or empty directories, some more work needs to be done. This is usually accomplished by adding @dir lines for those directories. Subdirectories must be deleted before deleting parent directories.

```
[...-]
@dir /var/games/oneko/saved-games
@dir /var/games/oneko
```

8.2.2. Creating Empty Directories

Empty directories created during port installation need special attention. They must be present when the package is created. If they are not created by the port code, create them in the Makefile:

```
post-install:
 ${MKDIR} ${STAGEDIR}${PREFIX}/some/directory
```

Add the directory to pkg-plist like any other. For example:

```
@dir some/directory
```

8.3. Configuration Files

If the port installs configuration files to PREFIX/etc (or elsewhere) do *not* list them in pkg-plist . That will cause pkg delete to remove files that have been carefully edited by the user, and a re-installation will wipe them out.

Instead, install sample files with a *filename*.sample extension. The @sample macro automates this, see Section 8.6.9, "@sample *file* [*file*]" for what it does exactly. For each sample file, add a line to pkg-plist :

```
@sample etc/orbit.conf.sample
```

If there is a very good reason not to install a working configuration file by default, only list the sample filename in pkg-plist , without the @sample followed by a space part, and add a message pointing out that the user must copy and edit the file before the software will work.

Tip

When a port installs its configuration in a subdirectory of ${PREFIX}/etc, use ETCDIR, which defaults to ${PREFIX}/etc/${PORTNAME} , it can be overridden in the ports Makefile if there is a convention for the port to use some other directory. The %%ETCDIR%% macro will be used in its stead in pkg-plist .

Note

The sample configuration files should always have the .sample suffix. If for some historical reason using the standard suffix is not possible, or if the sample files come from some other directory, use this construct:

```
@sample etc/orbit.conf-dist etc/orbit.conf
```

or

```
@sample %%EXAMPLESDIR%%/orbit.conf etc/orbit.conf
```

The format is @sample *sample-file actual-config-file*.

8.4. Dynamic Versus Static Package List

A *static package list* is a package list which is available in the Ports Collection either as `pkg-plist` (with or without variable substitution), or embedded into the `Makefile` via `PLIST_FILES` and `PLIST_DIRS`. Even if the contents are auto-generated by a tool or a target in the Makefile *before* the inclusion into the Ports Collection by a committer (for example, using `make makeplist>`), this is still considered a static list, since it is possible to examine it without having to download or compile the distfile.

A *dynamic package list* is a package list which is generated at the time the port is compiled based upon the files and directories which are installed. It is not possible to examine it before the source code of the ported application is downloaded and compiled, or after running a `make clean`.

While the use of dynamic package lists is not forbidden, maintainers should use static package lists wherever possible, as it enables users to grep(1) through available ports to discover, for example, which port installs a certain file. Dynamic lists should be primarily used for complex ports where the package list changes drastically based upon optional features of the port (and thus maintaining a static package list is infeasible), or ports which change the package list based upon the version of dependent software used. For example, ports which generate docs with Javadoc.

8.5. Automated Package List Creation

First, make sure the port is almost complete, with only `pkg-plist` missing. Running `make makeplist` will show an example for `pkg-plist`. The output of `makeplist` must be double checked for correctness as it tries to automatically guess a few things, and can get it wrong.

User configuration files should be installed as *filename*.sample, as it is described in Section 8.3, "Configuration Files". `info/dir` must not be listed and appropriate `install-info` lines must be added as noted in the info files section. Any libraries installed by the port must be listed as specified in the shared libraries section.

8.5.1. Expanding PLIST_SUB with Regular Expressions

Strings to be replaced sometimes need to be very specific to avoid undesired replacements. This is a common problem with shorter values.

To address this problem, for each *PLACEHOLDER=value*, a *PLACEHOLDER*_regex= *regex* can be set, with the *regex* part matching *value* more precisely.

Example 8.1. Using PLIST_SUB with Regular Expressions

Perl ports can install architecture dependent files in a specific tree. On FreeBSD to ease porting, this tree is called mach. For example, a port that installs a file whose path contains mach could have that part of the path string replaced with the wrong values. Consider this `Makefile`:

```
PORTNAME= Machine-Build
DISTVERSION= 1
```

```
CATEGORIES= devel perl5
MASTER_SITES= CPAN
PKGNAMEPREFIX= p5-

MAINTAINER= perl@FreeBSD.org
COMMENT= Building machine

USES=  perl5
USE_PERL5= configure

PLIST_SUB= PERL_ARCH=mach
```

The files installed by the port are:

```
/usr/local/bin/machine-build
/usr/local/lib/perl5/site_perl/man/man1/machine-build.1.gz
/usr/local/lib/perl5/site_perl/man/man3/Machine::Build.3.gz
/usr/local/lib/perl5/site_perl/Machine/Build.pm
/usr/local/lib/perl5/site_perl/mach/5.20/Machine/Build/Build.so
```

Running make makeplist wrongly generates:

```
bin/%%PERL_ARCH%%ine-build
%%PERL5_MAN1%%/%%PERL_ARCH%%ine-build.1.gz
%%PERL5_MAN3%%/Machine::Build.3.gz
%%SITE_PERL%%/Machine/Build.pm
%%SITE_PERL%%/%%PERL_ARCH%%/%%PERL_VER%%/Machine/Build/Build.so
```

Change the PLIST_SUB line from the Makefile to:

```
PLIST_SUB= PERL_ARCH=mach \
   PERL_ARCH_regex=\bmach\b
```

Now make makeplist correctly generates:

```
bin/machine-build
%%PERL5_MAN1%%/machine-build.1.gz
%%PERL5_MAN3%%/Machine::Build.3.gz
%%SITE_PERL%%/Machine/Build.pm
%%SITE_PERL%%/%%PERL_ARCH%%/%%PERL_VER%%/Machine/Build/Build.so
```

8.6. Expanding Package List with Keywords

All keywords can also take optional arguments in parentheses. The arguments are owner, group, and mode. This argument is used on the file or directory referenced. To change the owner, group, and mode of a configuration file, use:

```
@sample(games,games,640) etc/config.sample
```

The arguments are optional. If only the group and mode need to be changed, use:

```
@sample(,games,660) etc/config.sample
```

8.6.1. @desktop-file-utils

Will run update-desktop-database -q after installation and deinstallation.

8.6.2. @fc directory

Add a @dir entry for the directory passed as an argument, and run fc-cache -fs on that directory after installation and deinstallation.

8.6.3. `@fcfontsdir` **directory**

Add a `@dir` entry for the directory passed as an argument, and run `fc-cache -fs`, `mkfontscale` and `mkfontdir` on that directory after installation and deinstallation. Additionally, on deinstallation, it removes the `fonts.scale` and `fonts.dir` cache files if they are empty. This keyword is equivalent to adding both `@fc directory` and `@fontsdir directory`.

8.6.4. `@fontsdir` **directory**

Add a `@dir` entry for the directory passed as an argument, and run `mkfontscale` and `mkfontdir` on that directory after installation and deinstallation. Additionally, on deinstallation, it removes the `fonts.scale` and `fonts.dir` cache files if they are empty.

8.6.5. `@glib-schemas`

Runs `glib-compile-schemas` on installation and deinstallation.

8.6.6. `@info` **file**

Add the file passed as argument to the plist, and updates the info document index on installation and deinstallation. Additionally, it removes the index if empty on deinstallation. This should never be used manually, but always through `INFO`. See Section 5.12, "Info Files" for more information.

8.6.7. `@kld` **directory**

Runs `kldxref` on the directory on installation and deinstallation. Additionally, on deinstallation, it will remove the directory if empty.

8.6.8. `@rmtry` **file**

Will remove the file on deinstallation, and not give an error if the file is not there.

8.6.9. `@sample` **file [file]**

This is used to handle installation of configuration files, through example files bundled with the package. The "actual", non-sample, file is either the second filename, if present, or the first filename without the `.sample` extension.

This does three things. First, add the first file passed as argument, the sample file, to the plist. Then, on installation, if the actual file is not found, copy the sample file to the actual file. And finally, on deinstallation, remove the actual file if it has not been modified. See Section 8.3, "Configuration Files" for more information.

8.6.10. `@shared-mime-info` **directory**

Runs `update-mime-database` on the directory on installation and deinstallation.

8.6.11. `@shell` **file**

Add the file passed as argument to the plist.

On installation, add the full path to `file` to `/etc/shells`, while making sure it is not added twice. On deinstallation, remove it from `/etc/shells`.

8.6.12. `@terminfo`

Do not use by itself. If the port installs `*.terminfo` files, add USES=terminfo to its `Makefile`.

On installation and deinstallation, if `tic` is present, refresh `${PREFIX}/share/misc/terminfo.db` from the `*.terminfo` files in `${PREFIX}/share/misc`.

8.6.13. Base Keywords

There are a few keywords that are hardcoded, and documented in pkg-create(8). For the sake of completeness, they are also documented here.

8.6.13.1. @ [file]

The empty keyword is a placeholder to use when the file's owner, group, or mode need to be changed. For example, to set the group of the file to games and add the setgid bit, add:

```
@(,games,2755) sbin/daemon
```

8.6.13.2. @preexec command, @postexec command, @preunexec command, @postunexec command

Execute *command* as part of the package installation or deinstallation process.

@preexec *command*
    Execute *command* as part of the pre-install scripts.

@postexec *command*
    Execute *command* as part of the post-install scripts.

@preunexec *command*
    Execute *command* as part of the pre-deinstall scripts.

@postunexec *command*
    Execute *command* as part of the post-deinstall scripts.

If *command* contains any of these sequences somewhere in it, they are expanded inline. For these examples, assume that @cwd is set to /usr/local and the last extracted file was bin/emacs.

%F
    Expand to the last filename extracted (as specified). In the example case bin/emacs.

%D
    Expand to the current directory prefix, as set with @cwd. In the example case /usr/local.

%B
    Expand to the basename of the fully qualified filename, that is, the current directory prefix plus the last file-spec, minus the trailing filename. In the example case, that would be /usr/local/bin.

%f
    Expand to the filename part of the fully qualified name, or the converse of %B. In the example case, emacs.

8.6.13.3. @mode mode

Set default permission for all subsequently extracted files to *mode*. Format is the same as that used by chmod(1). Use without an arg to set back to default permissions (mode of the file while being packed).

> **Important**
>
> This must be a numeric mode, like 644, 4755, or 600. It cannot be a relative mode like u+s.

8.6.13.4. @owner user

Set default ownership for all subsequent files to *user*. Use without an argument to set back to default ownership (root).

8.6.13.5. @group group

Set default group ownership for all subsequent files to *group*. Use without an arg to set back to default group ownership (wheel).

8.6.13.6. @comment string

This line is ignored when packing.

8.6.13.7. @dir directory

Declare directory name. By default, directories created under PREFIX by a package installation are automatically removed. Use this when an empty directory under PREFIX needs to be created, or when the directory needs to have non default owner, group, or mode. Directories outside of PREFIX need to be registered. For example, /var/db/${PORTNAME} needs to have a @dir entry whereas ${PREFIX}/share/${PORTNAME} does not if it contains files or uses the default owner, group, and mode.

8.6.13.8. @exec command, @unexec command (Deprecated)

Execute *command* as part of the installation or deinstallation process. Please use Section 8.6.13.2, "@preexec *command*, @postexec *command*, @preunexec *command*, @postunexec *command*" instead.

8.6.13.9. @dirrm directory (Deprecated)

Declare directory name to be deleted at deinstall time. By default, directories created under PREFIX by a package installation are deleted when the package is deinstalled.

8.6.13.10. @dirrmtry directory (Deprecated)

Declare directory name to be removed, as for @dirrm, but does not issue a warning if the directory cannot be removed.

8.6.14. Creating New Keywords

Package list files can be extended by keywords that are defined in the ${PORTSDIR}/Keywords directory. The settings for each keyword are stored in a UCL file named *keyword*.ucl. The file must contain at least one of these sections:

- attributes

- action

- pre-install

- post-install

- pre-deinstall

- post-deinstall

- pre-upgrade

- post-upgrade

8.6.14.1. attributes

Changes the owner, group, or mode used by the keyword. Contains an associative array where the possible keys are owner, group, and mode. The values are, respectively, a user name, a group name, and a file mode. For example:

```
attributes: { owner: "games", group: "games", mode: 0555 }
```

8.6.14.2. action

Defines what happens to the keyword's parameter. Contains an array where the possible values are:

setprefix
> Set the prefix for the next plist entries.

dir
> Register a directory to be created on install and removed on deinstall.

dirrm
> Register a directory to be deleted on deinstall. Deprecated.

dirrmtry
> Register a directory to try and deleted on deinstall. Deprecated.

file
> Register a file.

setmode
> Set the mode for the next plist entries.

setowner
> Set the owner for the next plist entries.

setgroup
> Set the group for the next plist entries.

comment
> Does not do anything, equivalent to not entering an action section.

ignore_next
> Ignore the next entry in the plist.

8.6.14.3. arguments

If set to true, adds argument handling, splitting the whole line, %@, into numbered arguments, %1, %2, and so on. For example, for this line:

```
@foo some.content other.content
```

%1 and %2 will contain:

```
some.content
other.content
```

It also affects how the action entry works. When there is more than one argument, the argument number must be specified. For example:

```
actions: [file(1)]
```

8.6.14.4. pre-install, post-install, pre-deinstall, post-deinstall, pre-upgrade, post-upgrade

These keywords contains a sh(1) script to be executed before or after installation, deinstallation, or upgrade of the package. In addition to the usual @exec %foo placeholders described in Section 8.6.13.2, "@preexec *command*, @postexec *command*, @preunexec *command*, @postunexec *command*", there is a new one, %@, which represents the argument of the keyword.

8.6.14.5. Custom Keyword Examples

Example 8.2. Example of a `@dirrmtryecho` Keyword

This keyword does two things, it adds a `@dirrmtry` *directory* line to the packing list, and echoes the fact that the directory is removed when deinstalling the package.

```
actions: [dirrmtry]
post-deinstall: <<EOD
  echo "Directory %D/%@ removed."
EOD
```

Example 8.3. Real Life Example, How `@sample` is Implemented

This keyword does three things. It adds the first *filename* passed as an argument to `@sample` to the packing list, it adds to the `post-install` script instructions to copy the sample to the actual configuration file if it does not already exist, and it adds to the `post-deinstall` instructions to remove the configuration file if it has not been modified.

```
actions: [file(1)]
arguments: true
post-install: <<EOD
  case "%1" in
  /*) sample_file="%1" -;;
  *) sample_file="%D/%1" -;;
  esac
  target_file="${sample_file%.sample}"
  set -- %@
  if [ $# -eq 2 -]; then
      target_file=${2}
  fi
  case "${target_file}" in
  /*) target_file="${target_file}" -;;
  *) target_file="%D/${target_file}" -;;
  esac
  if ! [ -f "${target_file}" -]; then
    /bin/cp -p "${sample_file}" "${target_file}" && \
      /bin/chmod u+w "${target_file}"
  fi
EOD
pre-deinstall: <<EOD
  case "%1" in
  /*) sample_file="%1" -;;
  *) sample_file="%D/%1" -;;
  esac
  target_file="${sample_file%.sample}"
  set -- %@
  if [ $# -eq 2 -]; then
      set -- %@
      target_file=${2}
  fi
  case "${target_file}" in
  /*) target_file="${target_file}" -;;
  *) target_file="%D/${target_file}" -;;
  esac
  if cmp -s "${target_file}" "${sample_file}"; then
    rm -f "${target_file}"
  else
```

```
        echo "You may need to manually remove ${target_file} if it is no longer ↲
needed."
    fi
EOD
```

Chapter 9. pkg-*

There are some tricks we have not mentioned yet about the pkg-* files that come in handy sometimes.

9.1. pkg-message

To display a message when the package is installed, place the message in pkg-message. This capability is often useful to display additional installation steps to be taken after a pkg install or to display licensing information.

When some lines about the build-time knobs or warnings have to be displayed, use ECHO_MSG. pkg-message is only for post-installation steps. Likewise, the distinction between ECHO_MSG is for printing informational text to the screen and ECHO_CMD is for command pipelining:

```
update-etc-shells:
 @${ECHO_MSG} "updating /etc/shells"
 @${CP} /etc/shells /etc/shells.bak
 @( ${GREP} -v ${PREFIX}/bin/bash /etc/shells.bak; \
  ${ECHO_CMD} ${PREFIX}/bin/bash) >/etc/shells
 @${RM} /etc/shells.bak
```

Note

Do not add an entry for pkg-message in pkg-plist.

9.2. pkg-install

If the port needs to execute commands when the binary package is installed with pkg add or pkg install, use pkg-install. This script will automatically be added to the package. It will be run twice by pkg, the first time as ${SH} pkg-install ${PKGNAME} PRE-INSTALL before the package is installed, and the second time as ${SH} pkg-install ${PKGNAME} POST-INSTALL after it has been installed. $2 can be tested to determine which mode the script is being run in. The PKG_PREFIX environmental variable will be set to the package installation directory.

9.3. pkg-deinstall

This script executes when a package is removed.

This script will be run twice by pkg delete The first time as ${SH} pkg-deinstall ${PKGNAME} DEINSTALL before the port is de-installed and the second time as ${SH} pkg-deinstall ${PKGNAME} POST-DEINSTALL after the port has been de-installed. $2 can be tested to determine which mode the script is being run in. The PKG_PREFIX environmental variable will be set to the package installation directory

9.4. Changing the Names of pkg-*

All the names of pkg-* are defined using variables that can be changed in the Makefile if needed. This is especially useful when sharing the same pkg-* files among several ports or when it is necessary to write to one of these files. See writing to places other than WRKDIR for why it is a bad idea to write directly into the directory containing the pkg-* files.

Here is a list of variable names and their default values. (PKGDIR defaults to ${MASTERDIR}.)

Variable	Default value
DESCR	${PKGDIR}/pkg-descr
PLIST	${PKGDIR}/pkg-plist
PKGINSTALL	${PKGDIR}/pkg-install
PKGDEINSTALL	${PKGDIR}/pkg-deinstall
PKGMESSAGE	${PKGDIR}/pkg-message

9.5. Making Use of SUB_FILES and SUB_LIST

SUB_FILES and SUB_LIST are useful for dynamic values in port files, such as the installation PREFIX in pkg-message.

SUB_FILES specifies a list of files to be automatically modified. Each *file* in the SUB_FILES list must have a corresponding *file*.in present in FILESDIR. A modified version will be created as ${WRKDIR}/ *file*. Files defined as a value of USE_RC_SUBR are automatically added to SUB_FILES. For the files pkg-message, pkg-install, and pkg-deinstall, the corresponding Makefile variable is automatically set to point to the processed version.

SUB_LIST is a list of VAR=VALUE pairs. For each pair, %%VAR%% will be replaced with VALUE in each file listed in SUB_FILES. Several common pairs are automatically defined: PREFIX, LOCALBASE, DATADIR, DOCSDIR, EXAMPLESDIR, WWWDIR, and ETCDIR. Any line beginning with @comment followed by a space, will be deleted from resulting files after a variable substitution.

This example replaces %%ARCH%% with the system architecture in a pkg-message:

```
SUB_FILES= pkg-message
SUB_LIST= ARCH=${ARCH}
```

Note that for this example, pkg-message.in must exist in FILESDIR.

Example of a good pkg-message.in:

```
Now it is time to configure this package.
Copy %%PREFIX%%/share/examples/putsy/%%ARCH%%.conf into your home directory
as .putsy.conf and edit it.
```

Chapter 10. Testing the Port

10.1. Running `make describe`

Several of the FreeBSD port maintenance tools, such as portupgrade(1), rely on a database called `/usr/ports/INDEX` which keeps track of such items as port dependencies. `INDEX` is created by the top-level `ports/Makefile` via `make index`, which descends into each port subdirectory and executes `make describe` there. Thus, if `make describe` fails in any port, no one can generate `INDEX`, and many people will quickly become unhappy.

 Note

It is important to be able to generate this file no matter what options are present in `make.conf`, so please avoid doing things such as using `.error` statements when (for instance) a dependency is not satisfied. (See Section 13.16, "Avoid Use of the `.error` Construct".)

If `make describe` produces a string rather than an error message, everything is probably safe. See `bsd.port.mk` for the meaning of the string produced.

Also note that running a recent version of `portlint` (as specified in the next section) will cause `make describe` to be run automatically.

10.2. Portlint

Do check the port with `portlint` before submitting or committing it. `portlint` warns about many common errors, both functional and stylistic. For a new (or repocopied) port, `portlint -A` is the most thorough; for an existing port, `portlint -C` is sufficient.

Since `portlint` uses heuristics to try to figure out errors, it can produce false positive warnings. In addition, occasionally something that is flagged as a problem really cannot be done in any other way due to limitations in the ports framework. When in doubt, the best thing to do is ask on FreeBSD ports mailing list.

10.3. Port Tools

The ports-mgmt/porttools program is part of the Ports Collection.

`port` is the front-end script, which can help simplify the testing job. Whenever a new port or an update to an existing one needs testing, use `port test` to test the port, including the `portlint` checking. This command also detects and lists any files that are not listed in `pkg-plist`. For example:

```
# port test /usr/ports/net/csup
```

10.4. `PREFIX` and `DESTDIR`

`PREFIX` determines where the port will be installed. It defaults to `/usr/local`, but can be set by the user to a custom path like `/opt`. The port must respect the value of this variable.

`DESTDIR`, if set by the user, determines the complete alternative environment, usually a jail or an installed system mounted somewhere other than `/`. A port will actually install into `DESTDIR/PREFIX`, and register with the package database in DESTDIR/var/db/pkg . As DESTDIR is handled automatically by the ports infrastructure with chroot(8). There is no need for modifications or any extra care to write DESTDIR-compliant ports.

The value of PREFIX will be set to LOCALBASE (defaulting to /usr/local). If USE_LINUX_PREFIX is set, PREFIX will be LINUXBASE (defaulting to /compat/linux).

Avoiding hard-coded /usr/local paths in the source makes the port much more flexible and able to cater to the needs of other sites. Often, this can be accomplished by replacing occurrences of /usr/local in the port's various Makefiles with ${PREFIX}. This variable is automatically passed down to every stage of the build and install processes.

Make sure the application is not installing things in /usr/local instead of PREFIX. A quick test for such hard-coded paths is:

```
% make clean; make package PREFIX=/var/tmp/`make -V PORTNAME`
```

If anything is installed outside of PREFIX, the package creation process will complain that it cannot find the files.

In addition, it is worth checking the same with the stage directory support (see Section 6.1, "Staging"):

```
% make stage && make check-plist && make stage-qa && make package
```

- check-plist checks for files missing from the plist, and files in the plist that are not installed by the port.

- stage-qa checks for common problems like bad shebang, symlinks pointing outside the stage directory, setuid files, and non-stripped libraries...

These tests will not find hard-coded paths inside the port's files, nor will it verify that LOCALBASE is being used to correctly refer to files from other ports. The temporarily-installed port in /var/tmp/`make -V PORTNAME` must be tested for proper operation to make sure there are no problems with paths.

PREFIX must not be set explicitly in a port's Makefile. Users installing the port may have set PREFIX to a custom location, and the port must respect that setting.

Refer to programs and files from other ports with the variables mentioned above, not explicit pathnames. For instance, if the port requires a macro PAGER to have the full pathname of less, do not use a literal path of /usr/local/bin/less . Instead, use ${LOCALBASE}:

```
-DPAGER=\"${LOCALBASE}/bin/less\"
```

The path with LOCALBASE is more likely to still work if the system administrator has moved the whole /usr/local tree somewhere else.

 Tip

All these tests are done automatically when running poudriere testport or poudriere bulk -t. It is highly recommended that every ports contributor install and test their ports with it. See Section 10.5, "Poudriere" for more information.

10.5. Poudriere

For a ports contributor, Poudriere is one of the most important and helpful testing and build tools. Its main features include:

- Bulk building of the entire ports tree, specific subsets of the ports tree, or a single port including its dependencies

- Automatic packaging of build results

- Generation of build log files per port

- Providing a signed pkg(8) repository

- Testing of port builds before submitting a patch to the FreeBSD bug tracker or committing to the ports tree

- Testing for successful ports builds using different options

Because Poudriere performs its building in a clean jail(8) environment and uses zfs(8) features, it has several advantages over traditional testing on the host system:

- No pollution of the host environment: No leftover files, no accidental removals, no changes of existing configuration files.

- Verify `pkg-plist` for missing or superfluous entries

- Ports committers sometimes ask for a Poudriere log alongside a patch submission to assess whether the patch is ready for integration into the ports tree

It is also quite straightforward to set up and use, has no dependencies, and will run on any supported FreeBSD release. This section shows how to install, configure, and run Poudriere as part of the normal workflow of a ports contributor.

The examples in this section show a default file layout, as standard in FreeBSD. Substitute any local changes accordingly. The ports tree, represented by `${PORTSDIR}` , is located in `/usr/ports` . Both `${LOCALBASE}` and `${PREFIX}` are `/usr/local` by default.

10.5.1. Installing Poudriere

Poudriere is available in the ports tree in ports-mgmt/poudriere. It can be installed using pkg(8) or from ports:

```
# pkg install poudriere
```

or

```
# make -C /usr/ports/ports-mgmt/poudriere install clean
```

There is also a work-in-progress version of Poudriere which will eventually become the next release. It is available in ports-mgmt/poudriere-devel. This development version is used for the official FreeBSD package builds, so it is well tested. It often has newer interesting features. A ports committer will want to use the development version because it is what is used in production, and has all the new features that will make sure everything is exactly right. A contributor will not necessarily need those as the most important fixes are backported to released version. The main reason for the use of the development version to build the official package is because it is faster, in a way that will shorten a full build from 18 hours to 17 hours when using a high end 32 CPU server with 128GB of RAM. Those optimizations will not matter a lot when building ports on a desktop machine.

10.5.2. Setting Up Poudriere

The port installs a default configuration file, `/usr/local/etc/poudriere.conf` . Each parameter is documented in the configuration file and in poudriere(8). Here is a minimal example config file:

```
ZPOOL=tank
ZROOTFS=/poudriere
BASEFS=/poudriere
DISTFILES_CACHE=/usr/ports/distfiles
RESOLV_CONF=/etc/resolv.conf
FREEBSD_HOST=ftp://ftp.freebsd.org
SVN_HOST=svn.FreeBSD.org
```

ZPOOL
    The name of the ZFS storage pool which Poudriere shall use. Must be listed in the output of `zpool status` .

ZROOTFS

The root of Poudriere-managed file systems. This entry will cause Poudriere to create zfs(8) file systems under `tank/poudriere`.

BASEFS

The root mount point for Poudriere file systems. This entry will cause Poudriere to mount `tank/poudriere` to `/poudriere`.

DISTFILES_CACHE

Defines where distfiles are stored. In this example, Poudriere and the host share the distfiles storage directory. This avoids downloading tarballs which are already present on the system.

RESOLV_CONF

Use the host `/etc/resolv.conf` inside jails for DNS. This is needed so jails can resolve the URLs of distfiles when downloading. It is not needed when using a proxy. Refer to the default configuration file for proxy configuration.

FREEBSD_HOST

The FTP/HTTP server to use when the jails are installed from FreeBSD releases and updated with freebsd-update(8). Choose a server location which is close, for example if the machine is located in Australia, use `ftp.au.freebsd.org`.

SVN_HOST

The server from where jails are installed and updated when using Subversion. Also used for ports tree when not using portsnap(8). Again, choose a nearby location. A list of official Subversion mirrors can be found in the FreeBSD Handbook Subversion section.

10.5.3. Creating Poudriere Jails

Create the base jails which Poudriere will use for building:

```
# poudriere jail -c -j 93Ramd64 -v 9.3-RELEASE -a amd64
```

Fetch a `9.3-RELEASE` for `amd64` from the FTP server given by `FREEBSD_HOST` in `poudriere.conf`, create the zfs file system `tank/poudriere/jails/93Ramd64`, mount it on `/poudriere/jails/93Ramd64` and extract the `9.3-RELEASE` tarballs into this file system.

```
# poudriere jail -c -j 10i386 -v stable/10 -a i386 -m svn+https
```

Create `tank/poudriere/jails/10i386`, mount it on `/poudriere/jails/10i386`, then check out the tip of the Subversion branch of `FreeBSD-10-STABLE` from `SVN_HOST` in `poudriere.conf` into `/poudriere/jails/10i386/usr/src`, then complete a `buildworld` and install it into `/poudriere/jails/10i386`.

Tip

If a specific Subversion revision is needed, append it to the version string. For example:

```
# poudriere jail -c -j 10i386 -v stable/10@123456 -a i386 -m svn+https
```

Note

While it is possible to build a newer version of FreeBSD on an older version, most of the time it will not run. For example, if a `stable/10` jail is needed, the host will have to run `stable/10` too. Running `10.0-RELEASE` is not enough.

Caution

The default svn protocol works but is not very secure. Using svn+https along with verifying the remote server's SSL fingerprint is advised. It will ensure that the files used for building the jail are from a trusted source.

A list of jails currently known to Poudriere can be shown with `poudriere jail -l` :

```
# poudriere jail -l
JAILNAME             VERSION           ARCH     METHOD
93Ramd64             9.3-RELEASE       amd64    ftp
10i386               10.0-STABLE       i386     svn+https
```

10.5.4. Keeping Poudriere Jails Updated

Managing updates is very straightforward. The command:

```
# poudriere jail -u -j JAILNAME
```

updates the specified jail to the latest version available. For FreeBSD releases, update to the latest patchlevel with freebsd-update(8). For FreeBSD versions built from source, update to the latest Subversion revision in the branch.

Tip

For jails employing a svn+* method, it is helpful to add -J NumberOfParallelBuildJobs to speed up the build by increasing the number of parallel compile jobs used. For example, if the building machine has 6 CPUs, use:

```
# poudriere jail -u -J 6 -j JAILNAME
```

10.5.5. Setting Up Ports Trees for Use with Poudriere

There are multiple ways to use ports trees in Poudriere. The most straightforward way is to have Poudriere create a default ports tree for itself:

```
# poudriere ports -c
```

This command creates tank/poudriere/ports/default , mount it on /poudriere/ports/default , and populate it using portsnap(8). Afterward it is included in the list of known ports trees:

```
# poudriere ports -l
PORTSTREE       METHOD       PATH
default         portsnap     /poudriere/ports/default
```

Note

Note that the "default" ports tree is special. Each of the build commands explained later will implicitly use this ports tree unless specifically specified otherwise. To use another tree, add -p treename to the commands.

While useful for regular bulk builds, having this default ports tree with the portsnap(8) method may not be the best way to deal with local modifications for a ports contributor. As with the creation of jails, it is possible to use a different method for creating the ports tree. To add an additional ports tree for testing local modifications and ports development, checking out the tree via Subversion is possible:

```
# poudriere ports -c -m svn+https -p subversive
```

Note

The http and https methods need devel/subversion built with the SERF option enabled. It is enabled by default.

Creates tank/poudriere/ports/subversive and mounts it on /poudriere/ports/subversive . It is then populated using Subversion. Finally, it is added to the list of known ports trees:

```
# poudriere ports -l
PORTSTREE          METHOD      PATH
default            portsnap    /poudriere/ports/default
subversive         svn+https   /poudriere/ports/subversive
```

Tip

The svn method allows extra qualifiers to tell Subversion exactly how to fetch data. This is explained in poudriere(8). For instance, poudriere ports -c -m svn+ssh -p subversive uses SSH for the checkout.

10.5.6. Using Manually Managed Ports Trees with Poudriere

Depending on the workflow, it can be extremely helpful to use ports trees which are maintained manually. For instance, if there is a local copy of the ports tree in /work/ports , point Poudriere to the location:

```
# poudriere ports -c -F -f none -M /work/ports -p development
```

This will be listed in the table of known trees:

```
# poudriere ports -l
PORTSTREE     METHOD    PATH
development   -         /work/ports
```

Note

The dash in the METHOD column means that Poudriere will not update or change this ports tree, ever. It is completely up to the user to maintain this tree, including all local modifications that may be used for testing new ports and submitting patches.

10.5.7. Keeping Poudriere Ports Trees Updated

As straightforward as with jails described earlier:

```
# poudriere ports -u -p PORTSTREE
```

Will update the given *PORTSTREE* , one tree given by the output of poudriere -l , to the latest revision available on the official servers.

> **Note**
>
> Ports trees without a method, see Section 10.5.6, "Using Manually Managed Ports Trees with Poudriere", cannot be updated like this. They must be updated manually by the porter.

10.5.8. Testing Ports

After jails and ports trees have been set up, the result of a contributor's modifications to the ports tree can be tested.

For example, local modifications to the www/firefox port located in `/work/ports/www/firefox` can be tested in the previously created 9.3-RELEASE jail:

```
# poudriere testport -j 93Ramd64 -p development -o www/firefox
```

This will build all dependencies of Firefox. If a dependency has been built previously and is still up-to-date, the pre-built package is installed. If a dependency has no up-to-date package, one will be built with default options in a jail. Then Firefox itself is built.

The complete build of every port is logged to `/poudriere/data/logs/bulk/93Ri386-development/` *build-time*`/logs`.

The directory name `93Ri386-development` is derived from the arguments to -j and -p, respectively. For convenience, a symbolic link `/poudriere/data/logs/bulk/93Ri386-development/latest` is also maintained. The link points to the latest *build-time* directory. Also in this directory is an `index.html` for observing the build process with a web browser.

By default, Poudriere cleans up the jails and leaves log files in the directories mentioned above. To ease investigation, jails can be kept running after the build by adding `-i` to `testport`:

```
# poudriere testport -j 93Ramd64 -p development -i -o www/firefox
```

After the build completes, and regardless of whether it was successful, a shell is provided within the jail. The shell is used to investigate further. Poudriere can be told to leave the jail running after the build finishes with `-I`. Poudriere will show the command to run when the jail is no longer needed. It is then possible to jexec(8) into it:

```
# poudriere testport -j 93Ramd64 -p development -I -o www/firefox
[...]
=====>> Installing local Pkg repository to /usr/local/etc/pkg/repos
=====>> Leaving jail 93Ramd64-development-n running, mounted at /poudriere/data/.↵
m/93Ramd64-development/ref for interactive run testing
=====>> To enter jail: jexec 93Ramd64-development-n env -i TERM=$TERM /usr/bin/login -fp ↵
root
=====>> To stop jail: poudriere jail -k -j 93Ramd64 -p development
# jexec 93Ramd64-development-n env -i TERM=$TERM /usr/bin/login -fp root
# [do some stuff in the jail]
# exit
# poudriere jail -k -j 93Ramd64 -p development
=====>> Umounting file systems
```

An integral part of the FreeBSD ports build infrastructure is the ability to tweak ports to personal preferences with options. These can be tested with Poudriere as well. Adding the `-c`:

```
# poudriere testport -c -o www/firefox
```

Presents the port configuration dialog before the port is built. The ports given after -o in the format *category/portname* will use the specified options, all dependencies will use the default options. Testing dependent ports with non-default options can be accomplished using sets, see Section 10.5.9, "Using Sets".

Tip

When testing ports where pkg-plist is altered during build depending on the selected options, it is recommended to perform a test run with all options selected *and* one with all options deselected.

10.5.9. Using Sets

For all actions involving builds, a so-called *set* can be specified using -z *setname*. A set refers to a fully independent build. This allows, for instance, usage of testport with non-standard options for the dependent ports.

To use sets, Poudriere expects an existing directory structure similar to PORT_DBDIR, defaults to /var/db/ports in its configuration directory. This directory is then nullfs-mounted into the jails where the ports and their dependencies are built. Usually a suitable starting point can be obtained by recursively copying the existing PORT_DBDIR to / usr/local/etc/poudriere.d/ *jailname*-*portname*-*setname*-options. This is described in detail in poudriere(8). For instance, testing www/firefox in a specific set named devset, add the -z devset parameter to the testport command:

```
# poudriere testport -j 93Ramd64 -p development -z devset -o www/firefox
```

This will look for the existence of these directories in this order:

- /usr/local/etc/poudriere.d/93Ramd64-development-devset-options

- /usr/local/etc/poudriere.d/93Ramd64-devset-options

- /usr/local/etc/poudriere.d/93Ramd64-development-options

- /usr/local/etc/poudriere.d/devset-options

- /usr/local/etc/poudriere.d/development-options

- /usr/local/etc/poudriere.d/93Ramd64-options

- /usr/local/etc/poudriere.d/options

From this list, Poudriere nullfs-mounts the *first existing* directory tree into the /var/db/ports directory of the build jails. Hence, all custom options are used for all the ports during this run of testport.

After the directory structure for a set is provided, the options for a particular port can be altered. For example:

```
# poudriere options -c www/firefox -z devset
```

The configuration dialog for www/firefox is shown, and options can be edited. The selected options are saved to the devset set.

Note

Poudriere is very flexible in the option configuration. They can be set for particular jails, ports trees, and for multiple ports by one command. Refer to poudriere(8) for details.

10.5.10. Providing a Custom make.conf File

Similar to using sets, Poudriere will also use a custom make.conf if it is provided. No special command line argument is necessary. Instead, Poudriere looks for existing files matching a name scheme derived from the command line. For instance:

```
# poudriere testport -j 93Ramd64 -p development -z devset -o www/firefox
```

causes Poudriere to check for the existence of these files in this order:

- `/usr/local/etc/poudriere.d/make.conf`

- `/usr/local/etc/poudriere.d/devset-make.conf`

- `/usr/local/etc/poudriere.d/development-make.conf`

- `/usr/local/etc/poudriere.d/93Ramd64-make.conf`

- `/usr/local/etc/poudriere.d/93Ramd64-development-make.conf`

- `/usr/local/etc/poudriere.d/93Ramd64-devset-make.conf`

- `/usr/local/etc/poudriere.d/93Ramd64-development-devset-make.conf`

Unlike with sets, all of the found files will be appended, *in that order*, into one make.conf inside the build jails. It is hence possible to have general make variables, intended to affect all builds in /usr/local/etc/poudriere.d/make.conf. Special variables, intended to affect only certain jails or sets can be set in specialised make.conf files, such as /usr/local/etc/poudriere.d/93Ramd64-development-devset-make.conf .

Example 10.1. Using **make.conf** to Change Default Perl

To build a set with a non default Perl version, for example, 5.20, using a set named perl5-20 , create a perl5-20-make.conf with this line:

```
DEFAULT_VERSIONS+= perl=5.20
```

Note

Note the use of += so that if the variable is already set in the default make.conf its content will not be overwritten.

10.5.11. Pruning no Longer Needed Distfiles

Poudriere comes with a built-in mechanism to remove outdated distfiles that are no longer used by any port of a given tree. The command

```
# poudriere distclean -p portstree
```

will scan the distfiles folder, DISTFILES_CACHE in poudriere.conf , versus the ports tree given by the -p *portstree* argument and prompt for removal of those distfiles. To skip the prompt and remove all unused files unconditionally, the -y argument can be added:

```
# poudriere distclean -p portstree -y
```

10.6. Tinderbox

As an avid ports contributor, take a look at Tinderbox. It is a powerful system for building and testing ports. Install Tinderbox using ports-mgmt/tinderbox port. Be sure to read supplied documentation since the configuration is not trivial.

Visit the Tinderbox website for more details.

Chapter 11. Upgrading a Port

When a port is not the most recent version available from the authors, update the local working copy of /usr/ports. The port might have already been updated to the new version.

When working with more than a few ports, it will probably be easier to use Subversion to keep the whole ports collection up-to-date, as described in the Handbook. This will have the added benefit of tracking all the port's dependencies.

The next step is to see if there is an update already pending. To do this, there are two options. There is a searchable interface to the FreeBSD Problem Report (PR) or bug database. Select Ports & Packages in the Product multiple select menu, and enter the name of the port in the Summary field.

However, sometimes people forget to put the name of the port into the Summary field in an unambiguous fashion. In that case, try searching in the Comment field in the Detailled Bug Information section, or try the FreeBSD Ports Monitoring System (also known as portsmon). This system attempts to classify port PRs by portname. To search for PRs about a particular port, use the Overview of One Port.

If there is no pending PR, the next step is to send an email to the port's maintainer, as shown by make maintainer. That person may already be working on an upgrade, or have a reason to not upgrade the port right now (because of, for example, stability problems of the new version), and there is no need to duplicate their work. Note that unmaintained ports are listed with a maintainer of ports@FreeBSD.org, which is just the general ports mailing list, so sending mail there probably will not help in this case.

If the maintainer asks you to do the upgrade or there is no maintainer, then help out FreeBSD by preparing the update! Please do this by using the diff(1) command in the base system.

To create a suitable diff for a single patch, copy the file that needs patching to *something*.orig, save the changes to *something* and then create the patch:

```
% diff -u something.orig something > something.diff
```

Otherwise, either use the svn diff method (Section 11.1, "Using Subversion to Make Patches") or copy the contents of the port to an entire different directory and use the result of the recursive diff(1) output of the new and old ports directories (for example, if the modified port directory is called superedit and the original is in our tree as superedit.bak, then save the result of diff -ruN superedit.bak superedit). Either unified or context diff is fine, but port committers generally prefer unified diffs. Note the use of the -N option—this is the accepted way to force diff to properly deal with the case of new files being added or old files being deleted. Before sending us the diff, please examine the output to make sure all the changes make sense. (In particular, make sure to first clean out the work directories with make clean).

> **Note**
>
> If some files have been added, copied, moved, or removed, add this information to the problem report so that the committer picking up the patch will know what svn(1) commands to run.

To simplify common operations with patch files, use make makepatch as described in Section 4.4, "Patching". Other tools exists, like /usr/ports/Tools/scripts/patchtool.py . Before using it, please read /usr/ports/Tools/scripts/README.patchtool .

If the port is unmaintained, and you are actively using it, please consider volunteering to become its maintainer. FreeBSD has over 4000 ports without maintainers, and this is an area where more volunteers are always needed. (For a detailed description of the responsibilities of maintainers, refer to the section in the Developer's Handbook.)

To submit the diff, use the bug submit form (product `Ports & Packages`, component `Individual Port(s)`). If the submitter is also maintaining the port, be sure to put `[MAINTAINER]` at the beginning of the `Summary` line. Always include the category with the port name, followed by colon, and brief descripton of the issue. For example: *category/portname*: *add FOO option*, or if maintaining the port, `[MAINTAINER]` *category/portname*: *Update to X.Y*. Please mention any added or deleted files in the message, as they have to be explicitly specified to svn(1) when doing a commit. Do not compress or encode the diff.

Before submitting the bug, review the Writing the problem report section in the Problem Reports article. It contains far more information about how to write useful problem reports.

Important

If the upgrade is motivated by security concerns or a serious fault in the currently committed port, please notify the Ports Management Team <portmgr@FreeBSD.org> to request immediate rebuilding and redistribution of the port's package. Unsuspecting users of pkg will otherwise continue to install the old version via `pkg install` for several weeks.

Note

Please use diff(1) or `svn diff` to create updates to existing ports. Other formats include the whole file and make it impossible to see just what has changed. When diffs are not included, the entire update might be ignored.

Now that all of that is done, read about how to keep up-to-date in Chapter 16, *Keeping Up*.

11.1. Using Subversion to Make Patches

When possible, please submit a svn(1) diff. They are easier to handle than diffs between "new and old" directories. It is easier to see what has changed, and to update the diff if something was modified in the Ports Collection since the work on it began, or if the committer asks for something to be fixed. Also, a patch generated with `svn diff` can be easily applied with `svn patch` and will save some time to the committer.

```
% cd ~/my_wrkdir ❶
% svn co https://svn.FreeBSD.org /ports/head/dns/pdnsd ❷
% cd ~/my_wrkdir/pdnsd
```

❶   This can be anywhere, of course. Building ports is not limited to within /usr/ports/ .
❷   svn.FreeBSD.org is the FreeBSD public Subversion server. See Subversion mirror sites for more information.

While in the port directory, make any changes that are needed. If adding, copying, moving, or removing a file, use svn to track these changes:

```
% svn add new_file
% svn copy some_file file_copy
% svn move old_name new_name
% svn remove deleted_file
```

Make sure to check the port using the checklist in Section 3.4, "Testing the Port" and Section 3.5, "Checking the Port with portlint".

```
% svn status
% svn update ❶
```

❶   This will attempt to merge the differences between the patch and current repository version. Watch the output carefully. The letter in front of each file name indicates what was done with it. See Table 11.1, "Subversion Update File Prefixes" for a complete list.

Table 11.1. Subversion Update File Prefixes

U	The file was updated without problems.
G	The file was updated without problems (only when working against a remote repository).
M	The file had been modified, and was merged without conflicts.
C	The file had been modified, and was merged with conflicts.

If C is displayed as a result of svn update, it means something changed in the Subversion repository and svn(1) was not able to merge the local changes with those from the repository. It is always a good idea to inspect the changes anyway, since svn(1) does not know anything about the structure of a port, so it might (and probably will) merge things that do not make sense.

The last step is to make a unified diff(1) of the changes:

```
% svn diff > ../`make -VPKGNAME`.diff
```

Note

If files have been added, copied, moved, or removed, include the svn(1) add, copy, move, and remove commands that were used. svn move or svn copy must be run before the patch can be applied. svn add or svn remove must be run after the patch is applied.

Send the patch following the problem report submission guidelines.

Tip

The patch can be automatically generated and the PR pre-filled with the contact information by using port submit. See Section 10.3, "Port Tools" for more details.

11.2. UPDATING and MOVED

11.2.1. /usr/ports/UPDATING

If upgrading the port requires special steps like changing configuration files or running a specific program, it must be documented in this file. The format of an entry in this file is:

```
YYYYMMDD:
  AFFECTS: users of portcategory/portname
  AUTHOR: Your name <Your email address>

  Special instructions
```

Tip

When including exact portmaster, portupgrade, and/or pkg instructions, please make sure to get the shell escaping right. For example, do *not* use:

```
# pkg delete -g -f docbook-xml* docbook-sk* docbook[2345]??-* docbook-4*
```

As shown, the command will only work with bourne shells. Instead, use the form shown below, which will work with both bourne shell and c-shell:

```
# pkg delete -g -f docbook-xml\* docbook-sk\* docbook\[2345\]\?\?-\* ↵
docbook-4\*
```

Note

It is recommended that the AFFECTS line contains a glob matching all the ports affected by the entry so that automated tools can parse it as easily as possible. If an update concerns all the existing BIND 9 versions the AFFECTS content must be users of dns/bind9* , it must *not* be users of BIND 9

11.2.2. /usr/ports/MOVED

This file is used to list moved or removed ports. Each line in the file is made up of the name of the port, where the port was moved, when, and why. If the port was removed, the section detailing where it was moved can be left blank. Each section must be separated by the | (pipe) character, like so:

```
old name|new name (blank for deleted)|date of move|reason
```

The date must be entered in the form YYYY-MM-DD . New entries are added to the end of the list to keep it in chronological order, with the oldest entry at the top of the list.

If a port was removed but has since been restored, delete the line in this file that states that it was removed.

If a port was renamed and then renamed back to its original name, add a new one with the intermediate name to the old name, and remove the old entry as to not create a loop.

Note

Any changes must be validated with Tools/scripts/MOVEDlint.awk .

If using a ports directory other than /usr/ports , use:

```
% cd /home/user/ports
% env PORTSDIR=$PWD Tools/scripts/MOVEDlint.awk
```

Chapter 12. Security

12.1. Why Security is So Important

Bugs are occasionally introduced to the software. Arguably, the most dangerous of them are those opening security vulnerabilities. From the technical viewpoint, such vulnerabilities are to be closed by exterminating the bugs that caused them. However, the policies for handling mere bugs and security vulnerabilities are very different.

A typical small bug affects only those users who have enabled some combination of options triggering the bug. The developer will eventually release a patch followed by a new version of the software, free of the bug, but the majority of users will not take the trouble of upgrading immediately because the bug has never vexed them. A critical bug that may cause data loss represents a graver issue. Nevertheless, prudent users know that a lot of possible accidents, besides software bugs, are likely to lead to data loss, and so they make backups of important data; in addition, a critical bug will be discovered really soon.

A security vulnerability is all different. First, it may remain unnoticed for years because often it does not cause software malfunction. Second, a malicious party can use it to gain unauthorized access to a vulnerable system, to destroy or alter sensitive data; and in the worst case the user will not even notice the harm caused. Third, exposing a vulnerable system often assists attackers to break into other systems that could not be compromised otherwise. Therefore closing a vulnerability alone is not enough: notify the audience of it in the most clear and comprehensive manner, which will allow them to evaluate the danger and take appropriate action.

12.2. Fixing Security Vulnerabilities

While on the subject of ports and packages, a security vulnerability may initially appear in the original distribution or in the port files. In the former case, the original software developer is likely to release a patch or a new version instantly. Update the port promptly with respect to the author's fix. If the fix is delayed for some reason, either mark the port as FORBIDDEN or introduce a patch file to the port. In the case of a vulnerable port, just fix the port as soon as possible. In either case, follow the standard procedure for submitting changes unless having rights to commit it directly to the ports tree.

> **Important**
>
> Being a ports committer is not enough to commit to an arbitrary port. Remember that ports usually have maintainers, must be respected.

Please make sure that the port's revision is bumped as soon as the vulnerability has been closed. That is how the users who upgrade installed packages on a regular basis will see they need to run an update. Besides, a new package will be built and distributed over FTP and WWW mirrors, replacing the vulnerable one. Bump PORTREVISION unless DISTVERSION has changed in the course of correcting the vulnerability. That is, bump PORTREVISION if adding a patch file to the port, but do not bump it if updating the port to the latest software version and thus already touched DISTVERSION . Please refer to the corresponding section for more information.

12.3. Keeping the Community Informed

12.3.1. The VuXML Database

A very important and urgent step to take as early after a security vulnerability is discovered as possible is to notify the community of port users about the jeopardy. Such notification serves two purposes. First, if the danger is really severe it will be wise to apply an instant workaround. For example, stop the affected network service or even deinstall the port completely until the vulnerability is closed. Second, a lot of users tend to upgrade installed packages only occasionally. They will know from the notification that they *must* update the package without delay as soon as a corrected version is available.

Given the huge number of ports in the tree, a security advisory cannot be issued on each incident without creating a flood and losing the attention of the audience when it comes to really serious matters. Therefore security vulnerabilities found in ports are recorded in the FreeBSD VuXML database. The Security Officer Team members also monitor it for issues requiring their intervention.

Committers can update the VuXML database themselves, assisting the Security Officer Team and delivering crucial information to the community more quickly. Those who are not committers or have discovered an exceptionally severe vulnerability should not hesitate to contact the Security Officer Team directly, as described on the FreeBSD Security Information page.

The VuXML database is an XML document. Its source file `vuln.xml` is kept right inside the port security/vuxml. Therefore the file's full pathname will be `PORTSDIR/security/vuxml/vuln.xml` . Each time a security vulnerability is discovered in a port, please add an entry for it to that file. Until familiar with VuXML, the best thing to do is to find an existing entry fitting the case at hand, then copy it and use it as a template.

12.3.2. A Short Introduction to VuXML

The full-blown XML format is complex, and far beyond the scope of this book. However, to gain basic insight on the structure of a VuXML entry only the notion of tags is needed. XML tag names are enclosed in angle brackets. Each opening <tag> must have a matching closing </tag>. Tags may be nested. If nesting, the inner tags must be closed before the outer ones. There is a hierarchy of tags, that is, more complex rules of nesting them. This is similar to HTML. The major difference is that XML is eXtensible, that is, based on defining custom tags. Due to its intrinsic structure XML puts otherwise amorphous data into shape. VuXML is particularly tailored to mark up descriptions of security vulnerabilities.

Now consider a realistic VuXML entry:

```
<vuln vid="f4bc80f4-da62-11d8-90ea-0004ac98a7b9"> ❶
  <topic>Several vulnerabilities found in Foo</topic> ❷
  <affects>
    <package>
      <name>foo</name> ❸
      <name>foo-devel</name>
      <name>ja-foo</name>
      <range><ge>1.6</ge><lt>1.9</lt></range> ❹
      <range><ge>2.*</ge><lt>2.4_1</lt></range>
      <range><eq>3.0b1</eq></range>
    </package>
    <package>
      <name>openfoo</name> ❺
      <range><lt>1.10_7</lt></range> ❻
      <range><ge>1.2,1</ge><lt>1.3_1,1</lt></range>
    </package>
  </affects>
  <description>
    <body xmlns="http://www.w3.org/1999/xhtml">
      <p>J. Random Hacker reports:</p> ❼
      <blockquote
        cite="http://j.r.hacker.com/advisories/1">
        <p>Several issues in the Foo software may be exploited
          via carefully crafted QUUX requests.  These requests will
          permit the injection of Bar code, mumble theft, and the
          readability of the Foo administrator account.</p>
      </blockquote>
    </body>
  </description>
```

```
  <references> ❽
    <freebsdsa>SA-10:75.foo</freebsdsa> ❾
    <freebsdpr>ports/987654</freebsdpr> ❿
    <cvename>CAN-2010-0201</cvename> ⓫
    <cvename>CAN-2010-0466</cvename>
    <bid>96298</bid> ⓬
    <certsa>CA-2010-99</certsa> ⓭
    <certvu>740169</certvu> ⓮
    <uscertsa>SA10-99A</uscertsa> ⓯
    <uscertta>SA10-99A</uscertta> ⓰
    <mlist msgid="201075606@hacker.com">http://marc.theaimsgroup.com/?
l=bugtraq&amp;m=203886607825605</mlist> ⓱
    <url>http://j.r.hacker.com/advisories/1</url> ⓲
  </references>
  <dates>
    <discovery>2010-05-25</discovery> ⓳
    <entry>2010-07-13</entry> ⓴
    <modified>2010-09-17</modified> ㉑
  </dates>
</vuln>
```

The tag names are supposed to be self-explanatory so we shall take a closer look only at fields which needs to be filled in:

❶   This is the top-level tag of a VuXML entry. It has a mandatory attribute, vid, specifying a universally unique identifier (UUID) for this entry (in quotes). Generate a UUID for each new VuXML entry (and do not forget to substitute it for the template UUID unless writing the entry from scratch). use uuidgen(1) to generate a VuXML UUID.

❷   This is a one-line description of the issue found.

❸   The names of packages affected are listed there. Multiple names can be given since several packages may be based on a single master port or software product. This may include stable and development branches, localized versions, and slave ports featuring different choices of important build-time configuration options.

Important

It is the submitter's responsibility to find all such related packages when writing a VuXML entry. Keep in mind that `make search name=foo` is helpful. The primary points to look for are:

- the `foo-devel` variant for a `foo` port;

- other variants with a suffix like `-a4` (for print-related packages), `-without-gui` (for packages with X support disabled), or similar;

- `jp-`, `ru-`, `zh-`, and other possible localized variants in the corresponding national categories of the ports collection.

---

❹   Affected versions of the package(s) are specified there as one or more ranges using a combination of `<lt>`, `<le>`, `<eq>`, `<ge>`, and `<gt>` elements. Check that the version ranges given do not overlap.

In a range specification, `*` (asterisk) denotes the smallest version number. In particular, `2.*` is less than `2.a`. Therefore an asterisk may be used for a range to match all possible alpha, beta, and RC versions. For instance, `<ge>2.*</ge><lt>3.*</lt>` will selectively match every `2.x` version while `<ge>2.0</ge><lt>3.0</lt>` will not since the latter misses `2.r3` and matches `3.b`.

The above example specifies that affected are versions from `1.6` to `1.9` inclusive, versions `2.x` before `2.4_1`, and version `3.0b1`.

❺ Several related package groups (essentially, ports) can be listed in the <affected> section. This can be used if several software products (say FooBar, FreeBar and OpenBar) grow from the same code base and still share its bugs and vulnerabilities. Note the difference from listing multiple names within a single <package> section.

❻ The version ranges have to allow for PORTEPOCH and PORTREVISION if applicable. Please remember that according to the collation rules, a version with a non-zero PORTEPOCH is greater than any version without PORTEPOCH, for example, 3.0,1 is greater than 3.1 or even than 8.9.

❼ This is a summary of the issue. XHTML is used in this field. At least enclosing <p> and </p> has to appear. More complex mark-up may be used, but only for the sake of accuracy and clarity: No eye candy please.

❽ This section contains references to relevant documents. As many references as apply are encouraged.

❾ This is a FreeBSD security advisory.

❿ This is a FreeBSD problem report.

⓫ This is a MITRE CVE identifier.

⓬ This is a SecurityFocus Bug ID.

⓭ This is a US-CERT security advisory.

⓮ This is a US-CERT vulnerability note.

⓯ This is a US-CERT Cyber Security Alert.

⓰ This is a US-CERT Technical Cyber Security Alert.

⓱ This is a URL to an archived posting in a mailing list. The attribute msgid is optional and may specify the message ID of the posting.

⓲ This is a generic URL. Only it if none of the other reference categories apply.

⓳ This is the date when the issue was disclosed (*YYYY-MM-DD*).

⓴ This is the date when the entry was added (*YYYY-MM-DD*).

㉑ This is the date when any information in the entry was last modified (*YYYY-MM-DD*). New entries must not include this field. Add it when editing an existing entry.

12.3.3. Testing Changes to the VuXML Database

This example describes a new entry for a vulnerability in the package dropbear that has been fixed in version dropbear-2013.59.

As a prerequisite, install a fresh version of security/vuxml port.

First, check whether there already is an entry for this vulnerability. If there were such an entry, it would match the previous version of the package, 2013.58:

```
% pkg audit dropbear-2013.58
```

If there is none found, add a new entry for this vulnerability.

```
% cd ${PORTSDIR}/security/vuxml
% make newentry
```

Verify its syntax and formatting:

```
% make validate
```

> **Note**
>
> At least one of these packages needs to be installed: textproc/libxml2, textproc/jade.

Verify that the <affected> section of the entry will match the correct packages:

```
% pkg audit -f ${PORTSDIR}/security/vuxml/vuln.xml dropbear-2013.58
```

Make sure that the entry produces no spurious matches in the output.

Now check whether the right package versions are matched by the entry:

```
% pkg audit -f ${PORTSDIR}/security/vuxml/vuln.xml dropbear-2013.58 dropbear-2013.59
dropbear-2012.58 is vulnerable:
dropbear -- exposure of sensitive information, DoS
CVE: CVE-2013-4434
CVE: CVE-2013-4421
WWW: http://portaudit.FreeBSD.org/8c9b48d1-3715-11e3-a624-00262d8b701d.html

1 problem(s) in the installed packages found.
```

The former version matches while the latter one does not.

Chapter 13. Dos and Don'ts

13.1. Introduction

Here is a list of common dos and don'ts that are encountered during the porting process. Check the port against this list, but also check ports in the PR database that others have submitted. Submit any comments on ports as described in Bug Reports and General Commentary. Checking ports in the PR database will both make it faster for us to commit them, and prove that you know what you are doing.

13.2. WRKDIR

Do not write anything to files outside WRKDIR. WRKDIR is the only place that is guaranteed to be writable during the port build (see installing ports from a CDROM for an example of building ports from a read-only tree). The pkg-* files can be modified by redefining a variable rather than overwriting the file.

13.3. WRKDIRPREFIX

Make sure the port honors WRKDIRPREFIX. Most ports do not have to worry about this. In particular, when referring to a WRKDIR of another port, note that the correct location is WRKDIRPREFIXPORTSDIR/*subdir*/*name*/work not PORTSDIR/*subdir*/*name*/work or .CURDIR/../../*subdir*/*name*/work or some such.

Also, if defining WRKDIR, make sure to prepend ${WRKDIRPREFIX}${.CURDIR} in the front.

13.4. Differentiating Operating Systems and OS Versions

Some code needs modifications or conditional compilation based upon what version of FreeBSD Unix it is running under. The preferred way to tell FreeBSD versions apart are the __FreeBSD_version and __FreeBSD__ macros defined in sys/param.h. If this file is not included add the code,

```
#include <sys/param.h>
```

to the proper place in the .c file.

__FreeBSD__ is defined in all versions of FreeBSD as their major version number. For example, in FreeBSD 9.x, __FreeBSD__ is defined to be 9.

```
#if __FreeBSD__ >= 9
#  if __FreeBSD_version >= 901000
  /* 9.1+ release specific code here */
#  endif
#endif
```

A complete list of __FreeBSD_version values is available in Chapter 18, *__FreeBSD_version Values*.

13.5. Writing Something After bsd.port.mk

Do not write anything after the .include <bsd.port.mk> line. It usually can be avoided by including bsd.port.pre.mk somewhere in the middle of the Makefile and bsd.port.post.mk at the end.

Important

Include either the bsd.port.pre.mk/bsd.port.post.mk pair or bsd.port.mk only; do not mix these two usages.

bsd.port.pre.mk only defines a few variables, which can be used in tests in the Makefile, bsd.port.post.mk defines the rest.

Here are some important variables defined in bsd.port.pre.mk (this is not the complete list, please read bsd.port.mk for the complete list).

Variable	Description
ARCH	The architecture as returned by uname -m (for example, i386)
OPSYS	The operating system type, as returned by uname -s (for example, FreeBSD)
OSREL	The release version of the operating system (for example, 2.1.5 or 2.2.7)
OSVERSION	The numeric version of the operating system; the same as __FreeBSD_version.
LOCALBASE	The base of the "local" tree (for example, /usr/local)
PREFIX	Where the port installs itself (see more on PREFIX).

Note

When MASTERDIR is needed, always define it before including bsd.port.pre.mk.

Here are some examples of things that can be added after bsd.port.pre.mk:

```
# no need to compile lang/perl5 if perl5 is already in system
.if ${OSVERSION} > 300003
BROKEN= perl is in system
.endif
```

Always use tab instead of spaces after BROKEN=.

13.6. Use the exec Statement in Wrapper Scripts

If the port installs a shell script whose purpose is to launch another program, and if launching that program is the last action performed by the script, make sure to launch the program using the exec statement, for instance:

```
#!/bin/sh
exec %%LOCALBASE%%/bin/java -jar %%DATADIR%%/foo.jar "$@"
```

The exec statement replaces the shell process with the specified program. If exec is omitted, the shell process remains in memory while the program is executing, and needlessly consumes system resources.

13.7. Do Things Rationally

The Makefile should do things in a simple and reasonable manner. Making it a couple of lines shorter or more readable is always better. Examples include using a make `.if` construct instead of a shell `if` construct, not redefining `do-extract` if redefining `EXTRACT*` is enough, and using `GNU_CONFIGURE` instead of `CONFIGURE_ARGS += --prefix=${PREFIX}`.

If a lot of new code is needed to do something, there may already be an implementation of it in `bsd.port.mk`. While hard to read, there are a great many seemingly-hard problems for which `bsd.port.mk` already provides a shorthand solution.

13.8. Respect Both cc and cxx

The port must respect both CC and CXX. What we mean by this is that the port must not set the values of these variables absolutely, overriding existing values; instead, it may append whatever values it needs to the existing values. This is so that build options that affect all ports can be set globally.

If the port does not respect these variables, please add `NO_PACKAGE=ignores either cc or cxx` to the Makefile.

Here is an example of a Makefile respecting both CC and CXX. Note the `?=`:

```
CC?= gcc
```

```
CXX?= g++
```

Here is an example which respects neither CC nor CXX:

```
CC= gcc
```

```
CXX= g++
```

Both CC and CXX can be defined on FreeBSD systems in `/etc/make.conf`. The first example defines a value if it was not previously set in `/etc/make.conf`, preserving any system-wide definitions. The second example clobbers anything previously defined.

13.9. Respect cflags

The port must respect CFLAGS. What we mean by this is that the port must not set the value of this variable absolutely, overriding the existing value. Instead, it may append whatever values it needs to the existing value. This is so that build options that affect all ports can be set globally.

If it does not, please add `NO_PACKAGE=ignores cflags` to the Makefile.

Here is an example of a Makefile respecting CFLAGS. Note the `+=`:

```
CFLAGS+= -Wall -Werror
```

Here is an example which does not respect CFLAGS:

```
CFLAGS= -Wall -Werror
```

CFLAGS is defined on FreeBSD systems in `/etc/make.conf`. The first example appends additional flags to CFLAGS, preserving any system-wide definitions. The second example clobbers anything previously defined.

Remove optimization flags from the third party Makefiles. The system CFLAGS contains system-wide optimization flags. An example from an unmodified Makefile:

```
CFLAGS= -O3 -funroll-loops -DHAVE_SOUND
```

Using system optimization flags, the `Makefile` would look similar to this example:

```
CFLAGS+= -DHAVE_SOUND
```

13.10. Verbose Build Logs

Make the port build system display all commands executed during the build stage. Complete build logs are crucial to debugging port problems.

Non-informative build log example (bad):

```
CC      source1.o
CC      source2.o
CCLD    someprogram
```

Verbose build log example (good):

```
cc -O2 -pipe -I/usr/local/include -c -o source1.o source1.c
cc -O2 -pipe -I/usr/local/include -c -o source2.o source2.c
cc -o someprogram source1.o source2.o -L/usr/local/lib -lsomelib
```

Some build systems such as CMake, ninja, and GNU configure are set up for verbose logging by the ports framework. In other cases, ports might need individual tweaks.

13.11. Feedback

Do send applicable changes and patches to the upstream maintainer for inclusion in the next release of the code. This makes updating to the next release that much easier.

13.12. README.html

`README.html` is not part of the port, but generated by `make readme`. Do not include this file in patches or commits.

> **Note**
>
> If `make readme` fails, make sure that the default value of `ECHO_MSG` has not been modified by the port.

13.13. Marking a Port as Architecture Neutral

Ports that do not have any architecture-dependent files or requirements are identified by setting `NO_ARCH=yes`.

13.14. Marking a Port Not Installable with BROKEN, FORBIDDEN, or IGNORE

In certain cases, users must be prevented from installing a port. There are several variables that can be used in a port's `Makefile` to tell the user that the port cannot be installed. The value of these make variables will be the reason that is shown to users for why the port refuses to install itself. Please use the correct make variable. Each variable conveys radically different meanings, both to users and to automated systems that depend on `Makefiles`, such as the ports build cluster, FreshPorts, and portsmon.

13.14.1. Variables

- BROKEN is reserved for ports that currently do not compile, install, deinstall, or run correctly. Use it for ports where the problem is believed to be temporary.

  If instructed, the build cluster will still attempt to try to build them to see if the underlying problem has been resolved. (However, in general, the cluster is run without this.)

  For instance, use BROKEN when a port:

  - does not compile

  - fails its configuration or installation process

  - installs files outside of ${PREFIX}

  - does not remove all its files cleanly upon deinstall (however, it may be acceptable, and desirable, for the port to leave user-modified files behind)

  - has runtime issues on systems where it is supposed to run fine.

- FORBIDDEN is used for ports that contain a security vulnerability or induce grave concern regarding the security of a FreeBSD system with a given port installed (for example, a reputably insecure program or a program that provides easily exploitable services). Mark ports as FORBIDDEN as soon as a particular piece of software has a vulnerability and there is no released upgrade. Ideally upgrade ports as soon as possible when a security vulnerability is discovered so as to reduce the number of vulnerable FreeBSD hosts (we like being known for being secure), however sometimes there is a noticeable time gap between disclosure of a vulnerability and an updated release of the vulnerable software. Do not mark a port FORBIDDEN for any reason other than security.

- IGNORE is reserved for ports that must not be built for some other reason. Use it for ports where the problem is believed to be structural. The build cluster will not, under any circumstances, build ports marked as IGNORE. For instance, use IGNORE when a port:

  - does not work on the installed version of FreeBSD

  - has a distfile which may not be automatically fetched due to licensing restrictions

  - does not work with some other currently installed port (for instance, the port depends on www/apache20 but www/apache22 is installed)

  ### Note

  If a port would conflict with a currently installed port (for example, if they install a file in the same place that performs a different function), use CONFLICTS instead. CONFLICTS will set IGNORE by itself.

- To mark a port as IGNOREd only on certain architectures, there are two other convenience variables that will automatically set IGNORE: ONLY_FOR_ARCHS and NOT_FOR_ARCHS . Examples:

```
ONLY_FOR_ARCHS= i386 amd64
```

```
NOT_FOR_ARCHS= ia64 sparc64
```

A custom IGNORE message can be set using ONLY_FOR_ARCHS_REASON and NOT_FOR_ARCHS_REASON . Per architecture entries are possible with ONLY_FOR_ARCHS_REASON_*ARCH* and NOT_FOR_ARCHS_REASON_ *ARCH*.

- If a port fetches i386 binaries and installs them, set IA32_BINARY_PORT. If this variable is set, /usr/lib32 must be present for IA32 versions of libraries and the kernel must support IA32 compatibility. If one of these two dependencies is not satisfied, IGNORE will be set automatically.

13.14.2. Implementation Notes

Do not quote the values of BROKEN, IGNORE, and related variables. Due to the way the information is shown to the user, the wording of messages for each variable differ:

```
BROKEN= fails to link with base -lcrypto
```

```
IGNORE= unsupported on recent versions
```

resulting in this output from make describe:

```
===>  foobar-0.1 is marked as broken: fails to link with base -lcrypto.
```

```
===>  foobar-0.1 is unsupported on recent versions.
```

13.15. Marking a Port for Removal with DEPRECATED or EXPIRATION_DATE

Do remember that BROKEN and FORBIDDEN are to be used as a temporary resort if a port is not working. Permanently broken ports will be removed from the tree entirely.

When it makes sense to do so, users can be warned about a pending port removal with DEPRECATED and EXPIRATION_DATE. The former is a string stating why the port is scheduled for removal; the latter is a string in ISO 8601 format (YYYY-MM-DD). Both will be shown to the user.

It is possible to set DEPRECATED without an EXPIRATION_DATE (for instance, recommending a newer version of the port), but the converse does not make any sense.

There is no set policy on how much notice to give. Current practice seems to be one month for security-related issues and two months for build issues. This also gives any interested committers a little time to fix the problems.

13.16. Avoid Use of the .error Construct

The correct way for a Makefile to signal that the port cannot be installed due to some external factor (for instance, the user has specified an illegal combination of build options) is to set a non-blank value to IGNORE. This value will be formatted and shown to the user by make install.

It is a common mistake to use .error for this purpose. The problem with this is that many automated tools that work with the ports tree will fail in this situation. The most common occurrence of this is seen when trying to build /usr/ports/INDEX (see Section 10.1, "Running make describe"). However, even more trivial commands such as make maintainer also fail in this scenario. This is not acceptable.

Example 13.1. How to Avoid Using .error

The first of the next two Makefile snippets will cause make index to fail, while the second one will not:

```
.error "option is not supported"
```

```
IGNORE=option is not supported
```

13.17. Usage of `sysctl`

The usage of `sysctl` is discouraged except in targets. This is because the evaluation of any `makevars`, such as used during `make index`, then has to run the command, further slowing down that process.

Only use sysctl(8) through `SYSCTL`, as it contains the fully qualified path and can be overridden, if one has such a special need.

13.18. Rerolling Distfiles

Sometimes the authors of software change the content of released distfiles without changing the file's name. Verify that the changes are official and have been performed by the author. It has happened in the past that the distfile was silently altered on the download servers with the intent to cause harm or compromise end user security.

Put the old distfile aside, download the new one, unpack them and compare the content with diff(1). If there is nothing suspicious, update `distinfo`.

> **Important**
>
> Be sure to summarize the differences in the PR and commit log, so that other people know that nothing bad has happened.

Contact the authors of the software and confirm the changes with them.

13.19. Use POSIX Standards

FreeBSD ports generally expect POSIX compliance. Some software and build systems make assumptions based on a particular operating system or environment that can cause problems when used in a port.

Do not use `/proc` if there are any other ways of getting the information. For example, `setprogname(argv[0])` in `main()` and then getprogname(3) to know the executable name.

Do not rely on behavior that is undocumented by POSIX.

Do not record timestamps in the critical path of the application if it also works without. Getting timestamps may be slow, depending on the accuracy of timestamps in the OS. If timestamps are really needed, determine how precise they have to be and use an API which is documented to just deliver the needed precision.

A number of simple syscalls (for example gettimeofday(2), getpid(2)) are much faster on Linux® than on any other operating system due to caching and the vsyscall performance optimizations. Do not rely on them being cheap in performance-critical applications. In general, try hard to avoid syscalls if possible.

Do not rely on Linux®-specific socket behavior. In particular, default socket buffer sizes are different (call setsockopt(2) with `SO_SNDBUF` and `SO_RCVBUF`, and while Linux®'s send(2) blocks when the socket buffer is full, FreeBSD's will fail and set `ENOBUFS` in errno.

If relying on non-standard behavior is required, encapsulate it properly into a generic API, do a check for the behavior in the configure stage, and stop if it is missing.

Check the man pages to see if the function used is a POSIX interface (in the "STANDARDS" section of the man page).

Do not assume that `/bin/sh` is bash. Ensure that a command line passed to system(3) will work with a POSIX compliant shell.

A list of common bashisms is available here.

Check that headers are included in the POSIX or man page recommended way. For example, `sys/types.h` is often forgotten, which is not as much of a problem for Linux® as it is for FreeBSD.

13.20. Miscellanea

Always double-check `pkg-descr` and `pkg-plist` . If reviewing a port and a better wording can be achieved, do so.

Do not copy more copies of the GNU General Public License into our system, please.

Please be careful to note any legal issues! Do not let us illegally distribute software!

Chapter 14. A Sample Makefile

Here is a sample `Makefile` that can be used to create a new port. Make sure to remove all the extra comments (ones between brackets).

The format shown is the recommended one for ordering variables, empty lines between sections, and so on. This format is designed so that the most important information is easy to locate. We recommend using portlint to check the `Makefile`.

```
[the header...just to make it easier for us to identify the ports.-]
# $FreeBSD$
[ ^^^^^^^^^ This will be automatically replaced with RCS ID string by SVN
when it is committed to our repository.  If upgrading a port, do not alter
this line back to "$FreeBSD$".  SVN deals with it automatically.-]

[section to describe the port itself and the master site - PORTNAME
 and PORTVERSION or the DISTVERSION* variables are always first,
 followed by CATEGORIES, and then MASTER_SITES, which can be followed
 by MASTER_SITE_SUBDIR.  PKGNAMEPREFIX and PKGNAMESUFFIX, if needed,
 will be after that.  Then comes DISTNAME, EXTRACT_SUFX and/or
 DISTFILES, and then EXTRACT_ONLY, as necessary.-]
PORTNAME= xdvi
DISTVERSION= 18.2
CATEGORIES= print
[do not forget the trailing slash ("/")!
 if not using MASTER_SITE_* macros]
MASTER_SITES= ${MASTER_SITE_XCONTRIB}
MASTER_SITE_SUBDIR= applications
PKGNAMEPREFIX= ja-
DISTNAME= xdvi-pl18
[set this if the source is not in the standard ".tar.gz" form]
EXTRACT_SUFX= .tar.Z

[section for distributed patches -- can be empty]
PATCH_SITES= ftp://ftp.sra.co.jp/pub/X11/japanese/
PATCHFILES= xdvi-18.patch1.gz xdvi-18.patch2.gz
[If the distributed patches were not made relative to ${WRKSRC},
 this may need to be tweaked]
PATCH_DIST_STRIP= -p1

[maintainer; *mandatory*!  This is the person who is volunteering to
 handle port updates, build breakages, and to whom a users can direct
 questions and bug reports.  To keep the quality of the Ports Collection
 as high as possible, we do not accept new ports that are assigned to
 "ports@FreeBSD.org".-]
MAINTAINER= asami@FreeBSD.org
COMMENT= DVI Previewer for the X Window System

[license -- should not be empty]
LICENSE= BSD2CLAUSE
LICENSE_FILE= ${WRKSRC}/LICENSE

[dependencies -- can be empty]
RUN_DEPENDS= gs:print/ghostscript

[If it requires GNU make, not /usr/bin/make, to build...-]
USES= gmake
[If it is an X application and requires "xmkmf -a" to be run...-]
USES= imake
[If the source is obtained from github, remove MASTER_SITE* and...-]
USE_GITHUB= yes
GH_ACCOUNT= example

[this section is for other standard bsd.port.mk variables that do not]
```

```
 belong to any of the above]
[If it asks questions during configure, build, install...-]
IS_INTERACTIVE= yes
[If it extracts to a directory other than ${DISTNAME}...-]
WRKSRC=  ${WRKDIR}/xdvi-new
[If it requires a "configure" script generated by GNU autoconf to be run]
GNU_CONFIGURE= yes
[et cetera.-]

[If it requires options, this section is for options]
OPTIONS_DEFINE= DOCS EXAMPLES FOO
OPTIONS_DEFAULT= FOO
[If options will change the files in plist]
OPTIONS_SUB=yes

FOO_DESC=  Enable foo support

FOO_CONFIGURE_ENABLE= foo

[non-standard variables to be used in the rules below]
MY_FAVORITE_RESPONSE= "yeah, right"

[then the special rules, in the order they are called]
pre-fetch:
 i go fetch something, yeah

post-patch:
 i need to do something after patch, great

pre-install:
 and then some more stuff before installing, wow

[and then the epilogue]

.include <bsd.port.mk>
```

Chapter 15. Order of Variables in Port Makefiles

The first sections of the `Makefile` must always come in the same order. This standard makes it so everyone can easily read any port without having to search for variables in a random order.

The first line of a `Makefile` is always a comment containing the Subversion version control ID, followed by an empty line. In new ports, it looks like this:

```
# $FreeBSD$
```

In existing ports, Subversion has expanded it to look like this:

```
# $FreeBSD: head/ports-mgmt/pkg/Makefile 437007 2017-03-26 21:25:47Z bapt $
```

> ### Note
>
> The sections and variables described here are mandatory in a ordinary port. In a slave port, many sections variables and can be skipped.

> ### Important
>
> Each following block must be separated from the previous block by a single blank line.
>
> In the following blocks, only set the variables that are required by the port. Define these variables in the order they are shown here.

15.1. PORTNAME Block

This block is the most important. It defines the port name, version, distribution file location, and category. The variables must be in this order:

- PORTNAME

- PORTVERSION

- DISTVERSIONPREFIX

- DISTVERSION

- DISTVERSIONSUFFIX

- PORTREVISION

- PORTEPOCH

- CATEGORIES

- MASTER_SITES

- `MASTER_SITE_SUBDIR` (deprecated)

- `PKGNAMEPREFIX`

- `PKGNAMESUFFIX`

- `DISTNAME`

- `EXTRACT_SUFX`

- `DISTFILES`

- `DIST_SUBDIR`

- `EXTRACT_ONLY`

Important

Only one of `PORTVERSION` and `DISTVERSION` can be used.

15.2. PATCHFILES **Block**

This block is optional. The variables are:

- `PATCH_SITES`

- `PATCHFILES`

- `PATCH_DIST_STRIP`

15.3. MAINTAINER **Block**

This block is mandatory. The variables are:

- `MAINTAINER`

- `COMMENT`

15.4. LICENSE **Block**

This block is optional, although it is highly recommended. The variables are:

- `LICENSE`

- `LICENSE_COMB`

- `LICENSE_GROUPS` or **LICENSE_GROUPS_NAME**

- `LICENSE_NAME` or **LICENSE_NAME_NAME**

- `LICENSE_TEXT` or **LICENSE_TEXT_NAME**

- `LICENSE_FILE` or **LICENSE_FILE_NAME**

- LICENSE_PERMS or **LICENSE_PERMS_*NAME***

- LICENSE_DISTFILES or **LICENSE_DISTFILES_*NAME***

If there are multiple licenses, sort the different LICENSE_*VAR_NAME* variables by license name.

15.5. Generic BROKEN/IGNORE/DEPRECATED Messages

This block is optional. The variables are:

- DEPRECATED

- EXPIRATION_DATE

- FORBIDDEN

- BROKEN

- BROKEN_*

- IGNORE

- IGNORE_*

- ONLY_FOR_ARCHS

- ONLY_FOR_ARCHS_REASON*

- NOT_FOR_ARCHS

- NOT_FOR_ARCHS_REASON*

Note

BROKEN* and IGNORE* can be any generic variables, for example, IGNORE_amd64, BRO-KEN_FreeBSD_10, BROKEN_SSL, etc.

If the port is marked BROKEN when some conditions are met, and such conditions can only be tested after including bsd.port.options.mk or bsd.port.pre.mk, then those variables should be set later, in Section 15.11, "The Rest of the Variables".

15.6. The Dependencies Block

This block is optional. The variables are:

- FETCH_DEPENDS

- EXTRACT_DEPENDS

- PATCH_DEPENDS

- BUILD_DEPENDS

- LIB_DEPENDS

- RUN_DEPENDS

• TEST_DEPENDS

15.7. Flavors

This block is optional.

Start this section with defining FLAVORS. Continue with the possible Flavors helpers. See Section 7.2, "Using FLAVORS" for more Information.

Constructs setting variables not available as helpers using `.if ${FLAVOR:U} == foo` should go in their respective sections below.

15.8. USES **and** USE_x

Start this section with defining USES, and then possible USE_x.

Keep related variables close together. For example, if using USE_GITHUB, always put the GH_* variables right after it.

15.9. Standard `bsd.port.mk` Variables

This section block is for variables that can be defined in `bsd.port.mk` that do not belong in any of the previous section blocks.

Order is not important, however try to keep similar variables together. For example uid and gid variables USERS and GROUPS. Configuration variables CONFIGURE_* and *_CONFIGURE. List of files, and directories PORTDOCS and PORTEXAMPLES.

15.10. Options and Helpers

If the port uses the options framework, define OPTIONS_DEFINE and OPTIONS_DEFAULT first, then the other OPTIONS_* variables first, then the *_DESC descriptions, then the options helpers. Try and sort all of those alphabetically.

Example 15.1. Options Variables Order Example

The FOO and BAR options do not have a standard description, so one need to be written. The other options already have one in Mk/bsd.options.desc.mk so writing one is not needed. The DOCS and EXAMPLES use target helpers to install their files, they are shown here for completeness, though they belong in Section 15.12, "The Targets", so other variables and targets could be inserted before them.

```
OPTIONS_DEFINE= DOCS EXAMPLES FOO BAR
OPTIONS_DEFAULT= FOO
OPTIONS_RADIO= SSL
OPTIONS_RADIO_SSL=     OPENSSL GNUTLS
OPTIONS_SUB= yes

BAR_DESC=  Enable bar support
FOO_DESC=  Enable foo support

BAR_CONFIGURE_WITH= bar=${LOCALBASE}
FOO_CONFIGURE_ENABLE= foo
GNUTLS_CONFIGURE_ON= --with-ssl=gnutls
OPENSSL_CONFIGURE_ON= --with-ssl=openssl
```

```
post-install-DOCS-on:
        ${MKDIR} ${STAGEDIR}${DOCSDIR}
        cd ${WRKSRC}/doc && ${COPYTREE_SHARE} . ${STAGEDIR}${DOCSDIR}

post-install-EXAMPLES-on:
        ${MKDIR} ${STAGEDIR}${EXAMPLESDIR}
        cd ${WRKSRC}/ex && ${COPYTREE_SHARE} . ${STAGEDIR}${DOCSDIR}
```

15.11. The Rest of the Variables

And then, the rest of the variables that are not mentioned in the previous blocks.

15.12. The Targets

After all the variables are defined, the optional make(1) targets can be defined. Keep pre-* before post-* and in the same order as the different stages run:

- fetch

- extract

- patch

- configure

- build

- install

- test

Chapter 16. Keeping Up

The FreeBSD Ports Collection is constantly changing. Here is some information on how to keep up.

16.1. FreshPorts

One of the easiest ways to learn about updates that have already been committed is by subscribing to FreshPorts. Multiple ports can be monitored. Maintainers are strongly encouraged to subscribe, because they will receive notification of not only their own changes, but also any changes that any other FreeBSD committer has made. (These are often necessary to keep up with changes in the underlying ports framework—although it would be most polite to receive an advance heads-up from those committing such changes, sometimes this is overlooked or impractical. Also, in some cases, the changes are very minor in nature. We expect everyone to use their best judgement in these cases.)

To use FreshPorts, an account is required. Those with registered email addresses at @FreeBSD.org will see the opt-in link on the right-hand side of the web pages. Those who already have a FreshPorts account but are not using a @FreeBSD.org email address can change the email to @FreeBSD.org, subscribe, then change it back again.

FreshPorts also has a sanity test feature which automatically tests each commit to the FreeBSD ports tree. If subscribed to this service, a committer will receive notifications of any errors which FreshPorts detects during sanity testing of their commits.

16.2. The Web Interface to the Source Repository

It is possible to browse the files in the source repository by using a web interface. Changes that affect the entire port system are now documented in the CHANGES file. Changes that affect individual ports are now documented in the UPDATING file. However, the definitive answer to any question is undoubtedly to read the source code of bsd.port.mk, and associated files.

16.3. The FreeBSD Ports Mailing List

As a ports maintainer, consider subscribing to FreeBSD ports mailing list. Important changes to the way ports work will be announced there, and then committed to CHANGES.

If the volume of messages on this mailing list is too high, consider following FreeBSD ports announce mailing list which contains only announcements.

16.4. The FreeBSD Port Building Cluster

One of the least-publicized strengths of FreeBSD is that an entire cluster of machines is dedicated to continually building the Ports Collection, for each of the major OS releases and for each Tier-1 architecture.

Individual ports are built unless they are specifically marked with IGNORE. Ports that are marked with BROKEN will still be attempted, to see if the underlying problem has been resolved. (This is done by passing TRYBROKEN to the port's Makefile.)

16.5. Portscout: the FreeBSD Ports Distfile Scanner

The build cluster is dedicated to building the latest release of each port with distfiles that have already been fetched. However, as the Internet continually changes, distfiles can quickly go missing. Portscout, the FreeBSD Ports distfile scanner, attempts to query every download site for every port to find out if each distfile is still available. Portscout can generate HTML reports and send emails about newly available ports to those who request them. Unless not otherwise subscribed, maintainers are asked to check periodically for changes, either by hand or using the RSS feed.

Portscout's first page gives the email address of the port maintainer, the number of ports the maintainer is responsible for, the number of those ports with new distfiles, and the percentage of those ports that are out-of-date. The search function allows for searching by email address for a specific maintainer, and for selecting whether only out-of-date ports are shown.

Upon clicking on a maintainer's email address, a list of all of their ports is displayed, along with port category, current version number, whether or not there is a new version, when the port was last updated, and finally when it was last checked. A search function on this page allows the user to search for a specific port.

Clicking on a port name in the list displays the FreshPorts port information.

16.6. The FreeBSD Ports Monitoring System

Another handy resource is the FreeBSD Ports Monitoring System (also known as portsmon). This system comprises a database that processes information from several sources and allows it to be browsed via a web interface. Currently, the ports Problem Reports (PRs), the error logs from the build cluster, and individual files from the ports collection are used. In the future, this will be expanded to include the distfile survey, as well as other sources.

To get started, use the Overview of One Port search page to find all the information about a port.

This is the only resource available that maps PR entries to portnames. PR submitters do not always include the portname in their Synopsis, although we would prefer that they did. So, portsmon is a good place to find out whether an existing port has any PRs filed against it, any build errors, or if a new port the porter is considering creating has already been submitted.

Chapter 17. Using USES Macros

17.1. An Introduction to USES

USES macros make it easy to declare requirements and settings for a port. They can add dependencies, change building behavior, add metadata to packages, and so on, all by selecting simple, preset values..

Each section in this chapter describes a possible value for USES, along with its possible arguments. Arguments are appeneded to the value after a colon (:). Multiple arguments are separated by commas (,).

Example 17.1. Using Multiple Values

```
USES= bison perl
```

Example 17.2. Adding an Argument

```
USES= gmake:lite
```

Example 17.3. Adding Multiple Arguments

```
USES= drupal:7,theme
```

Example 17.4. Mixing it All Together

```
USES= pgsql:9.3+ cpe python:2.7,build
```

17.2. 7z

Possible arguments: (none), p7zip, partial

Extract using 7z(1) instead of bsdtar(1) and sets EXTRACT_SUFX=.7z. The p7zip option forces a dependency on the 7z from archivers/p7zip if the one from the base system is not able to extract the files. EXTRACT_SUFX is not changed if the partial option is used, this can be used if the main distribution file does not have a .7z extension.

17.3. ada

Possible arguments: (none), 5, 6

Depends on an Ada-capable compiler, and sets CC accordingly. Defaults to use gcc 5 from ports. Use the :*X* version option to force building with a different version.

17.4. `autoreconf`

Possible arguments: (none), `build`

Runs `autoreconf`. It encapsulates the `aclocal`, `autoconf`, `autoheader`, `automake`, `autopoint`, and `libtoolize` commands. Each command applies to `${AUTORECONF_WRKSRC}/configure.ac` or its old name, `${AUTORECONF_WRKSRC}/configure.in`. If `configure.ac` defines subdirectories with their own `configure.ac` using `AC_CONFIG_SUBDIRS`, `autoreconf` will recursively update those as well. The `:build` argument only adds build time dependencies on those tools but does not run `autoreconf`. A port can set `AUTORECONF_WRKSRC` if `WRKSRC` does not contain the path to `configure.ac`.

17.5. `blaslapack`

Possible arguments: (none), `atlas`, `netlib` (default), `gotoblas`, `openblas`

Adds dependencies on Blas / Lapack libraries.

17.6. `bdb`

Possible arguments: (none), `48`, `5` (default), `6`

Add dependency on the Berkeley DB library. Default to databases/db5. It can also depend on databases/db48 when using the `:48` argument or databases/db6 with `:6`. It is possible to declare a range of acceptable values, `:48+` finds the highest installed version, and falls back to 4.8 if nothing else is installed. `INVALID_BDB_VER` can be used to specify versions which do not work with this port. The framework exposes the following variables to the port:

`BDB_LIB_NAME`
> The name of the Berkeley DB library. For example, when using databases/db5, it contains `db-5.3`.

`BDB_LIB_CXX_NAME`
> The name of the Berkeley DB C++ library. For example, when using databases/db5, it contains `db_cxx-5.3` .

`BDB_INCLUDE_DIR`
> The location of the Berkeley DB include directory. For example, when using databases/db5, it will contain `${LOCALBASE}/include/db5`.

`BDB_LIB_DIR`
> The location of the Berkeley DB library directory. For example, when using databases/db5, it contains `${LOCALBASE}/lib`.

`BDB_VER`
> The detected Berkeley DB version. For example, if using `USES=bdb:48+` and Berkeley DB 5 is installed, it contains `5`.

 Important

databases/db48 is deprecated and unsupported. It must not be used by any port.

17.7. bison

Possible arguments: (none), build, run, both

Uses devel/bison By default, with no arguments or with the build argument, it implies bison is a build-time dependency, run implies a run-time dependency, and both implies both run-time and build-time dependencies.

17.8. charsetfix

Possible arguments: (none)

Prevents the port from installing charset.alias . This must be installed only by converters/libiconv. CHARSET-FIX_MAKEFILEIN can be set to a path relative to WRKSRC if charset.alias is not installed by ${WRKSRC}/Makefile.in.

17.9. cmake

Possible arguments: (none), outsource, run

Uses CMake for configuring and building. With the outsource argument, an out-of-source build will be performed. With the run argument, a run-time dependency is registered. For more information see Section 6.5.4, "Using cmake".

17.10. compiler

Possible arguments: (none), c++14-lang , c++11-lang , gcc-c++11-lib , c++11-lib , c++0x, c11, openmp, nested-fct, features

Determines which compiler to use based on any given wishes. Use c++14-lang if the port needs a C++14-capable compiler, gcc-c++11-lib if the port needs the g++ compiler with a C++11 library, or c++11-lib if the port needs a C++11-ready standard library. If the port needs a compiler understanding C++11, C++0X, C11, OpenMP, or nested functions, the corresponding parameters can be used. Use features to request a list of features supported by the default compiler. After including bsd.port.pre.mk the port can inspect the results using these variables:

- COMPILER_TYPE: the default compiler on the system, either gcc or clang

- ALT_COMPILER_TYPE: the alternative compiler on the system, either gcc or clang. Only set if two compilers are present in the base system.

- COMPILER_VERSION: the first two digits of the version of the default compiler.

- ALT_COMPILER_VERSION: the first two digits of the version of the alternative compiler, if present.

- CHOSEN_COMPILER_TYPE: the chosen compiler, either gcc or clang

- COMPILER_FEATURES: the features supported by the default compiler. It currently lists the C++ library.

17.11. cpe

Possible arguments: (none)

Include Common Platform Enumeration (CPE) information in package manifest as a CPE 2.3 formatted string. See the CPE specification for details. To add CPE information to a port, follow these steps:

1. Search for the official CPE para for the software product either by using the NVD's CPE search engine or in the official CPE dictionary (warning, very large XML file). *Do not ever make up CPE data.*

2. Add cpe to USES and compare the result of make -V CPE_STR to the CPE dictionary para. Continue one step at a time until make -V CPE_STR is correct.

3. If the product name (second field, defaults to PORTNAME) is incorrect, define CPE_PRODUCT.

4. If the vendor name (first field, defaults to CPE_PRODUCT) is incorrect, define CPE_VENDOR.

5. If the version field (third field, defaults to PORTVERSION) is incorrect, define CPE_VERSION .

6. If the update field (fourth field, defaults to empty) is incorrect, define CPE_UPDATE.

7. If it is still not correct, check Mk/Uses/cpe.mk for additional details, or contact the Ports Security Team <ports-secteam@FreeBSD.org>.

8. Derive as much as possible of the CPE name from existing variables such as PORTNAME and PORTVERSION . Use variable modifiers to extract the relevant portions from these variables rather than hardcoding the name.

9. *Always* run make -V CPE_STR and check the output before committing anything that changes PORTNAME or PORTVERSION or any other variable which is used to derive CPE_STR .

17.12. cran

Possible arguments: (none), auto-plist, compiles

Uses the Comprehensive R Archive Network. Specify auto-plist to automatically generate pkg-plist . Specify compiles if the port has code that need to be compiled.

17.13. desktop-file-utils

Possible arguments: (none)

Uses update-desktop-database from devel/desktop-file-utils. An extra post-install step will be run without interfering with any post-install steps already in the port Makefile. A line with @desktop-file-utils will be added to the plist.

17.14. desthack

Possible arguments: (none)

Changes the behavior of GNU configure to properly support DESTDIR in case the original software does not.

17.15. display

Possible arguments: (none), *ARGS*

Set up a virtual display environment. If the environment variable DISPLAY is not set, then Xvfb is added as a build dependency, and CONFIGURE_ENV is extended with the port number of the currently running instance of Xvfb. The *ARGS* parameter defaults to install and controls the phase around which to start and stop the virtual display.

17.16. dos2unix

Possible arguments: (none)

The port has files with line endings in DOS format which need to be converted. Several variables can be set to control which files will be converted. The default is to convert *all* files, including binaries. See Section 4.4.3, "Simple Automatic Replacements" for examples.

- `DOS2UNIX_REGEX` : match file names based on a regular expression.

- `DOS2UNIX_FILES` : match literal file names.

- `DOS2UNIX_GLOB` : match file names based on a glob pattern.

- `DOS2UNIX_WRKSRC` : the directory from which to start the conversions. Defaults to `${WRKSRC}` .

17.17. drupal

Possible arguments: `7`, `module`, `theme`

Automate installation of a port that is a Drupal theme or module. Use with the version of Drupal that the port is expecting. For example, `USES=drupal:7,module` says that this port creates a Drupal 6 module. A Drupal 7 theme can be specified with `USES=drupal:7,theme`.

17.18. fakeroot

Possible arguments: (none)

Changes some default behavior of build systems to allow installing as a user. See http://fakeroot.alioth.debian.org/ for more information on `fakeroot`.

17.19. fam

Possible arguments: (none), `fam`, `gamin`

Uses a File Alteration Monitor as a library dependency, either devel/fam or devel/gamin. End users can set WITH_FAM_SYSTEM to specify their preference.

17.20. firebird

Possible arguments: (none), `25`

Add a dependency to the client library of the Firebird database.

17.21. fonts

Possible arguments: (none), `fc`, `fcfontsdir` (default), `fontsdir`, `none`

Adds a runtime dependency on tools needed to register fonts. Depending on the argument, add a `@fc ${FONTSDIR}` line, `@fcfontsdir ${FONTSDIR}` line, `@fontsdir ${FONTSDIR}` line, or no line if the argument is none, to the plist. FONTSDIR defaults to `${PREFIX}/share/fonts/${FONTNAME}` and FONTNAME to `${PORTNAME}`. Add FONTSDIR to PLIST_SUB and SUB_LIST

17.22. fortran

Possible arguments: `gcc` (default)

Uses the GNU Fortran compiler.

17.23. fuse

Possible arguments: 2 (default), 3

The port will depend on the FUSE library and handle the dependency on the kernel module depending on the version of FreeBSD.

17.24. gecko

Possible arguments: `libxul` (default), `firefox`, `seamonkey`, `thunderbird`, `build`, *XY*, *XY+*

Add a dependency on different gecko based applications. If `libxul` is used, it is the only argument allowed. When the argument is not `libxul`, the `firefox`, `seamonkey`, or `thunderbird` arguments can be used, along with optional `build` and *XY/XY+* version arguments.

17.25. gem

Possible arguments: (none), `noautoplist`

Handle building with RubyGems. If `noautoplist` is used, the packing list is not generated automatically.

17.26. gettext

Possible arguments: (none)

Deprecated. Will include both gettext-runtime and gettext-tools.

17.27. gettext-runtime

Possible arguments: (none), `lib` (default), `build`, `run`

Uses devel/gettext-runtime. By default, with no arguments or with the `lib` argument, implies a library dependency on `libintl.so`. `build` and `run` implies, respectively a build-time and a run-time dependency on `gettext`.

17.28. gettext-tools

Possible arguments: (none), `build` (default), `run`

Uses devel/gettext-tools. By default, with no argument, or with the `build` argument, a build time dependency on `msgfmt` is registered. With the `run` argument, a run-time dependency is registered.

17.29. ghostscript

Possible arguments: *X*, `build`, `run`, `nox11`

A specific version *X* can be used. Possible versions are 7, 8, 9, and `agpl` (default). `nox11` indicates that the `-nox11` version of the port is required. `build` and `run` add build- and run-time dependencies on Ghostscript. The default is both build- and run-time dependencies.

17.30. gmake

Possible arguments: (none)

Uses devel/gmake as a build-time dependency and sets up the environment to use gmake as the default make for the build.

17.31. gnome

Possible arguments: (none)

Provides an easy way to depend on GNOME components. The components should be listed in USE_GNOME. The available components are:

- atk

- atkmm

- cairo

- cairomm

- dconf

- esound

- evolutiondataserver3

- gconf2

- gconfmm26

- gdkpixbuf

- gdkpixbuf2

- glib12

- glib20

- glibmm

- gnomecontrolcenter3

- gnomedesktop3

- gnomedocutils

- gnomemenus3

- gnomemimedata

- gnomeprefix

- gnomesharp20

- gnomevfs2

- gsound

- gtk-update-icon-cache

- gtk12

- gtk20

- gtk30

- gtkhtml3

- gtkhtml4

- gtkmm20

- gtkmm24

- gtkmm30

- gtksharp20

- gtksourceview

- gtksourceview2

- gtksourceview3

- gtksourceviewmm3

- gvfs

- intlhack

- intltool

- introspection

- libartlgpl2

- libbonobo

- libbonoboui

- libgda5

- libgda5-ui

- libgdamm5

- libglade2

- libgnome

- libgnomecanvas

- libgnomekbd

- libgnomeprint

- libgnomeprintui

- libgnomeui

- libgsf

- libgtkhtml

- libgtksourceviewmm

- libidl

- librsvg2

- libsigc++12

- libsigc++20

- libwnck

- libwnck3

- libxml++26

- libxml2

- libxslt

- metacity

- nautilus3

- orbit2

- pango

- pangomm

- pangox-compat

- py3gobject3

- pygnome2

- pygobject

- pygobject3

- pygtk2

- pygtksourceview

- referencehack

- vte

- vte3

The default dependency is build- and run-time, it can be changed with :build or :run. For example:

```
USES=   gnome
USE_GNOME= gnomemenus3:build intlhack
```

See Section 6.10, "Using GNOME" for more information.

17.32. go

Important

Ports should not be created for Go libs, see Section 6.30, "Go Libraries" for more information.

Possible arguments: (none)

Sets default values and targets used to build Go software. A build-time dependency on lang/go is added. The build process is controlled by several variables:

GO_PKGNAME
> The name of the Go package. This is the directory that will be created in GOPATH/src . The default value is ${PORTNAME}.

GO_TARGET
> The name of the packages to build. The default value is ${GO_PKGNAME}.

CGO_CFLAGS
> Additional CFLAGS values to be passed to the C compiler by go.

CGO_LDFLAGS
> Additional LDFLAGS values to be passed to the C compiler by go.

17.33. gperf

Possible arguments: (none)

Add a buildtime dependency on devel/gperf if gperf is not present in the base system.

17.34. grantlee

Possible arguments: 4, 5, selfbuild

Handle dependency on Grantlee. Specify 4 to depend on the Qt4 based version, devel/grantlee. Specify 5 to depend on the Qt5 based version, devel/grantlee5. selfbuild is used internally by devel/grantlee and devel/grantlee5 to get their versions numbers.

17.35. groff

Possible arguments: build, run, both

Registers a dependency on textproc/groff if not present in the base system.

17.36. gssapi

Possible arguments: (none), base (default), heimdal, mit, flags, bootstrap

Handle dependencies needed by consumers of the GSS-API. Only libraries that provide the Kerberos mechanism are available. By default, or set to base, the GSS-API library from the base system is used. Can also be set to heimdal to use security/heimdal, or mit to use security/krb5.

When the local Kerberos installation is not in LOCALBASE, set HEIMDAL_HOME (for heimdal) or KRB5_HOME (for krb5) to the location of the Kerberos installation.

These variables are exported for the ports to use:

- GSSAPIBASEDIR

- GSSAPICPPFLAGS

- GSSAPIINCDIR

- GSSAPILDFLAGS

- GSSAPILIBDIR

- GSSAPILIBS

- GSSAPI_CONFIGURE_ARGS

The flags option can be given alongside base, heimdal, or mit to automatically add GSSAPICPPFLAGS , GSSAPILD-FLAGS, and GSSAPILIBS to CFLAGS , LDFLAGS, and LDADD, respectively. For example, use base,flags .

The bootstrap option is a special prefix only for use by security/krb5 and security/heimdal. For example, use bootstrap,mit.

Example 17.5. Typical Use

```
OPTIONS_SINGLE= GSSAPI
OPTIONS_SINGLE_GSSAPI= GSSAPI_BASE GSSAPI_HEIMDAL GSSAPI_MIT GSSAPI_NONE

GSSAPI_BASE_USES= gssapi
GSSAPI_BASE_CONFIGURE_ON= --with-gssapi=${GSSAPIBASEDIR} ${GSSAPI_CONFIGURE_ARGS}
GSSAPI_HEIMDAL_USES= gssapi:heimdal
GSSAPI_HEIMDAL_CONFIGURE_ON= --with-gssapi=${GSSAPIBASEDIR} ↵
${GSSAPI_CONFIGURE_ARGS}
GSSAPI_MIT_USES= gssapi:mit
GSSAPI_MIT_CONFIGURE_ON= --with-gssapi=${GSSAPIBASEDIR} ${GSSAPI_CONFIGURE_ARGS}
GSSAPI_NONE_CONFIGURE_ON= --without-gssapi
```

17.37. horde

Possible arguments: (none)

Add buildtime and runtime dependencies on devel/pear-channel-horde. Other Horde dependencies can be added with USE_HORDE_BUILD and USE_HORDE_RUN . See Section 6.16.4.1, "Horde Modules" for more information.

17.38. iconv

Possible arguments: (none), lib, build, patch, translit , wchar_t

Uses `iconv` functions, either from the port converters/libiconv as a build-time and run-time dependency, or from the base system on 10-CURRENT after a native `iconv` was committed in 254273. By default, with no arguments or with the `lib` argument, implies `iconv` with build-time and run-time dependencies. `build` implies a build-time dependency, and `patch` implies a patch-time dependency. If the port uses the `WCHAR_T` or `//TRANSLIT` iconv extensions, add the relevant arguments so that the correct iconv is used. For more information see Section 6.23, "Using iconv".

17.39. imake

Possible arguments: (none), env, notall, noman

Add devel/imake as a build-time dependency and run `xmkmf -a` during the configure stage. If the env argument is given, the `configure` target is not set. If the `-a` flag is a problem for the port, add the `notall` argument. If `xmkmf` does not generate a `install.man` target, add the `noman` argument.

17.40. kde

Possible arguments: 4

Add dependency on KDE components. See Section 6.13, "Using KDE" for more information.

17.41. kmod

Possible arguments: (none), debug

Fills in the boilerplate for kernel module ports, currently:

- Add `kld` to `CATEGORIES`.

- Set `SSP_UNSAFE`.

- Set `IGNORE` if the kernel sources are not found in `SRC_BASE`.

- Define `KMODDIR` to `/boot/modules` by default, add it to `PLIST_SUB` and `MAKE_ENV`, and create it upon installation. If `KMODDIR` is set to `/boot/kernel`, it will be rewritten to `/boot/modules`. This prevents breaking packages when upgrading the kernel due to `/boot/kernel` being renamed to `/boot/kernel.old` in the process.

- Handle cross-referencing kernel modules upon installation and deinstallation, using `@kld`.

- If the debug argument is given, the port can install a debug version of the module into `KERN_DEBUGDIR/KMODDIR`. By default, `KERN_DEBUGDIR` is copied from `DEBUGDIR` and set to `/usr/lib/debug`. The framework will take care of creating and removing any required directories.

17.42. lha

Possible arguments: (none)

Set `EXTRACT_SUFX` to `.lzh`

17.43. libarchive

Possible arguments: (none)

Registers a dependency on archivers/libarchive. Any ports depending on libarchive must include USES=libarchive .

17.44. libedit

Possible arguments: (none)

Registers a dependency on devel/libedit. Any ports depending on libedit must include USES=libedit.

17.45. libtool

Possible arguments: (none), keepla , build

Patches libtool scripts. This must be added to all ports that use libtool . The keepla argument can be used to keep .la files. Some ports do not ship with their own copy of libtool and need a build time dependency on devel/libtool, use the :build argument to add such dependency.

17.46. linux

Possible arguments: c6, c7

Ports Linux compatibility framework. Specify c6 to depend on CentOS 6 packags. Specify c7 to depend on CentOS 7 packages. The available packages are:

- allegro

- alsa-plugins-oss

- alsa-plugins-pulseaudio

- alsalib

- atk

- avahi-libs

- base

- cairo

- cups-libs

- curl

- cyrus-sasl2

- dbusglib

- dbuslibs

- devtools

- dri

- expat

- flac

- fontconfig

- gdkpixbuf2

- gnutls

- graphite2

- gtk2

- harfbuzz

- jasper

- jbigkit

- jpeg

- libasyncns

- libaudiofile

- libelf

- libgcrypt

- libgfortran

- libgpg-error

- libmng

- libogg

- libpciaccess

- libsndfile

- libsoup

- libssh2

- libtasn1

- libthai

- libtheora

- libv4l

- libvorbis

- libxml2

- mikmod

- naslibs

- ncurses-base

- nspr

- nss

- openal

- openal-soft

- openldap

- openmotif

- openssl

- pango

- pixman

- png

- pulseaudio-libs

- qt

- qt-x11

- qtwebkit

- scimlibs

- sdl12

- sdlimage

- sdlmixer

- sqlite3

- tcl85

- tcp_wrappers-libs

- tiff

- tk85

- ucl

- xorglibs

17.47. localbase

Possible arguments: (none), ldflags

Ensures that libraries from dependencies in LOCALBASE are used instead of the ones from the base system. Specify ldflags to add -L${LOCALBASE}/lib to LDFLAGS instead of LIBS. Ports that depend on libraries that are also present in the base system should use this. It is also used internally by a few other USES.

17.48. lua

Possible arguments: (none), *XY+*, *XY*, build, run

Adds a dependency on Lua. By default this is a library dependency, unless overridden by the build or run option. The default version is 5.2, unless set by the *XY* parameter (for example, 51 or 52+).

17.49. lxqt

Possible arguments: (none)

Handle dependencies for the LXQt Desktop Environment. Use USE_LXQT to select the components needed for the port. See Section 6.14, "Using LXQt" for more information.

17.50. makeinfo

Possible arguments: (none)

Add a build-time dependency on makeinfo if it is not present in the base system.

17.51. makeself

Possible arguments: (none)

Indicates that the distribution files are makeself archives and sets the appropriate dependencies.

17.52. mate

Possible arguments: (none)

Provides an easy way to depend on MATE components. The components should be listed in USE_MATE . The available components are:

- autogen
- caja
- common
- controlcenter
- desktop
- dialogs
- docutils
- icontheme
- intlhack
- intltool
- libmatekbd
- libmateweather

- marco

- menus

- notificationdaemon

- panel

- pluma

- polkit

- session

- settingsdaemon

The default dependency is build- and run-time, it can be changed with :build or :run. For example:

```
USES= mate
USE_MATE= menus:build intlhack
```

17.53. meson

Possible arguments: (none)

Provide support for Meson based projects.

17.54. metaport

Possible arguments: (none)

Sets the following variables to make it easier to create a metaport: MASTER_SITES , DISTFILES, EXTRACT_ONLY, NO_BUILD , NO_INSTALL, NO_MTREE , NO_ARCH .

17.55. mysql

Possible arguments: (none), *version*, client (default), server, embedded

Provide support for MySQL. If no version is given, try to find the current installed version. Fall back to the default version, MySQL-5.6. The possible versions are 55, 55m, 55p, 56, 56p, 56w, 57, 57p, 80, 100m, 101m, and 102m. The m and p suffixes are for the MariaDB and Percona variants of MySQL. server and embedded add a build- and run-time dependency on the MySQL server. When using server or embedded, add client to also add a dependency on libmysqlclient.so. A port can set IGNORE_WITH_MYSQL if some versions are not supported.

The framework sets MYSQL_VER to the detected MySQL version.

17.56. mono

Possible arguments: (none), nuget

Adds a dependency on the Mono (currently only C#) framework by setting the appropriate dependencies.

Specify nuget when the port uses nuget packages. NUGET_DEPENDS needs to be set with the names and versions of the nuget packages in the format *name=version*. An optional package origin can be added using *name=version:origin*.

The helper target, buildnuget, will output the content of the NUGET_DEPENDS based on the provided packages.config.

17.57. motif

Possible arguments: (none)

Uses x11-toolkits/open-motif as a library dependency. End users can set WANT_LESSTIF for the dependency to be on x11-toolkits/lesstif instead of x11-toolkits/open-motif.

17.58. ncurses

Possible arguments: (none), base, port

Uses ncurses, and causes some useful variables to be set.

17.59. ninja

Possible arguments: (none)

Uses ninja to build the port.

17.60. objc

Possible arguments: (none)

Add objective C dependencies (compiler, runtime library) if the base system does not support it.

17.61. openal

Possible arguments: al, soft (default), si, alut

Uses OpenAL. The backend can be specified, with the software implementation as the default. The user can specify a preferred backend with WANT_OPENAL. Valid values for this knob are soft (default) and si.

17.62. pathfix

Possible arguments: (none)

Look for Makefile.in and configure in PATHFIX_WRKSRC (defaults to WRKSRC) and fix common paths to make sure they respect the FreeBSD hierarchy. For example, it fixes the installation directory of pkgconfig's .pc files to ${PREFIX}/libdata/pkgconfig. If the port uses USES=autoreconf, Makefile.am will be added to PATHFIX_MAKEFILEIN automatically.

If the port USES=cmake it will look for CMakeLists.txt in PATHFIX_WRKSRC. If needed, that default filename can be changed with PATHFIX_CMAKELISTSTXT.

17.63. pear

Possible arguments: (none)

Adds a dependency on devel/pear. It will setup default behavior for software using the PHP Extension and Application Repository. See Section 6.16.4, "PEAR Modules" for more information.

17.64. perl5

Possible arguments: (none)

Depends on Perl. The configuration is done using USE_PERL5.

USE_PERL5 can contain the phases in which to use Perl, can be extract, patch, build, run, or test.

USE_PERL5 can also contain configure, modbuild, or modbuildtiny when Makefile.PL, Build.PL, or Module::Build::Tiny's flavor of Build.PL is required.

USE_PERL5 defaults to build run. When using configure, modbuild, or modbuildtiny, build and run are implied.

See Section 6.8, "Using Perl" for more information.

17.65. pgsql

Possible arguments: (none), *X.Y*, *X.Y+*, *X.Y-*

Provide support for PostgreSQL. Maintainer can set version required. Minimum and maximum versions can be specified; for example, 9.0-, 8.4+.

Add PostgreSQL component dependency, using WANT_PGSQL=component[:target]. for example, WANT_PGSQL=server:configure pltcl plperl For the full list use make -V _USE_PGSQL_DEP .

17.66. php

Possible arguments: (none), phpize, ext, zend, build, cli, cgi, mod, web, embed, pecl

Provide support for PHP. Add a runtime dependency on the default PHP version, lang/php56.

phpize
    Use to build a PHP extension.

ext
    Use to build, install and register a PHP extension.

zend
    Use to build, install and register a Zend extension.

build
    Set PHP also as a build-time dependency.

cli
    Needs the CLI version of PHP.

cgi
    Needs the CGI version of PHP.

mod
    Needs the Apache module for PHP.

web
> Needs the Apache module or the CGI version of PHP.

embed
> Needs the embedded library version of PHP.

pecl
> Provide defaults for fetching PHP extensions from the PECL repository.

Variables are used to specify which PHP modules are required, as well as which version of PHP are supported.

USE_PHP
> The list of required PHP extensions at run-time. Add :build to the extension name to add a build-time dependency. Example: pcre xml:build gettext

DEFAULT_PHP_VER
> Selects which major version of PHP will be installed as a dependency when no PHP is installed yet. Default is 56. Possible values: 55, 56, and 70.

IGNORE_WITH_PHP
> The port does not work with PHP of the given version. Possible values: 55, 56, and 7.

When building a PHP or Zend extension with :ext or :zend, these variables can be set:

PHP_MODNAME
> The name of the PHP or Zend extension. Default value is ${PORTNAME}.

PHP_HEADER_DIRS
> A list of subdirectories from which to install header files. The framework will always install the header files that are present in the same directory as the extension.

PHP_MOD_PRIO
> The priority at which to load the extension. It is a number between 00 and 99.
>
> For extensions that do not depend on any extension, the priority is automatically set to 20, for extensions that depend on another extension, the priority is automatically set to 30. Some extensions may need to be loaded before every other extension, for example www/php56-opcache. Some may need to be loaded after an extension with a priority of 30. In that case, add PHP_MOD_PRIO=XX in the port's Makefile. For example:

```
USES=   php:ext
USE_PHP= wddx
PHP_MOD_PRIO= 40
```

17.67. pkgconfig

Possible arguments: (none), build (default), run, both

Uses devel/pkgconf. With no arguments or with the build argument, it implies pkg-config as a build-time dependency. run implies a run-time dependency and both implies both run-time and build-time dependencies.

17.68. pure

Possible arguments: (none), ffi

Uses lang/pure. Largely used for building related pure ports. With the ffi argument, it implies devel/pure-ffi as a run-time dependency.

17.69. pyqt

Possible arguments: (none), 4, 5

Uses PyQt. If the port is part of PyQt itself, set PYQT_DIST . Use USE_PYQT to select the components the port needs. The available components are:

- core

- dbus

- dbussupport

- demo

- designer

- designerplugin

- doc

- gui

- multimedia

- network

- opengl

- qscintilla2

- sip

- sql

- svg

- test

- webkit

- xml

- xmlpatterns

These components are only available with PyQT4:

- assistant

- declarative

- help

- phonon

- script

- scripttools

These components are only available with PyQT5:

- multimediawidgets

- printsupport

- qml

- serialport

- webkitwidgets

- widgets

The default dependency for each component is build- and run-time, to select only build or run, add _build or _run to the component name. For example:

```
USES= pyqt
USE_PYQT= core doc_build designer_run
```

17.70. python

Possible arguments: (none), *X.Y*, *X.Y+*, *-X.Y*, *X.Y-Z.A*, patch, build, run, test

Uses Python. A supported version or version range can be specified. If Python is only needed at build time, run time or for the tests, it can be set as a build, run or test dependency with build, run, or test. If Python is also needed during the patch phase, use patch. See Section 6.17, "Using Python" for more information.

PYTHON_NO_DEPENDS=yes can be used when the variables exported by the framework are needed but a dependency on Python is not. It can happen when using with USES=shebangfix, and the goal is only to fix the shebangs but not add a dependency on Python.

17.71. qmail

Possible arguments: (none), build, run, both, vars

Uses mail/qmail. With the build argument, it implies qmail as a build-time dependency. run implies a run-time dependency. Using no argument or the both argument implies both run-time and build-time dependencies. vars will only set QMAIL variables for the port to use.

17.72. qmake

Possible arguments: (none), norecursive, outsource

Uses QMake for configuring. For more information see Section 6.12.3, "Using qmake".

17.73. readline

Possible arguments: (none), port

Uses readline as a library dependency, and sets CPPFLAGS and LDFLAGS as necessary. If the port argument is used or if readline is not present in the base system, add a dependency on devel/readline

17.74. samba

Possible arguments: build, env, lib, run

Handle dependency on Samba. `env` will not add any dependency and only set up the variables. `build` and `run` will add build-time and run-time dependency on `smbd`. `lib` will add a dependency on `libsmbclient.so`. The variables that are exported are:

SAMBAPORT
> The origin of the default Samba port.

SAMBAINCLUDES
> The location of the Samba header files.

SAMBALIBS
> The directory where the Samba shared libraries are available.

17.75. scons

Possible arguments: (none)

Provide support for the use of devel/scons. See Section 6.5.5, "Using scons" for more information.

17.76. shared-mime-info

Possible arguments: (none)

Uses update-mime-database from misc/shared-mime-info. This uses will automatically add a post-install step in such a way that the port itself still can specify there own post-install step if needed. It also add an @shared-mime-info para to the plist.

17.77. shebangfix

Possible arguments: (none)

A lot of software uses incorrect locations for script interpreters, most notably `/usr/bin/perl` and `/bin/bash`. The shebangfix macro fixes shebang lines in scripts listed in SHEBANG_REGEX, SHEBANG_GLOB, or SHEBANG_FILES.

SHEBANG_REGEX
> Contains *one* extended regular expressions, and is used with the `-iregex` argument of find(1). See Example 17.9, "USES=shebangfix with SHEBANG_REGEX".

SHEBANG_GLOB
> Contains a list of patterns used with the `-name` argument of find(1). See Example 17.10, "USES=shebangfix with SHEBANG_GLOB".

SHEBANG_FILES
> Contains a list of files or sh(1) globs. The shebangfix macro is run from `${WRKSRC}`, so SHEBANG_FILES can contain paths that are relative to `${WRKSRC}`. It can also deal with absolute paths if files outside of `${WRKSRC}` require patching. See Example 17.11, "USES=shebangfix with SHEBANG_FILES".

Currently Bash, Java, Ksh, Lua, Perl, PHP, Python, Ruby, Tcl, and Tk are supported by default.

There are three configuration variables:

SHEBANG_LANG
> The list of supported interpreters.

*interp*_CMD
> The path to the command interpreter on FreeBSD. The default value is ${LOCALBASE}/bin/*interp*.

*interp*_OLD_CMD

The list of wrong invocations of interpreters. These are typically obsolete paths, or paths used on other operating systems that are incorrect on FreeBSD. They will be replaced by the correct path in *interp*_CMD.

Note

These will *always* be part of *interp*_OLD_CMD: "/usr/bin/env *interp*" /bin/*interp* /usr/bin/ *interp* /usr/local/bin/ *interp*.

Tip

*interp*_OLD_CMD contain multiple values. Any entry with spaces must be quoted. See Example 17.7, "Specifying all the Paths When Adding an Interpreter to USES=shebangfix".

Important

The fixing of shebangs is done during the patch phase. If scripts are created with incorrect shebangs during the build phase, the build process (for example, the configure script, or the Makefiles) must be patched or given the right path (for example, with CONFIGURE_ENV, CONFIGURE_ARGS, MAKE_ENV , or MAKE_ARGS) to generate the right shebangs.

Correct paths for supported interpreters are available in *interp*_CMD.

Tip

When used with USES=python , and the aim is only to fix the shebangs but a dependency on Python itself is not wanted, use PYTHON_NO_DEPENDS=yes.

Example 17.6. Adding Another Interpreter to USES=shebangfix

To add another interpreter, set SHEBANG_LANG. For example:

```
SHEBANG_LANG= lua
```

Example 17.7. Specifying all the Paths When Adding an Interpreter to USES=shebangfix

If it was not already defined, and there were no default values for *interp*_OLD_CMD and *interp*_CMD the Ksh entry could be defined as:

```
SHEBANG_LANG= ksh
```

```
ksh_OLD_CMD= "/usr/bin/env ksh" /bin/ksh /usr/bin/ksh
ksh_CMD= ${LOCALBASE}/bin/ksh
```

Example 17.8. Adding a Strange Location for an Interpreter

Some software uses strange locations for an interpreter. For example, an application might expect Python to be located in /opt/bin/python2.7 . The strange path to be replaced can be declared in the port Makefile:

```
python_OLD_CMD= /opt/bin/python2.7
```

Example 17.9. USES=shebangfix with SHEBANG_REGEX

To fix all the files in ${WRKSRC}/scripts ending in .pl, .sh, or .cgi do:

```
USES= shebangfix
SHEBANG_REGEX= ./scripts/.*\.(sh|pl|cgi)
```

Note

SHEBANG_REGEX is used by running find -E, which uses modern regular expressions also known as extended regular expressions. See re_format(7) for more information.

Example 17.10. USES=shebangfix with SHEBANG_GLOB

To fix all the files in ${WRKSRC} ending in .pl or .sh, do:

```
USES= shebangfix
SHEBANG_GLOB= *.sh *.pl
```

Example 17.11. USES=shebangfix with SHEBANG_FILES

To fix the files script/foobar.pl and script/*.sh in ${WRKSRC} , do:

```
USES= shebangfix
SHEBANG_FILES= scripts/foobar.pl scripts/*.sh
```

17.78. sqlite

Possible arguments: (none), 2, 3

Add a dependency on SQLite. The default version used is 3, but version 2 is also possible using the :2 modifier.

17.79. ssl

Possible arguments: (none), build, run

Provide support for OpenSSL. A build- or run-time only dependency can be specified using build or run. These variables are available for the port's use, they are also added to MAKE_ENV:

OPENSSLBASE
   Path to the OpenSSL installation base.

OPENSSLDIR
   Path to OpenSSL's configuration files.

OPENSSLLIB
   Path to the OpenSSL libraries.

OPENSSLINC
   Path to the OpenSSL includes.

OPENSSLRPATH
   If defined, the path the linker needs to use to find the OpenSSL libraries.

> **Tip**
>
> If a port does not build with an OpenSSL flavor, set the BROKEN_SSL variable, and possibly the BROKEN_SSL_REASON_*flavor*:
>
> ```
> BROKEN_SSL= libressl
> BROKEN_SSL_REASON_libressl= needs features only available in OpenSSL
> ```

17.80. tar

Possible arguments: (none), Z, bz2, bzip2, lzma, tbz, tbz2, tgz, txz, xz

Set EXTRACT_SUFX to .tar, .tar.Z, .tar.bz2, .tar.bz2, .tar.lzma, .tbz, .tbz2, .tgz, .txz or .tar.xz respectively.

17.81. tcl

Possible arguments: *version*, wrapper, build, run, tea

Add a dependency on Tcl. A specific version can be requested using *version*. The version can be empty, one or more exact version numbers (currently 84, 85, or 86), or a minimal version number (currently 84+, 85+ or 86+). To only request a non version specific wrapper, use wrapper. A build- or run-time only dependency can be specified using build or run. To build the port using the Tcl Extension Architecture, use tea. After including bsd.port.pre.mk the port can inspect the results using these variables:

- `TCL_VER`: chosen major.minor version of Tcl

- `TCLSH`: full path of the Tcl interpreter

- `TCL_LIBDIR`: path of the Tcl libraries

- `TCL_INCLUDEDIR`: path of the Tcl C header files

- `TK_VER`: chosen major.minor version of Tk

- `WISH`: full path of the Tk interpreter

- `TK_LIBDIR`: path of the Tk libraries

- `TK_INCLUDEDIR`: path of the Tk C header files

17.82. `terminfo`

Possible arguments: (none)

Adds @terminfo to the `plist`. Use when the port installs *.terminfo files in `${PREFIX}/share/misc` .

17.83. `tk`

Same as arguments for `tcl`

Small wrapper when using both Tcl and Tk. The same variables are returned as when using Tcl.

17.84. `uidfix`

Possible arguments: (none)

Changes some default behavior (mostly variables) of the build system to allow installing this port as a normal user. Try this in the port before using USES=fakeroot or patching.

17.85. `uniquefiles`

Possible arguments: (none), `dirs`

Make files or directories 'unique', by adding a prefix or suffix. If the `dirs` argument is used, the port needs a prefix (a only a prefix) based on `UNIQUE_PREFIX` for standard directories `DOCSDIR` , `EXAMPLESDIR`, `DATADIR` , `WWWDIR`, `ETCDIR`. These variables are available for ports:

- `UNIQUE_PREFIX`: The prefix to be used for directories and files. Default: `${PKGNAMEPREFIX}`.

- `UNIQUE_PREFIX_FILES`: A list of files that need to be prefixed. Default: empty.

- `UNIQUE_SUFFIX`: The suffix to be used for files. Default: `${PKGNAMESUFFIX}`.

- `UNIQUE_SUFFIX_FILES`: A list of files that need to be suffixed. Default: empty.

17.86. `varnish`

Possible arguments: 4, 5

Handle dependencies on Varnish Cache. 4 will add a dependency on www/varnish4. 5 will add a dependency on www/varnish5.

17.87. webplugin

Possible arguments: (none), ARGS

Automatically create and remove symbolic links for each application that supports the webplugin framework. ARGS can be one of:

- gecko: support plug-ins based on Gecko

- native: support plug-ins for Gecko, Opera, and WebKit-GTK

- linux: support Linux plug-ins

- all (default, implicit): support all plug-in types

- (individual entries): support only the browsers listed

These variables can be adjusted:

- WEBPLUGIN_FILES: No default, must be set manually. The plug-in files to install.

- WEBPLUGIN_DIR: The directory to install the plug-in files to, default *PREFIX*/lib/browser_plugins/ *WEB-PLUGIN_NAME*. Set this if the port installs plug-in files outside of the default directory to prevent broken symbolic links.

- WEBPLUGIN_NAME: The final directory to install the plug-in files into, default PKGBASE.

17.88. xfce

Possible arguments: (none), gtk3

Provide support for Xfce related ports. See Section 6.24, "Using Xfce" for details.

The gtk3 argument specifies that the port requires GTK3 support. It adds additional features provided by some core components, for example, x11/libxfce4menu and x11-wm/xfce4-panel.

17.89. zip

Possible arguments: (none), infozip

Indicates that the distribution files use the ZIP compression algorithm. For files using the InfoZip algorithm the infozip argument must be passed to set the appropriate dependencies.

17.90. zope

Possible arguments: (none)

Uses www/zope *XY*. Mostly used for building zope related ports. ZOPE_VERSION can be used by a port to indicate that a specific version of zope shall be used.

Chapter 18. __FreeBSD_version Values

Here is a convenient list of __FreeBSD_version values as defined in sys/param.h:

18.1. FreeBSD 12 Versions

Table 18.1. FreeBSD 12 __FreeBSD_version Values

Value	Revision	Date	Release
1200000	302409	July 7, 2016	12.0-CURRENT.
1200001	302628	July 12, 2016	12.0-CURRENT after removing collation from [a-z]-type ranges.
1200002	304395	August 18, 2016	12.0-CURRENT after removing unused and obsolete openbsd_poll system call.
1200003	304608	August 22, 2016	12.0-CURRENT after adding C++11 thread_local support in rev 303795.
1200004	304752	August 24, 2016	12.0-CURRENT after fixing LC_*_MASK for newlocale(3) and querylocale(3) (rev 304703).
1200005	304789	August 25, 2016	12.0-CURRENT after changing some ioctl interfaces in rev 304787 between the iSCSI userspace programs and the kernel.
1200006	305256	September 1, 2016	12.0-CURRENT after crunchgen(1) META_MODE fix in 305254.
1200007	305421	September 5, 2016	12.0-CURRENT after resolving a deadlock between device_detach() and usb-d_do_request_flags(9).
1200008	305833	September 15, 2016	12.0-CURRENT after removing the 4.3BSD compatible macro m_copy() in 305824.
1200009	306077	September 21, 2016	12.0-CURRENT after removing bio_taskqueue() in 305988.
1200010	306276	September 23, 2016	12.0-CURRENT after mounting msdosfs(5) with longnames support by default.

Value	Revision	Date	Release
1200011	306556	October 1, 2016	12.0-CURRENT after adding fb_memattr field to fb_info in 306555.
1200012	306592	October 2, 2016	12.0-CURRENT after net80211(4) changes (rev 306590, 306591).
1200013	307140	October 12, 2016	12.0-CURRENT after installing header files required development with libzfs_core.
1200014	307529	October 17, 2016	12.0-CURRENT after merging common code in rtwn(4) and urtwn(4), and adding support for 802.11ac devices.
1200015	308874	November 20, 2016	12.0-CURRENT after some ABI change for unbreaking powerpc.
1200016	309017	November 22, 2016	12.0-CURRENT after removing PG_CACHED -related fields from vmmeter.
1200017	309124	November 25, 2016	12.0-CURRENT after upgrading our copies of clang, llvm, lldb, compiler-rt and libc++ to 3.9.0 release, and adding lld 3.9.0.
1200018	309676	December 7, 2016	12.0-CURRENT after adding the ki_moretdname member to struct kinfo_proc and struct kinfo_proc32 to export the whole thread name to user-space utilities.
1200019	310149	December 16, 2016	12.0-CURRENT after starting to lay down the foundation for 11ac support.
1200020	312087	January 13, 2017	12.0-CURRENT after removing fgetsock and fputsock.
1200021	313858	February 16, 2017	12.0-CURRENT after removing MCA and EISA support.
1200022	314040	February 21, 2017	12.0-CURRENT after making the LinuxKPI task struct persistent across system calls.
(not changed)	314373	March 2, 2017	12.0-CURRENT after removing System V Release

Value	Revision	Date	Release
			4 binary compatibility support.
1200023	314564	March 2, 2017	12.0-CURRENT after upgrading our copies of clang, llvm, lld, lldb, compiler-rt and libc++ to 4.0.0.
1200024	314865	March 7, 2017	12.0-CURRENT after removal of pcap-int.h
1200025	315430	March 16, 2017	12.0-CURRENT after addition of the <dev/mmc/mmc_ioctl.h> header.
1200026	315662	March 16, 2017	12.0-CURRENT after hiding struct inpcb and struct tcpcb from userland.
1200027	315673	March 21, 2017	12.0-CURRENT after making CAM SIM lock optional.
1200028	316683	April 10, 2017	12.0-CURRENT after renaming smp_no_rendevous_barrier() to smp_no_rendezvous_barrier() in 316648.
1200029	317176	April 19, 2017	12.0-CURRENT after the removal of struct vmmeter from struct pcpu from 317061.
1200030	317383	April 24, 2017	12.0-CURRENT after removing NATM support including en(4), fatm(4), hatm(4), and patm(4).
1200031	318736	May 23, 2017	12.0-CURRENT after types ino_t, dev_t, nlink_t were extended to 64bit and struct dirent changed layout (also known as ino64).
1200032	319664	June 8, 2017	12.0-CURRENT after removal of groff.
1200033	320043	June 17, 2017	12.0-CURRENT after the type of the struct event member data was increased to 64bit, and ext structure members added.
1200034	320085	June 19, 2017	12.0-CURRENT after the NFS client and server were changed so that they actually use the 64bit ino_t.
1200035	320317	June 24, 2017	12.0-CURRENT after the MAP_GUARD mmap(2) flag was added.

Value	Revision	Date	Release
1200036	320347	June 26, 2017	12.0-CURRENT after changing `time_t` to 64 bits on powerpc (32-bit version).
1200037	320545	July 1, 2017	12.0-CURRENT after the cleanup and inlining of `bus_dmamap*` functions (320528).
1200038	320879	July 10, 2017	12.0-CURRENT after MMC CAM committed. (320844).
1200039	r321369	July 22, 2017	12.0-CURRENT after upgrade of copies of clang, llvm, lld, lldb, compiler-rt and libc++ to 5.0.0 (trunk r308421).
1200040	r321688	July 29, 2017	12.0-CURRENT after adding NFS client forced dismount support `umount -N`.
1200041	r322762	August 21, 2017	12.0-CURRENT after WRFSBASE instruction become operational on amd64.
1200042	r322900	August 25, 2017	12.0-CURRENT after PLPMTUD counters were changed to use counter(9).
1200043	r322989	August 28, 2017	12.0-CURRENT after dropping x86 CACHE_LINE_SIZE down to 64 bytes.
1200044	r323349	September 8, 2017	12.0-CURRENT after implementing poll_wait() in the LinuxKPI.
1200045	r323706	September 18, 2017	12.0-CURRENT after adding shared memory support to LinuxKPI. (r323703).
1200046	r323910	September 22, 2017	12.0-CURRENT after adding support for 32-bit compatibility IOCTLs to LinuxKPI.
1200047	r324053	September 26, 2017	12.0-CURRENT after removing M_HASHTYPE_RSS_UDP_IPV4_EX. (r324052).
1200048	r324227	October 2, 2017	12.0-CURRENT after hiding `struct socket` and `struct unpcb` from userland.
1200049	r324281	October 4, 2017	12.0-CURRENT after adding the `value.u16` field to `struct diocgattr_arg`.
1200050	r324342	October 5, 2017	12.0-CURRENT after adding the `armv7 MACHINE_ARCH`. (r324340).

Value	Revision	Date	Release
1200051	r324455	October 9, 2017	12.0-CURRENT after removing libstand.a as a public interface. (r324454).
1200052	r325028	October 26, 2017	12.0-CURRENT after fixing ptrace() to always clear the correct thread event when resuming.
1200053	r325506	November 7, 2017	12.0-CURRENT after changing struct mbuf layout to add optional hardware timestamps for receive packets.
1200054	r325852	November 15, 2017	12.0-CURRENT after changing the layout of struct vmtotal to allow for reporting large memory counters.
1200055	r327740	January 9, 2018	12.0-CURRENT after adding cpucontrol -e support.
1200056	r327952	January 14, 2018	12.0-CURRENT after upgrading clang, llvm, lld, lldb, compiler-rt and libc++ to 6.0.0 (branches/release_60 r321788).
1200057	r329033	February 8, 2018	12.0-CURRENT after applying a clang 6.0.0 fix to make the wine ports build correctly.

18.2. FreeBSD 11 Versions

Table 18.2. FreeBSD 11 __FreeBSD_version Values

Value	Revision	Date	Release
1100000	256284	October 10, 2013	11.0-CURRENT.
1100001	256776	October 19, 2013	11.0-CURRENT after addition of support for "first boot" rc.d scripts, so ports can make use of this.
1100002	257696	November 5, 2013	11.0-CURRENT after dropping support for historic ioctls.
1100003	258284	November 17, 2013	11.0-CURRENT after iconv changes.
1100004	259424	December 15, 2013	11.0-CURRENT after the behavior change of gss_pseudo_random introduced in 259286.

Value	Revision	Date	Release
1100005	260010	December 28, 2013	11.0-CURRENT after 259951 - Do not coalesce entries in vm_map_stack(9).
1100006	261246	January 28, 2014	11.0-CURRENT after upgrades of libelf and libdwarf.
1100007	261283	January 30, 2014	11.0-CURRENT after upgrade of libc++ to 3.4 release.
1100008	261881	February 14, 2014	11.0-CURRENT after libc++ 3.4 ABI compatibility fix.
1100009	261991	February 16, 2014	11.0-CURRENT after upgrade of llvm/clang to 3.4 release.
1100010	262630	February 28, 2014	11.0-CURRENT after upgrade of ncurses to 5.9 release (rev 262629).
1100011	263102	March 13, 2014	11.0-CURRENT after ABI change in struct if_data.
1100012	263140	March 14, 2014	11.0-CURRENT after removal of Novell IPX protocol support.
1100013	263152	March 14, 2014	11.0-CURRENT after removal of AppleTalk protocol support.
1100014	263235	March 16, 2014	11.0-CURRENT after renaming <sys/capability.h> to <sys/capsicum.h> to avoid a clash with similarly named headers in other operating systems. A compatibility header is left in place to limit build breakage, but will be deprecated in due course.
1100015	263620	March 22, 2014	11.0-CURRENT after cnt rename to vm_cnt.
1100016	263660	March 23, 2014	11.0-CURRENT after addition of armv6hf TARGET_ARCH.
1100017	264121	April 4, 2014	11.0-CURRENT after GCC support for __block definition.
1100018	264212	April 6, 2014	11.0-CURRENT after support for UDP-Lite protocol (RFC 3828).

Value	Revision	Date	Release
1100019	264289	April 8, 2014	11.0-CURRENT after Free-BSD-SA-14:06.openssl (rev 264265).
1100020	265215	May 1, 2014	11.0-CURRENT after removing lindev in favor of having /dev/full by default (rev 265212).
1100021	266151	May 6, 2014	11.0-CURRENT after src.opts.mk changes, decoupling make.conf(5) from buildworld (rev 265419).
1100022	266904	May 30, 2014	11.0-CURRENT after changes to strcasecmp(3), moving strcasecmp_l(3) and strncasecmp_l(3) from <string.h> to <strings.h> for POSIX 2008 compliance (rev 266865).
1100023	267440	June 13, 2014	11.0-CURRENT after the CUSE library and kernel module have been attached to the build by default.
1100024	267992	June 27, 2014	11.0-CURRENT after sysctl(3) API change.
1100025	268066	June 30, 2014	11.0-CURRENT after regex(3) library update to add ">" and "<" delimiters.
1100026	268118	July 1, 2014	11.0-CURRENT after the internal interface between the NFS modules, including the krpc, was changed by (rev 268115).
1100027	268441	July 8, 2014	11.0-CURRENT after Free-BSD-SA-14:17.kmem (rev 268431).
1100028	268945	July 21, 2014	11.0-CURRENT after hdestroy(3) compliance fix changed ABI.
1100029	270173	August 3, 2014	11.0-CURRENT after SOCK_DGRAM bug fix (rev 269489).
1100030	270929	September 1, 2014	11.0-CURRENT after SOCK_RAW sockets were changed to not modify packets at all.
1100031	271341	September 9, 2014	11.0-CURRENT after Free-BSD-SA-14:18.openssl (rev 269686).

Value	Revision	Date	Release
1100032	271438	September 11, 2014	11.0-CURRENT after API changes to `ifa_ifwith-broadaddr`, `ifa_ifwith-dstaddr`, `ifa_ifwithnet`, and `ifa_ifwithroute`.
1100033	271657	September 9, 2014	11.0-CURRENT after changing access, eaccess, and faccessat to validate the mode argument.
1100034	271686	September 16, 2014	11.0-CURRENT after Free-BSD-SA-14:19.tcp (rev 271666).
1100035	271705	September 17, 2014	11.0-CURRENT after i915 HW context support.
1100036	271724	September 17, 2014	Version bump to have ABI note distinguish binaries ready for strict mmap(2) flags checking (rev 271724).
1100037	272674	October 6, 2014	11.0-CURRENT after addition of explicit_bzero(3) (rev 272673).
1100038	272951	October 11, 2014	11.0-CURRENT after cleanup of TCP wrapper headers.
1100039	273250	October 18, 2014	11.0-CURRENT after removal of `MAP_RENAME` and `MAP_NORESERVE` .
1100040	273432	October 21, 2014	11.0-CURRENT after Free-BSD-SA-14:23 (rev 273146).
1100041	273875	October 30, 2014	11.0-CURRENT after API changes to `syscall_reg-ister`, `syscall32_reg-ister`, `syscall_regis-ter_helper` and `syscal-l32_register_helper` (rev 273707).
1100042	274046	November 3, 2014	11.0-CURRENT after a change to struct `tcpcb` .
1100043	274085	November 4, 2014	11.0-CURRENT after enabling vt(4) by default.
1100044	274116	November 4, 2014	11.0-CURRENT after adding new libraries/utilities (dpv and figpar) for data throughput visualization.
1100045	274162	November 4, 2014	11.0-CURRENT after Free-BSD-SA-14:23, Free-BSD-SA-14:24, and Free-BSD-SA-14:25.

Value	Revision	Date	Release
1100046	274470	November 13, 2014	11.0-CURRENT after kern_poll signature change (rev 274462).
1100047	274476	November 13, 2014	11.0-CURRENT after removal of no-at version of VFS syscalls helpers, like kern_open .
1100048	275358	December 1, 2014	11.0-CURRENT after starting the process of removing the use of the deprecated "M_FLOWID" flag from the network code.
1100049	275633	December 9, 2014	11.0-CURRENT after importing an important fix to the LLVM vectorizer, which could lead to buffer overruns in some cases.
1100050	275732	December 12, 2014	11.0-CURRENT after adding AES-ICM and AES-GCM to OpenCrypto.
1100051	276096	December 23, 2014	11.0-CURRENT after removing old NFS client and server code from the kernel.
1100052	276479	December 31, 2014	11.0-CURRENT after upgrade of clang, llvm and lldb to 3.5.0 release.
1100053	276781	January 7, 2015	11.0-CURRENT after MCLGET(9) gained a return value (rev 276750).
1100054	277213	January 15, 2015	11.0-CURRENT after rewrite of callout subsystem.
1100055	277528	January 22, 2015	11.0-CURRENT after reverting callout changes in 277213.
1100056	277610	January 23, 2015	11.0-CURRENT after addition of futimens and utimensat system calls.
1100057	277897	January 29, 2015	11.0-CURRENT after removal of d_thread_t.
1100058	278228	February 5, 2015	11.0-CURRENT after addition of support for probing the SCSI VPD Extended Inquiry page (0x86).
1100059	278442	February 9, 2015	11.0-CURRENT after import of xz 5.2.0, which added multi-threaded compres-

Value	Revision	Date	Release
			sion and lzma gained libthr dependency (rev 278433).
1100060	278846	February 16, 2015	11.0-CURRENT after forwarding `FBIO_BLANK` to framebuffer clients.
1100061	278964	February 18, 2015	11.0-CURRENT after `CDAI_FLAG_NONE` addition.
1100062	279221	February 23, 2015	11.0-CURRENT after mtio(4) and sa(4) API and ioctl(2) additions.
1100063	279728	March 7, 2015	11.0-CURRENT after adding mutex support to the pps_ioctl() API in the kernel.
1100064	279729	March 7, 2015	11.0-CURRENT after adding PPS support to USB serial drivers.
1100065	280031	March 15, 2015	11.0-CURRENT after upgrading clang, llvm and lldb to 3.6.0.
1100066	280306	March 20, 2015	11.0-CURRENT after removal of SSLv2 support from OpenSSL.
1100067	280630	March 25, 2015	11.0-CURRENT after removal of SSLv2 support from fetch(1) and fetch(3).
1100068	281172	April 6, 2015	11.0-CURRENT after change to net.inet6.ip6.mif6table sysctl.
1100069	281550	April 15, 2015	11.0-CURRENT after removal of const qualifier from iconv(3).
1100070	281613	April 16, 2015	11.0-CURRENT after moving ALTQ from `contrib` to `net/altq`.
1100071	282256	April 29, 2015	11.0-CURRENT after API/ABI change to smb(4) (rev 281985).
1100072	282319	May 1, 2015	11.0-CURRENT after adding reallocarray(3) in libc (rev 282314).
1100073	282650	May 8, 2015	11.0-CURRENT after extending the maximum number of allowed PCM channels in a PCM stream to 127 and decreasing the maximum number of subchannels to 1.

Value	Revision	Date	Release
1100074	283526	May 25, 2015	11.0-CURRENT after adding preliminary support for x86-64 Linux binaries (rev 283424), and upgrading clang and llvm to 3.6.1.
1100075	283623	May 27, 2015	11.0-CURRENT after dounmount()requiring a reference on the passed struct mount (rev 283602).
1100076	283983	June 4, 2015	11.0-CURRENT after disabled generation of legacy formatted password databases entries by default.
1100077	284233	June 10, 2015	11.0-CURRENT after API changes to lim_cur, lim_max, and lim_rlimit (rev 284215).
1100078	286672	August 12, 2015	11.0-CURRENT after crunchgen(1) changes from 284356 to 285986.
1100079	286874	August 18, 2015	11.0-CURRENT after import of jemalloc 4.0.0 (rev 286866).
1100080	288943	October 5, 2015	11.0-CURRENT after upgrading clang, llvm, lldb, compiler-rt and libc++ to 3.7.0.
1100081	289415	October 16, 2015	11.0-CURRENT after undating ZFS to support resumable send/receive (rev 289362).
1100082	289594	October 19, 2015	11.0-CURRENT after Linux KPI updates.
1100083	289749	October 22, 2015	11.0-CURRENT after renaming linuxapi.ko to linuxkpi.ko.
1100084	290135	October 29, 2015	11.0-CURRENT after moving the LinuxKPI module into the default kernel build.
1100085	290207	October 30, 2015	11.0-CURRENT after import of OpenSSL 1.0.2d.
1100086	290275	November 2, 2015	11.0-CURRENT after making figpar(3) macros more unique.
1100087	290479	November 7, 2015	11.0-CURRENT after changing sysctl_add_oid(9)'s ABI.

Value	Revision	Date	Release
1100088	290495	November 7, 2015	11.0-CURRENT after string collation and locales rework.
1100089	290505	November 7, 2015	11.0-CURRENT after API change to sysctl_add_oid(9) (rev 290475).
1100090	290715	November 10, 2015	11.0-CURRENT after API change to callout_stop macro; (rev 290664).
1100091	291537	November 30, 2015	11.0-CURRENT after changing the interface between the nfsd.ko and nfscommon.ko modules in 291527.
1100092	292499	December 19, 2015	11.0-CURRENT after removal of vm_pageout_grow_cache (rev 292469).
1100093	292966	December 30, 2015	11.0-CURRENT after removal of sys/crypto/sha2.h (rev 292782).
1100094	294086	January 15, 2016	11.0-CURRENT after LinuxKPI PCI changes (rev 294086).
1100095	294327	January 19, 2016	11.0-CURRENT after LRO optimizations.
1100096	294505	January 21, 2016	11.0-CURRENT after LinuxKPI idr_* additions.
1100097	294860	January 26, 2016	11.0-CURRENT after API change to dpv(3).
1100098	295682	February 16, 2016	11.0-CURRENT after API change to rman (rev 294883).
1100099	295739	February 18, 2016	11.0-CURRENT after allowing drivers to set the TCP ACK/data segment aggregation limit.
1100100	296136	February 26, 2016	11.0-CURRENT after bus_alloc_resource_any(9) API addition.
1100101	296417	March 5, 2016	11.0-CURRENT after upgrading our copies of clang, llvm, lldb and compiler-rt to 3.8.0 release.
1100102	296749	March 12, 2016	11.0-CURRENT after libelf cross-endian fix in rev 296685.
1100103	297000	March 18, 2016	11.0-CURRENT after using uintmax_t for rman ranges.

Value	Revision	Date	Release
1100104	297156	March 21, 2016	11.0-CURRENT after tracking filemon usage via a proc.p_filemon pointer rather than its own lists.
1100105	297602	April 6, 2016	11.0-CURRENT after fixing sed functions i and a from discarding leading white space.
1100106	298486	April 22, 2016	11.0-CURRENT after fixes for using IPv6 addresses with RDMA.
1100107	299090	May 4, 2016	11.0-CURRENT after improving performance and functionality of the bitstring(3) api.
1100108	299530	May 12, 2016	11.0-CURRENT after fixing handling of IOCTLs in the LinuxKPI.
1100109	299933	May 16, 2016	11.0-CURRENT after implementing more Linux device related functions in the LinuxKPI.
1100110	300207	May 19, 2016	11.0-CURRENT after adding support for managing Shingled Magnetic Recording (SMR) drives.
1100111	300303	May 20, 2016	11.0-CURRENT after removing brk and sbrk from arm64.
1100112	300539	May 23, 2016	11.0-CURRENT after adding bit_count to the bitstring(3) API.
1100113	300701	May 26, 2016	11.0-CURRENT after disabling alignment faults on armv6.
1100114	300806	May 26, 2016	11.0-CURRENT after fixing crunchgen(1) usage with MAKEOBJDIRPREFIX.
1100115	300982	May 30, 2016	11.0-CURRENT after adding an mbuf flag for M_HASHTYPE_.
1100116	301011	May 31, 2016	11.0-CURRENT after SHA-512t256 (rev 300903) and Skein (rev 300966) where added to libmd, libcrypt, the kernel, and ZFS (rev 301010).
1100117	301892	June 6, 2016	11.0-CURRENT after libpam was synced with stock

Value	Revision	Date	Release
			301602, bumping library version.
1100118	302071	June 21, 2016	11.0-CURRENT after breaking binary compatibility of struct disk 302069.
1100119	302150	June 23, 2016	11.0-CURRENT after switching geom_disk to using a pool mutex.
1100120	302153	June 23, 2016	11.0-CURRENT after adding spares to struct ifnet.
1100121	303979	August 12, 2015	11-STABLE after releng/11.0 branched from 11-STABLE (rev 303975).
1100500	303979	August 12, 2016	11.0-STABLE adding branched 303976.
1100501	304609	August 22, 2016	11.0-STABLE after adding C++11 thread_local support.
1100502	304865	August 26, 2016	11.0-STABLE after LC_*_MASK fix.
1100503	305733	September 12, 2016	11.0-STABLE after resolving a deadlock between device_detach() and usbd_do_request_flags(9).
1100504	307330	October 14, 2016	11.0-STABLE after ZFS merges.
1100505	307590	October 19, 2016	11.0-STABLE after struct fb_info change.
1100506	308048	October 28, 2016	11.0-STABLE after installing header files required development with libzfs_core.
1100507	310120	December 15, 2016	11.0-STABLE after adding the ki_moretdname member to struct kinfo_proc and struct kinfo_proc32 to export the whole thread name to user-space utilities.
1100508	310618	December 26, 2016	11.0-STABLE after upgrading our copies of clang, llvm, lldb, compiler-rt and libc++ to 3.9.1 release, and adding lld 3.9.1.
1100509	311186	January 3, 2017	11.0-STABLE after crunchgen(1) META_MODE fix (rev r311185).

Value	Revision	Date	Release
1100510	315312	March 15, 2017	11.0-STABLE after MFC of `fget_cap`, `getsock_cap`, and related changes.
1100511	316423	April 2, 2017	11.0-STABLE after multiple MFCs updating clang, llvm, lld, lldb, compiler-rt and libc++ to 4.0.0 release.
1100512	316498	April 4, 2017	11.0-STABLE after making CAM SIM lock optional (revs 315673, 315674).
1100513	318197	May 11, 2017	11-STABLE after merging the addition of the `<dev/mmc/mmc_ioctl.h>` header.
1100514	319279	May 31, 2017	11.0-STABLE after multiple MFCs of `libpcap`, `WITHOUT_INET6`, and a few other minor changes.
1101000	320486	June 30, 2017	`releng/11.1` branched from `stable/11`.
1101001	320763	June 30, 2017	11.1-RC1 After merging the `MAP_GUARD` mmap(2) flag addition.
1101500	320487	June 30, 2017	11-STABLE after `releng/11.1` branched.
1101501	320666	July 5, 2017	11-STABLE after merging the `MAP_GUARD` mmap(2) flag addition.
1101502	r321688	July 29, 2017	11-STABLE after merging the NFS client forced dismount support umount -N addition.
1101503	r323431	September 11, 2017	11-STABLE after merging changes making the WRFSBASE instruction operational on amd64.
1101504	r324006	September 26, 2017	11-STABLE after merging libm from head, which adds cacoshl(3), cacosl(3), casinhl(3), casinl(3), catanl(3), catanhl(3), sincos(3), sincosf(3), and sincosl(3).
1101505	r324023	September 26, 2017	11-STABLE after merging clang, llvm, lld, lldb, compiler-rt and libc++ 5.0.0 release.
1101506	r325003	October 25, 2017	11-STABLE after merging r324281, adding the `value.u16` field to struct `diocgattr_arg`.

Value	Revision	Date	Release
1101507	r328379	January 24, 2018	11-STABLE after merging r325028, fixing ptrace() to always clear the correct thread event when resuming.
1101508	r328386	January 24, 2018	11-STABLE after merging r316648, renaming smp_no_rendevous_barrier() to smp_no_rendezvous_barrier().

18.3. FreeBSD 10 Versions

Table 18.3. FreeBSD 10 __FreeBSD_version Values

Value	Revision	Date	Release
1000000	225757	September 26, 2011	10.0-CURRENT.
1000001	227070	November 4, 2011	10-CURRENT after addition of the posix_fadvise(2) system call.
1000002	228444	December 12, 2011	10-CURRENT after defining boolean true/false in sys/types.h, sizeof(bool) may have changed (rev 228444). 10-CURRENT after xlocale.h was introduced (rev 227753).
1000003	228571	December 16, 2011	10-CURRENT after major changes to carp(4), changing size of struct in_aliasreq, struct in6_aliasreq (rev 228571) and straitening arguments check of SIOCAIFADDR (rev 228574).
1000004	229204	January 1, 2012	10-CURRENT after the removal of skpc() and the addition of memcchr(9) (rev 229200).
1000005	230207	January 16, 2012	10-CURRENT after the removal of support for SIOCSIFADDR, SIOCSIFNETMASK, SIOCSIFBRDADDR, SIOCSIFDSTADDR ioctls.
1000006	230590	January 26, 2012	10-CURRENT after introduction of read capacity data asynchronous notification in the cam(4) layer.
1000007	231025	February 5, 2012	10-CURRENT after introduction of new tcp(4) socket options: TCP_KEEPINIT,

Value	Revision	Date	Release
			TCP_KEEPIDLE, TCP_KEEP-INTVL, and TCP_KEEPCNT.
1000008	231505	February 11, 2012	10-CURRENT after introduction of the new extensible sysctl(3) interface NET_RT_IFLISTL to query address lists.
1000009	232154	February 25, 2012	10-CURRENT after import of libarchive 3.0.3 (rev 232153).
1000010	233757	March 31, 2012	10-CURRENT after xlocale cleanup.
1000011	234355	April 16, 2012	10-CURRENT import of LLVM/Clang 3.1 trunk 154661 (rev 234353).
1000012	234924	May 2, 2012	10-CURRENT jemalloc import.
1000013	235788	May 22, 2012	10-CURRENT after byacc import.
1000014	237631	June 27, 2012	10-CURRENT after BSD sort becoming the default sort (rev 237629).
1000015	238405	July 12, 2012	10-CURRENT after import of OpenSSL 1.0.1c.
(not changed)	238429	July 13, 2012	10-CURRENT after the fix for LLVM/Clang 3.1 regression.
1000016	239179	August 8, 2012	10-CURRENT after KBI change in ucom(4).
1000017	239214	August 8, 2012	10-CURRENT after adding streams feature to the USB stack.
1000018	240233	September 8, 2012	10-CURRENT after major rewrite of pf(4).
1000019	241245	October 6, 2012	10-CURRENT after pfil(9) KBI/KPI changed to supply packets in net byte order to AF_INET filter hooks.
1000020	241610	October 16, 2012	10-CURRENT after the network interface cloning KPI changed and struct if_clone becoming opaque.
1000021	241897	October 22, 2012	10-CURRENT after removal of support for non-MPSAFE filesystems and addition of support for FUSEFS (rev 241519).

Value	Revision	Date	Release
1000022	241913	October 22, 2012	10-CURRENT after the entire IPv4 stack switched to network byte order for IP packet header storage.
1000023	242619	November 5, 2012	10-CURRENT after jitter buffer in the common USB serial driver code, to temporarily store characters if the TTY buffer is full. Add flow stop and start signals when this happens.
1000024	242624	November 5, 2012	10-CURRENT after clang was made the default compiler on i386 and amd64.
1000025	243443	November 17, 2012	10-CURRENT after the sin6_scope_id member variable in struct sockaddr_in6 was changed to being filled by the kernel before passing the structure to the userland via sysctl or routing socket. This means the KAME-specific embedded scope id in sin6_addr.s6_addr[2] is always cleared in userland application.
1000026	245313	January 11, 2013	10-CURRENT after install gained the -N flag. May also be used to indicate the presence of nmtree.
1000027	246084	January 29, 2013	10-CURRENT after cat gained the -l flag (rev 246083).
1000028	246759	February 13, 2013	10-CURRENT after USB moved to the driver structure requiring a rebuild of all USB modules.
1000029	247821	March 4, 2013	10-CURRENT after the introduction of tickless callout facility which also changed the layout of struct callout (rev 247777).
1000030	248210	March 12, 2013	10-CURRENT after KPI breakage introduced in the VM subsystem to support read/write locking (rev 248084).
1000031	249943	April 26, 2013	10-CURRENT after the dst parameter of the ifnet

Value	Revision	Date	Release
			if_output method was changed to take const qualifier (rev 249925).
1000032	250163	May 1, 2013	10-CURRENT after the introduction of the accept4(2) (rev 250154) and pipe2(2) (rev 250159) system calls.
1000033	250881	May 21, 2013	10-CURRENT after flex 2.5.37 import.
1000034	251294	June 3, 2013	10-CURRENT after the addition of these functions to libm: cacos(3), cacosf(3), cacosh(3), cacoshf(3), casin(3), casinf(3), casinh(3), casinhf(3), catan(3), catanf(3), catanh(3), catanhf(3), logl(3), log2l(3), log10l(3), log1pl(3), expm1l(3).
1000035	251527	June 8, 2013	10-CURRENT after the introduction of the aio_mlock(2) system call (rev 251526).
1000036	253049	July 9, 2013	10-CURRENT after the addition of a new function to the kernel GSSAPI module's function call interface.
1000037	253089	July 9, 2013	10-CURRENT after the migration of statistics structures to PCPU counters. Changed structures include: ahstat, arpstat, espstat, icmp6_ifstat, icmp6stat, in6_ifstat, ip6stat, ipcompstat, ipipstat, ipsecstat, mrt6stat, mrtstat, pfkeystat, pim6stat, pimstat, rip6stat, udpstat (rev 253081).
1000038	253396	July 16, 2013	10-CURRENT after making ARM EABI the default ABI on arm, armeb, armv6, and armv6eb architectures.
1000039	253549	July 22, 2013	10-CURRENT after CAM and mps(4) driver scanning changes.
1000040	253638	July 24, 2013	10-CURRENT after addition of libusb pkgconf files.

Value	Revision	Date	Release
1000041	253970	August 5, 2013	10-CURRENT after change from time_second to time_uptime in PF_INET6 .
1000042	254138	August 9, 2013	10-CURRENT after VM subsystem change to unify soft and hard busy mechanisms.
1000043	254273	August 13, 2013	10-CURRENT after WITH_I-CONV is enabled by default. A new src.conf(5) option, WITH_LIBICONV_COMPAT (disabled by default) adds libiconv_open to provide compatibility with the libiconv port.
1000044	254358	August 15, 2013	10-CURRENT after libc.so conversion to an ld(1) script (rev 251668).
1000045	254389	August 15, 2013	10-CURRENT after devfs programming interface change by replacing the cdevsw flag D_UNMAPPED_IO with the struct cdev flag SI_UNMAPPED.
1000046	254537	August 19, 2013	10-CURRENT after addition of M_PROTO[9-12] and removal of M_FRAG|M_FIRST-FRAG|M_LASTFRAG mbuf flags (rev 254524, 254526).
1000047	254627	August 21, 2013	10-CURRENT after stat(2) update to allow storing some Windows/DOS and CIFS file attributes as stat(2) flags.
1000048	254672	August 22, 2013	10-CURRENT after modification of structure xsct-p_inpcb.
1000049	254760	August 24, 2013	10-CURRENT after physio(9) support for devices that do not function properly with split I/O, such as sa(4).
1000050	254844	August 24, 2013	10-CURRENT after modifications of structure mbuf (rev 254780, 254799, 254804, 254807 254842).
1000051	254887	August 25, 2013	10-CURRENT after Radeon KMS driver import (rev 254885).

Value	Revision	Date	Release
1000052	255180	September 3, 2013	10-CURRENT after import of NetBSD libexecinfo is connected to the build.
1000053	255305	September 6, 2013	10-CURRENT after API and ABI changes to the Capsicum framework.
1000054	255321	September 6, 2013	10-CURRENT after gcc and libstdc++ are no longer built by default.
1000055	255449	September 6, 2013	10-CURRENT after addition of MMAP_32BIT mmap(2) flag (rev 255426).
1000100	259065	December 7, 2013	releng/10.0 branched from stable/10.
1000500	256283	October 10, 2013	10-STABLE after branch from head/.
1000501	256916	October 22, 2013	10-STABLE after addition of first-boot rc(8) support.
1000502	258398	November 20, 2013	10-STABLE after removal of iconv symbols from libc.so.7.
1000510	259067	December 7, 2013	releng/10.0 __FreeBSD_version update to prevent the value from going backwards.
1000700	259069	December 7, 2013	10-STABLE after releng/10.0 branch.
1000701	259447	December 15, 2013	10.0-STABLE after Heimdal encoding fix.
1000702	260135	December 31, 2013	10-STABLE after MAP_STACK fixes.
1000703	262801	March 5, 2014	10-STABLE after upgrade of libc++ to 3.4 release.
1000704	262889	March 7, 2014	10-STABLE after MFC of the vt(4) driver (rev 262861).
1000705	263508	March 21, 2014	10-STABLE after upgrade of llvm/clang to 3.4 release.
1000706	264214	April 6, 2014	10-STABLE after GCC support for __block definition.
1000707	264289	April 8, 2014	10-STABLE after FreeBSD-SA-14:06.openssl.
1000708	265122	April 30, 2014	10-STABLE after FreeBSD-SA-14:07.devfs, FreeBSD-SA-14:08.tcp, and FreeBSD-SA-14:09.openssl.

Value	Revision	Date	Release
1000709	265946	May 13, 2014	10-STABLE after support for UDP-Lite protocol (RFC 3828).
1000710	267465	June 13, 2014	10-STABLE after changes to strcasecmp(3), moving strcasecmp_l(3) and strncasecmp_l(3) from <string.h> to <strings.h> for POSIX 2008 compliance.
1000711	268442	July 8, 2014	10-STABLE after Free-BSD-SA-14:17.kmem (rev 268432).
1000712	269400	August 1, 2014	10-STABLE after nfsd(8) 4.1 merge (rev 269398).
1000713	269484	August 3, 2014	10-STABLE after regex(3) library update to add ">" and "<" delimiters.
1000714	270174	August 3, 2014	10-STABLE after SOCK_D-GRAM bug fix (rev 269490).
1000715	271341	September 9, 2014	10-STABLE after Free-BSD-SA-14:18 (rev 269686).
1000716	271686	September 16, 2014	10-STABLE after Free-BSD-SA-14:19 (rev 271667).
1000717	271816	September 18, 2014	10-STABLE after i915 HW context support.
1001000	272463	October 2, 2014	10.1-RC1 after releng/10.1 branch.
1001500	272464	October 2, 2014	10-STABLE after releng/10.1 branch.
1001501	273432	October 21, 2014	10-STABLE after Free-BSD-SA-14:20, Free-BSD-SA-14:22, and Free-BSD-SA-14:23 (rev 273411).
1001502	274162	November 4, 2014	10-STABLE after Free-BSD-SA-14:23, Free-BSD-SA-14:24, and Free-BSD-SA-14:25.
1001503	275040	November 25, 2014	10-STABLE after merging new libraries/utilities (dpv(1), dpv(3), and figpar(3)) for data throughput visualization.
1001504	275742	December 13, 2014	10-STABLE after merging an important fix to the LLVM vectorizer, which could lead to buffer overruns in some cases.

Value	Revision	Date	Release
1001505	276633	January 3, 2015	10-STABLE after merging some arm constants in 276312.
1001506	277087	January 12, 2015	10-STABLE after merging max table size update for yacc.
1001507	277790	January 27, 2015	10-STABLE after changes to the UDP tunneling callback to provide a context pointer and the source sockaddr.
1001508	278974	February 18, 2015	10-STABLE after addition of the CDAI_TYPE_EXT_INQ request type.
1001509	279287	February 25, 2015	10-STABLE after FreeBSD-EN-15:01.vt, FreeBSD-EN-15:02.openssl, FreeBSD-EN-15:03.freebsd-update, FreeBSD-SA-15:04.igmp, and FreeBSD-SA-15:05.bind.
1001510	279329	February 26, 2015	10-STABLE after MFC of rev 278964.
1001511	280246	19 March, 2015	10-STABLE after sys/capability.h is renamed to sys/capsicum.h (rev 280224/).
1001512	280438	24 March, 2015	10-STABLE after addition of new mtio(4), sa(4) ioctls.
1001513	281955	24 April, 2015	10-STABLE after starting the process of removing the use of the deprecated "M_FLOWID" flag from the network code.
1001514	282275	April 30, 2015	10-STABLE after MFC of iconv(3) fixes.
1001515	282781	May 11, 2015	10-STABLE after adding back M_FLOWID.
1001516	283341	May 24, 2015	10-STABLE after MFC of many USB things.
1001517	283950	June 3, 2015	10-STABLE after MFC of sound related things.
1001518	284204	June 10, 2015	10-STABLE after MFC of zfs vfs fixes (rev 284203).
1001519	284720	June 23, 2015	10-STABLE after reverting bumping MAXCPU on amd64.
1002000	285830	24 July, 2015	releng/10.2 branched from 10-STABLE.

Value	Revision	Date	Release
1002500	285831	24 July, 2015	10-STABLE after re-leng/10.2 branched from 10-STABLE.
1002501	289005	8 October, 2015	10-STABLE after merge of ZFS changes that affected the internal interface of zfeature_info structure (rev 288572).
1002502	291243	24 November, 2015	10-STABLE after merge of dump device changes that affected the arguments of g_dev_setdumpdev() (rev 291215).
1002503	292224	14 December, 2015	10-STABLE after merge of changes to the internal interface between the nfsd.ko and nfscommon.ko modules, requiring them to be upgraded together (rev 292223).
1002504	292589	22 December, 2015	10-STABLE after merge of xz 5.2.2 merge (multithread support) (rev 292588).
1002505	292908	30 December, 2015	10-STABLE after merge of changes to pci(4) (rev 292907).
1002506	293476	9 January, 2016	10-STABLE after merge of utimensat(2) (rev 293473).
1002507	293610	9 January, 2016	10-STABLE after merge of changes to linux(4) (rev 293477 through 293609).
1002508	293619	9 January, 2016	10-STABLE after merge of changes to figpar(3) types/macros (rev 290275).
1002509	295107	1 February, 2016	10-STABLE after merge of API change to dpv(3).
1003000	296373	4 March, 2016	releng/10.3 branched from 10-STABLE.
1003500	296374	4 March, 2016	10-STABLE after re-leng/10.3 branched from 10-STABLE.
1003501	298299	19 June, 2016	10-STABLE after adding kdbcontrol's -P option (rev 298297).
1003502	299966	19 June, 2016	10-STABLE after libcrypto.so was made position independent.

Value	Revision	Date	Release
1003503	300235	19 June, 2016	10-STABLE after allowing MK_ overrides (rev 300233).
1003504	302066	21 June, 2016	10-STABLE after MFC of filemon changes from 11-CURRENT.
1003505	302228	27 June, 2016	10-STABLE after converting sed to use REG_STARTEND, fixing a Mesa issue.
1003506	304611	August 22, 2016	10-STABLE after adding C++11 thread_local support.
1003507	304864	August 26, 2016	10-STABLE after LC_*_MASK fix.
1003508	305734	September 12, 2016	10-STABLE after resolving a deadlock between device_detach() and usbd_do_request_flags(9).
1003509	307331	October 14, 2016	10-STABLE after ZFS merges.
1003510	308047	October 28, 2016	10-STABLE after installing header files required development with libzfs_core.
1003511	310121	December 15, 2016	10-STABLE after exporting whole thread name in kinfo_proc (rev 309676).
1003512	315730	March 22, 2017	10-STABLE after libmd changes (rev 314143).
1003513	316499	April 4, 2017	10-STABLE after making CAM SIM lock optional (revs 315673, 315674).
1003514	318198	May 11, 2017	10-STABLE after merging the addition of the <dev/mmc/mmc_ioctl.h> header.
1003515	321222	July 19, 2017	10-STABLE after adding C++14 sized deallocation functions to libc++.
1003516	321717	July 30, 2017	10-STABLE after merging the MAP_GUARD mmap(2) flag addition.
1004000	323604	September 15, 2017	releng/10.4 branched from 10-STABLE.
1004500	323605	September 15, 2017	10-STABLE after releng/10.4 branched from 10-STABLE.
1004501	r328379	January 24, 2018	10-STABLE after merging r325028, fixing ptrace() to always clear the correct

Value	Revision	Date	Release
			thread event when resuming.

18.4. FreeBSD 9 Versions

Table 18.4. FreeBSD 9 `__FreeBSD_version` Values

Value	Revision	Date	Release
900000	196432	August 22, 2009	9.0-CURRENT.
900001	197019	September 8, 2009	9.0-CURRENT after importing x86emu, a software emulator for real mode x86 CPU from OpenBSD.
900002	197430	September 23, 2009	9.0-CURRENT after implementing the EVFILT_USER kevent filter functionality.
900003	200039	December 2, 2009	9.0-CURRENT after addition of sigpause(2) and PIE support in csu.
900004	200185	December 6, 2009	9.0-CURRENT after addition of libulog and its libutempter compatibility interface.
900005	200447	December 12, 2009	9.0-CURRENT after addition of sleepq_sleepcnt(9), which can be used to query the number of waiters on a specific waiting queue.
900006	201513	January 4, 2010	9.0-CURRENT after change of the scandir(3) and alphasort(3) prototypes to conform to SUSv4.
900007	202219	January 13, 2010	9.0-CURRENT after the removal of utmp(5) and the addition of utmpx (see getutxent(3)) for improved logging of user logins and system events.
900008	202722	January 20, 2010	9.0-CURRENT after the import of BSDL bc/dc and the deprecation of GNU bc/dc.
900009	203052	January 26, 2010	9.0-CURRENT after the addition of SIOCGIFDESCR and SIOCSIFDESCR ioctls to network interfaces. These ioctl can be used to manipulate interface description, as inspired by OpenBSD.

Value	Revision	Date	Release
900010	205471	March 22, 2010	9.0-CURRENT after the import of zlib 1.2.4.
900011	207410	April 24, 2010	9.0-CURRENT after adding soft-updates journalling.
900012	207842	May 10, 2010	9.0-CURRENT after adding liblzma, xz, xzdec, and lzmainfo.
900013	208486	May 24, 2010	9.0-CURRENT after bringing in USB fixes for linux(4).
900014	208973	June 10, 2010	9.0-CURRENT after adding Clang.
900015	210390	July 22, 2010	9.0-CURRENT after the import of BSD grep.
900016	210565	July 28, 2010	9.0-CURRENT after adding mti_zone to struct malloc_type_internal.
900017	211701	August 23, 2010	9.0-CURRENT after changing back default grep to GNU grep and adding WITH_BSD_GREP knob.
900018	211735	August 24, 2010	9.0-CURRENT after the pthread_kill(3) -generated signal is identified as SI_LWP in si_code. Previously, si_code was SI_USER.
900019	211937	August 28, 2010	9.0-CURRENT after addition of the MAP_PREFAULT_READ flag to mmap(2).
900020	212381	September 9, 2010	9.0-CURRENT after adding drain functionality to sbufs, which also changed the layout of struct sbuf.
900021	212568	September 13, 2010	9.0-CURRENT after DTrace has grown support for userland tracing.
900022	213395	October 2, 2010	9.0-CURRENT after addition of the BSDL man utilities and retirement of GNU/GPL man utilities.
900023	213700	October 11, 2010	9.0-CURRENT after updating xz to git 20101010 snapshot.
900024	215127	November 11, 2010	9.0-CURRENT after libgcc.a was replaced by libcompiler_rt.a.

Value	Revision	Date	Release
900025	215166	November 12, 2010	9.0-CURRENT after the introduction of the modularised congestion control.
900026	216088	November 30, 2010	9.0-CURRENT after the introduction of Serial Management Protocol (SMP) passthrough and the XPT_SMP_IO and XPT_GDEV_ADVINFO CAM CCBs.
900027	216212	December 5, 2010	9.0-CURRENT after the addition of log2 to libm.
900028	216615	December 21, 2010	9.0-CURRENT after the addition of the Hhook (Helper Hook), Khelp (Kernel Helpers) and Object Specific Data (OSD) KPIs.
900029	216758	December 28, 2010	9.0-CURRENT after the modification of the TCP stack to allow Khelp modules to interact with it via helper hook points and store per-connection data in the TCP control block.
900030	217309	January 12, 2011	9.0-CURRENT after the update of libdialog to version 20100428.
900031	218414	February 7, 2011	9.0-CURRENT after the addition of pthread_getthreadid_np(3).
900032	218425	February 8, 2011	9.0-CURRENT after the removal of the uio_yield prototype and symbol.
900033	218822	February 18, 2011	9.0-CURRENT after the update of binutils to version 2.17.50.
900034	219406	March 8, 2011	9.0-CURRENT after the struct sysvec (sv_schedtail) changes.
900035	220150	March 29, 2011	9.0-CURRENT after the update of base gcc and libstdc++ to the last GPLv2 licensed revision.
900036	220770	April 18, 2011	9.0-CURRENT after the removal of libobjc and Objective-C support from the base system.
900037	221862	May 13, 2011	9.0-CURRENT after importing the libprocstat(3) li-

Value	Revision	Date	Release
			brary and fuser(1) utility to the base system.
900038	222167	May 22, 2011	9.0-CURRENT after adding a lock flag argument to VFS_FHTOVP(9).
900039	223637	June 28, 2011	9.0-CURRENT after importing pf from OpenBSD 4.5.
900040	224217	July 19, 2011	Increase default MAXCPU for FreeBSD to 64 on amd64 and ia64 and to 128 for XLP (mips).
900041	224834	August 13, 2011	9.0-CURRENT after the implementation of Capsicum capabilities; fget(9) gains a rights argument.
900042	225350	August 28, 2011	Bump shared libraries' version numbers for libraries whose ABI has changed in preparation for 9.0.
900043	225350	September 2, 2011	Add automatic detection of USB mass storage devices which do not support the no synchronize cache SCSI command.
900044	225469	September 10, 2011	Re-factor auto-quirk. 9.0-RELEASE.
900045	229285	January 2, 2012	9-STABLE after MFC of true/false from 1000002.
900500	229318	January 2, 2012	9.0-STABLE.
900501	229723	January 6, 2012	9.0-STABLE after merging of addition of the posix_fadvise(2) system call.
900502	230237	January 16, 2012	9.0-STABLE after merging gperf 3.0.3
900503	231768	February 15, 2012	9.0-STABLE after introduction of the new extensible sysctl(3) interface NET_RT_IFLISTL to query address lists.
900504	232728	March 3, 2012	9.0-STABLE after changes related to mounting of filesystem inside a jail.
900505	232945	March 13, 2012	9.0-STABLE after introduction of new tcp(4) socket options: TCP_KEEPINIT, TCP_KEEPIDLE, TCP_KEEPINTVL, and TCP_KEEPCNT.

Value	Revision	Date	Release
900506	235786	May 22, 2012	9.0-STABLE after introduction of the quick_exit function and related changes required for C++11.
901000	239082	August 5, 2012	9.1-RELEASE.
901500	239081	August 6, 2012	9.1-STABLE after branching releng/9.1 (RELENG_9_1).
901501	240659	November 11, 2012	9.1-STABLE after LIST_PREV(3) added to queue.h (rev 242893) and KBI change in USB serial devices.
901502	243656	November 28, 2012	9.1-STABLE after USB serial jitter buffer requires rebuild of USB serial device modules.
901503	247090	February 21, 2013	9.1-STABLE after USB moved to the driver structure requiring a rebuild of all USB modules. Also indicates the presence of nmtree.
901504	248338	March 15, 2013	9.1-STABLE after install gained -l, -M, -N and related flags and cat gained the -l option.
901505	251687	June 13, 2013	9.1-STABLE after fixes in ctfmerge bootstrapping (rev 249243).
902001	253912	August 3, 2013	releng/9.2 branched from stable/9.
902501	253913	August 2, 2013	9.2-STABLE after creation of releng/9.2 branch.
902502	254938	August 26, 2013	9.2-STABLE after inclusion of the PIM_RESCAN CAM path inquiry flag.
902503	254979	August 27, 2013	9.2-STABLE after inclusion of the SI_UNMAPPED cdev flag.
902504	256917	October 22, 2013	9.2-STABLE after inclusion of support for "first boot" rc(8) scripts.
902505	259448	December 12, 2013	9.2-STABLE after Heimdal encoding fix.
902506	260136	December 31, 2013	9-STABLE after MAP_STACK fixes (rev 260082).
902507	262801	March 5, 2014	9-STABLE after upgrade of libc++ to 3.4 release.

Chapter 18. __FreeBSD_version Values

Value	Revision	Date	Release
902508	263171	March 14, 2014	9-STABLE after merge of the Radeon KMS driver (rev 263170).
902509	263509	March 21, 2014	9-STABLE after upgrade of llvm/clang to 3.4 release.
902510	263818	March 27, 2014	9-STABLE after merge of the vt(4) driver.
902511	264289	March 27, 2014	9-STABLE after Free-BSD-SA-14:06.openssl.
902512	265123	April 30, 2014	9-STABLE after Free-BSD-SA-14:08.tcp.
903000	267656	June 20, 2014	9-RC1 releng/9.3 branch.
903500	267657	June 20, 2014	9.3-STABLE releng/9.3 branch.
903501	268443	July 8, 2014	9-STABLE after Free-BSD-SA-14:17.kmem (rev 268433).
903502	270175	August 19, 2014	9-STABLE after SOCK_DGRAM bug fix (rev 269789).
903503	271341	September 9, 2014	9-STABLE after Free-BSD-SA-14:18 (rev 269687).
903504	271686	September 16, 2014	9-STABLE after Free-BSD-SA-14:19 (rev 271668).
903505	273432	October 21, 2014	9-STABLE after Free-BSD-SA-14:20, Free-BSD-SA-14:21, and Free-BSD-SA-14:22 (rev 273412).
903506	274162	November 4, 2014	9-STABLE after Free-BSD-SA-14:23, Free-BSD-SA-14:24, and Free-BSD-SA-14:25.
903507	275742	December 13, 2014	9-STABLE after merging an important fix to the LLVM vectorizer, which could lead to buffer overruns in some cases.
903508	279287	February 25, 2015	9-STABLE after Free-BSD-EN-15:01.vt, Free-BSD-EN-15:02.openssl, FreeBSD-EN-15:03.freeb-sd-update, Free-BSD-SA-15:04.igmp, and FreeBSD-SA-15:05.bind.
903509	296219	February 29, 2016	9-STABLE after bumping the default value of com-pat.linux.osrelease to 2.6.18 to support the lin-

Value	Revision	Date	Release
			ux-c6-* ports out of the box.
903510	300236	May 19, 2016	9-STABLE after System Binary Interface (SBI) page was moved in latest version of Berkeley Boot Loader (BBL) due to code size increase in 300234.
903511	305735	September 12, 2016	9-STABLE after resolving a deadlock between device_detach() and usbd_do_request_flags(9).

18.5. FreeBSD 8 Versions

Table 18.5. FreeBSD 8 __FreeBSD_version Values

Value	Revision	Date	Release
800000	172531	October 11, 2007	8.0-CURRENT. Separating wide and single byte ctype.
800001	172688	October 16, 2007	8.0-CURRENT after libpcap 0.9.8 and tcpdump 3.9.8 import.
800002	172841	October 21, 2007	8.0-CURRENT after renaming kthread_create(9) and friends to kproc_create(9) etc.
800003	172932	October 24, 2007	8.0-CURRENT after ABI backwards compatibility to the FreeBSD 4/5/6 versions of the PCIOCGET-CONF, PCIOCREAD and PCIOCWRITE IOCTLs was added, which required the ABI of the PCIOCGETCONF IOCTL to be broken again
800004	173573	November 12, 2007	8.0-CURRENT after agp(4) driver moved from src/sys/pci to src/sys/dev/agp
800005	174261	December 4, 2007	8.0-CURRENT after changes to the jumbo frame allocator (rev 174247).
800006	174399	December 7, 2007	8.0-CURRENT after the addition of callgraph capture functionality to hwpmc(4).
800007	174901	December 25, 2007	8.0-CURRENT after kdb_enter() gains a "why" argument.

Value	Revision	Date	Release
800008	174951	December 28, 2007	8.0-CURRENT after LK_EX-CLUPGRADE option removal.
800009	175168	January 9, 2008	8.0-CURRENT after introduction of lockmgr_disown(9)
800010	175204	January 10, 2008	8.0-CURRENT after the vn_lock(9) prototype change.
800011	175295	January 13, 2008	8.0-CURRENT after the VOP_LOCK(9) and VOP_UN-LOCK(9) prototype changes.
800012	175487	January 19, 2008	8.0-CURRENT after introduction of lockmgr_recursed(9), BUF_RE-CURSED(9) and BUF_ISLOCKED(9) and the removal of BUF_REFCNT().
800013	175581	January 23, 2008	8.0-CURRENT after introduction of the "ASCII" encoding.
800014	175636	January 24, 2008	8.0-CURRENT after changing the prototype of lockmgr(9) and removal of lockcount() and LOCKM-GR_ASSERT().
800015	175688	January 26, 2008	8.0-CURRENT after extending the types of the fts(3) structures.
800016	175872	February 1, 2008	8.0-CURRENT after adding an argument to MEX-TADD(9)
800017	176015	February 6, 2008	8.0-CURRENT after the introduction of LK_NODUP and LK_NOWITNESS options in the lockmgr(9) space.
800018	176112	February 8, 2008	8.0-CURRENT after the addition of m_collapse.
800019	176124	February 9, 2008	8.0-CURRENT after the addition of current working directory, root directory, and jail directory support to the kern.proc.filedesc sysctl.
800020	176251	February 13, 2008	8.0-CURRENT after introduction of lockmgr_as-

Value	Revision	Date	Release
			sert(9) and **BUF_ASSERT** functions.
800021	176321	February 15, 2008	8.0-CURRENT after introduction of lockmgr_args(9) and LK_INTERNAL flag removal.
800022	176556	(backed out)	8.0-CURRENT after changing the default system ar to BSD ar(1).
800023	176560	February 25, 2008	8.0-CURRENT after changing the prototypes of lockstatus(9) and VOP_ISLOCKED(9), more specifically retiring the struct thread argument.
800024	176709	March 1, 2008	8.0-CURRENT after axing out the lockwaiters and **BUF_LOCKWAITERS** functions, changing the return value of brelvp from void to int and introducing new flags for lockinit(9).
800025	176958	March 8, 2008	8.0-CURRENT after adding F_DUP2FD command to fcntl(2).
800026	177086	March 12, 2008	8.0-CURRENT after changing the priority parameter to cv_broadcastpri such that 0 means no priority.
800027	177551	March 24, 2008	8.0-CURRENT after changing the bpf monitoring ABI when zerocopy bpf buffers were added.
800028	177637	March 26, 2008	8.0-CURRENT after adding l_sysid to struct flock.
800029	177688	March 28, 2008	8.0-CURRENT after reintegration of the **BUF_LOCK-WAITERS** function and the addition of lockmgr_waiters(9).
800030	177844	April 1, 2008	8.0-CURRENT after the introduction of the rw_try_r-lock(9) and rw_try_wlock(9) functions.
800031	177958	April 6, 2008	8.0-CURRENT after the introduction of the lockmgr_rw and lockmgr_args_rw functions.

Value	Revision	Date	Release
800032	178006	April 8, 2008	8.0-CURRENT after the implementation of the openat and related syscalls, introduction of the O_EXEC flag for the open(2), and providing the corresponding linux compatibility syscalls.
800033	178017	April 8, 2008	8.0-CURRENT after added write(2) support for psm(4) in native operation level. Now arbitrary commands can be written to /dev/psm %d and status can be read back from it.
800034	178051	April 10, 2008	8.0-CURRENT after introduction of the memrchr function.
800035	178256	April 16, 2008	8.0-CURRENT after introduction of the fdopendir function.
800036	178362	April 20, 2008	8.0-CURRENT after switchover of 802.11 wireless to multi-bss support (aka vaps).
800037	178892	May 9, 2008	8.0-CURRENT after addition of multi routing table support (aka setfib(1), setfib(2)).
800038	179316	May 26, 2008	8.0-CURRENT after removal of netatm and ISDN4BSD. Also, the addition of the Compact C Type (CTF) tools.
800039	179784	June 14, 2008	8.0-CURRENT after removal of sgtty.
800040	180025	June 26, 2008	8.0-CURRENT with kernel NFS lockd client.
800041	180691	July 22, 2008	8.0-CURRENT after addition of arc4random_buf(3) and arc4random_uniform(3).
800042	181439	August 8, 2008	8.0-CURRENT after addition of cpuctl(4).
800043	181694	August 13, 2008	8.0-CURRENT after changing bpf(4) to use a single device node, instead of device cloning.
800044	181803	August 17, 2008	8.0-CURRENT after the commit of the first step of

Value	Revision	Date	Release
			the vimage project renaming global variables to be virtualized with a V_ prefix with macros to map them back to their global names.
800045	181905	August 20, 2008	8.0-CURRENT after the integration of the MPSAFE TTY layer, including changes to various drivers and utilities that interact with it.
800046	182869	September 8, 2008	8.0-CURRENT after the separation of the GDT per CPU on amd64 architecture.
800047	182905	September 10, 2008	8.0-CURRENT after removal of VSVTX, VSGID and VSUID.
800048	183091	September 16, 2008	8.0-CURRENT after converting the kernel NFS mount code to accept individual mount options in the nmount(2) iovec, not just one big struct nfs_args.
800049	183114	September 17, 2008	8.0-CURRENT after the removal of suser(9) and suser_cred(9).
800050	184099	October 20, 2008	8.0-CURRENT after buffer cache API change.
800051	184205	October 23, 2008	8.0-CURRENT after the removal of the MALLOC(9) and FREE(9) macros.
800052	184419	October 28, 2008	8.0-CURRENT after the introduction of accmode_t and renaming of VOP_ACCESS 'a_mode' argument to 'a_accmode'.
800053	184555	November 2, 2008	8.0-CURRENT after the prototype change of vfs_busy(9) and the introduction of its MBF_NOWAIT and MBF_MNTLSTLOCK flags.
800054	185162	November 22, 2008	8.0-CURRENT after the addition of buf_ring, memory barriers and ifnet functions to facilitate multiple hardware transmit queues for cards that support them, and a lockless ring-buffer implementation to enable

Value	Revision	Date	Release
			drivers to more efficiently manage queuing of packets.
800055	185363	November 27, 2008	8.0-CURRENT after the addition of Intel™ Core, Core2, and Atom support to hw-pmc(4).
800056	185435	November 29, 2008	8.0-CURRENT after the introduction of multi-/no-IPv4/v6 jails.
800057	185522	December 1, 2008	8.0-CURRENT after the switch to the ath hal source code.
800058	185968	December 12, 2008	8.0-CURRENT after the introduction of the VOP_VPTOCNP operation.
800059	186119	December 15, 2008	8.0-CURRENT incorporates the new arp-v2 rewrite.
800060	186344	December 19, 2008	8.0-CURRENT after the addition of makefs.
800061	187289	January 15, 2009	8.0-CURRENT after TCP Appropriate Byte Counting.
800062	187830	January 28, 2009	8.0-CURRENT after removal of minor(), minor2unit(), unit2minor(), etc.
800063	188745	February 18, 2009	8.0-CURRENT after GENERIC config change to use the USB2 stack, but also the addition of fdevname(3).
800064	188946	February 23, 2009	8.0-CURRENT after the USB2 stack is moved to and replaces dev/usb.
800065	189092	February 26, 2009	8.0-CURRENT after the renaming of all functions in libmp(3).
800066	189110	February 27, 2009	8.0-CURRENT after changing USB devfs handling and layout.
800067	189136	February 28, 2009	8.0-CURRENT after adding getdelim(), getline(), stpncpy(), strnlen(), wcsnlen(), wcscasecmp(), and wcsncasecmp().
800068	189276	March 2, 2009	8.0-CURRENT after renaming the ushub devclass to uhub.

Value	Revision	Date	Release
800069	189585	March 9, 2009	8.0-CURRENT after libus-b20.so.1 was renamed to libusb.so.1.
800070	189592	March 9, 2009	8.0-CURRENT after merging IGMPv3 and Source-Specific Multicast (SSM) to the IPv4 stack.
800071	189825	March 14, 2009	8.0-CURRENT after gcc was patched to use C99 inline semantics in c99 and gnu99 mode.
800072	189853	March 15, 2009	8.0-CURRENT after the IFF_NEEDSGIANT flag has been removed; non-MPSAFE network device drivers are no longer supported.
800073	190265	March 18, 2009	8.0-CURRENT after the dynamic string token substitution has been implemented for rpath and needed paths.
800074	190373	March 24, 2009	8.0-CURRENT after tcpdump 4.0.0 and libpcap 1.0.0 import.
800075	190787	April 6, 2009	8.0-CURRENT after layout of structs vnet_net, vnet_inet and vnet_ipfw has been changed.
800076	190866	April 9, 2009	8.0-CURRENT after adding delay profiles in dummynet.
800077	190914	April 14, 2009	8.0-CURRENT after removing VOP_LEASE() and vop_vector.vop_lease.
800078	191080	April 15, 2009	8.0-CURRENT after struct rt_weight fields have been added to struct rt_metrics and struct rt_metrics_lite, changing the layout of struct rt_metrics_lite. A bump to RTM_VERSION was made, but backed out.
800079	191117	April 15, 2009	8.0-CURRENT after struct llentry pointers are added to struct route and struct route_in6.

Value	Revision	Date	Release
800080	191126	April 15, 2009	8.0-CURRENT after layout of struct inpcb has been changed.
800081	191267	April 19, 2009	8.0-CURRENT after the layout of struct malloc_type has been changed.
800082	191368	April 21, 2009	8.0-CURRENT after the layout of struct ifnet has changed, and with if_ref() and if_rele() ifnet refcounting.
800083	191389	April 22, 2009	8.0-CURRENT after the implementation of a low-level Bluetooth HCI API.
800084	191672	April 29, 2009	8.0-CURRENT after IPv6 SSM and MLDv2 changes.
800085	191688	April 30, 2009	8.0-CURRENT after enabling support for VIMAGE kernel builds with one active image.
800086	191910	May 8, 2009	8.0-CURRENT after adding support for input lines of arbitrarily length in patch(1).
800087	191990	May 11, 2009	8.0-CURRENT after some VFS KPI changes. The thread argument has been removed from the FSD parts of the VFS. VFS_* functions do not need the context any more because it always refers to curthread. In some special cases, the old behavior is retained.
800088	192470	May 20, 2009	8.0-CURRENT after net80211 monitor mode changes.
800089	192649	May 23, 2009	8.0-CURRENT after adding UDP control block support.
800090	192669	May 23, 2009	8.0-CURRENT after virtualizing interface cloning.
800091	192895	May 27, 2009	8.0-CURRENT after adding hierarchical jails and removing global securelevel.
800092	193011	May 29, 2009	8.0-CURRENT after changing sx_init_flags() KPI. The SX_ADAPTIVESPIN is retired and a new SX_NOAD-

Value	Revision	Date	Release
			APTIVE flag is introduced to handle the reversed logic.
800093	193047	May 29, 2009	8.0-CURRENT after adding mnt_xflag to struct mount.
800094	193093	May 30, 2009	8.0-CURRENT after adding VOP_ACCESSX(9).
800095	193096	May 30, 2009	8.0-CURRENT after changing the polling KPI. The polling handlers now return the number of packets processed. A new IF-CAP_POLLING_NOCOUNT is also introduced to specify that the return value is not significant and the counting should be skipped.
800096	193219	June 1, 2009	8.0-CURRENT after updating to the new netisr implementation and after changing the way we store and access FIBs.
800097	193731	June 8, 2009	8.0-CURRENT after the introduction of vnet destructor hooks and infrastructure.
(not changed)	194012	June 11, 2009	8.0-CURRENT after the introduction of netgraph outbound to inbound path call detection and queuing, which also changed the layout of struct thread.
800098	194210	June 14, 2009	8.0-CURRENT after OpenSSL 0.9.8k import.
800099	194675	June 22, 2009	8.0-CURRENT after NGROUPS update and moving route virtualization into its own VImage module.
800100	194920	June 24, 2009	8.0-CURRENT after SYSVIPC ABI change.
800101	195175	June 29, 2009	8.0-CURRENT after the removal of the /dev/net/* per-interface character devices.
800102	195634	July 12, 2009	8.0-CURRENT after padding was added to struct sackhint, struct tcpcb, and struct tcpstat.
800103	195654	July 13, 2009	8.0-CURRENT after replacing struct tcpopt with

Value	Revision	Date	Release
			struct toeopt in the TOE driver interface to the TCP syncache.
800104	195699	July 14, 2009	8.0-CURRENT after the addition of the linker-set based per-vnet allocator.
800105	195767	July 19, 2009	8.0-CURRENT after version bump for all shared libraries that do not have symbol versioning turned on.
800106	195852	July 24, 2009	8.0-CURRENT after introduction of OBJT_SG VM object type.
800107	196037	August 2, 2009	8.0-CURRENT after making the newbus subsystem Giant free by adding the newbus sxlock and 8.0-RELEASE.
800108	199627	November 21, 2009	8.0-STABLE after implementing EVFILT_USER kevent filter.
800500	201749	January 7, 2010	8.0-STABLE after __FreeBSD_version bump to make pkg_add -r use packages-8-stable.
800501	202922	January 24, 2010	8.0-STABLE after change of the scandir(3) and alphasort(3) prototypes to conform to SUSv4.
800502	203299	January 31, 2010	8.0-STABLE after addition of sigpause(2).
800503	204344	February 25, 2010	8.0-STABLE after addition of SIOCGIFDESCR and SIOCSIFDESCR ioctls to network interfaces. These ioctl can be used to manipulate interface description, as inspired by OpenBSD.
800504	204546	March 1, 2010	8.0-STABLE after MFC of importing x86emu, a software emulator for real mode x86 CPU from OpenBSD.
800505	208259	May 18, 2010	8.0-STABLE after MFC of adding liblzma, xz, xzdec, and lzmainfo.
801000	209150	June 14, 2010	8.1-RELEASE

Value	Revision	Date	Release
801500	209146	June 14, 2010	8.1-STABLE after 8.1-RELEASE.
801501	214762	November 3, 2010	8.1-STABLE after KBI change in struct sysentvec, and implementation of PL_FLAG_SCE/SCX/EXEC/SI and pl_siginfo for ptrace(PT_LWPINFO).
802000	216639	December 22, 2010	8.2-RELEASE
802500	216654	December 22, 2010	8.2-STABLE after 8.2-RELEASE.
802501	219107	February 28, 2011	8.2-STABLE after merging DTrace changes, including support for userland tracing.
802502	219324	March 6, 2011	8.2-STABLE after merging log2 and log2f into libm.
802503	221275	May 1, 2011	8.2-STABLE after upgrade of the gcc to the last GPLv2 version from the FSF gcc-4_2-branch.
802504	222401	May 28, 2011	8.2-STABLE after introduction of the KPI and supporting infrastructure for modular congestion control.
802505	222406	May 28, 2011	8.2-STABLE after introduction of Hhook and Khelp KPIs.
802506	222408	May 28, 2011	8.2-STABLE after addition of OSD to struct tcpcb.
802507	222741	June 6, 2011	8.2-STABLE after ZFS v28 import.
802508	222846	June 8, 2011	8.2-STABLE after removal of the schedtail event handler and addition of the sv_schedtail method to struct sysvec.
802509	224017	July 14, 2011	8.2-STABLE after merging the SSSE3 support into binutils.
802510	224214	July 19, 2011	8.2-STABLE after addition of RFTSIGZMB flag for rfork(2).
802511	225458	September 9, 2011	8.2-STABLE after addition of automatic detection of USB mass storage devices which do not support the

Value	Revision	Date	Release
			no synchronize cache SCSI command.
802512	225470	September 10, 2011	8.2-STABLE after merging of re-factoring of auto-quirk.
802513	226763	October 25, 2011	8.2-STABLE after merging of the MAP_PRE-FAULT_READ flag to mmap(2).
802514	227573	November 16, 2011	8.2-STABLE after merging of addition of posix_fallocate(2) syscall.
802515	229725	January 6, 2012	8.2-STABLE after merging of addition of the posix_fadvise(2) system call.
802516	230239	January 16, 2012	8.2-STABLE after merging gperf 3.0.3
802517	231769	February 15, 2012	8.2-STABLE after introduction of the new extensible sysctl(3) interface NET_RT_IFLISTL to query address lists.
803000	232446	March 3, 2012	8.3-RELEASE.
803500	232439	March 3, 2012	8.3-STABLE after branching releng/8.3 (RELENG_8_3).
803501	247091	February 21, 2013	8.3-STABLE after MFC of two USB fixes (rev 246616 and 246759).
804000	248850	March 28, 2013	8.4-RELEASE.
804500	248819	March 28, 2013	8.4-STABLE after 8.4-RELEASE.
804501	259449	December 16, 2013	8.4-STABLE after MFC of upstream Heimdal encoding fix.
804502	265123	April 30, 2014	8.4-STABLE after FreeBSD-SA-14:08.tcp.
804503	268444	July 9, 2014	8.4-STABLE after FreeBSD-SA-14:17.kmem.
804504	271341	September 9, 2014	8.4-STABLE after FreeBSD-SA-14:18 (rev 271305).
804505	271686	September 16, 2014	8.4-STABLE after FreeBSD-SA-14:19 (rev 271668).
804506	273432	October 21, 2014	8.4-STABLE after FreeBSD-SA-14:21 (rev 273413).
804507	274162	November 4, 2014	8.4-STABLE after FreeBSD-SA-14:23, Free-

Value	Revision	Date	Release
			BSD-SA-14:24, and Free-BSD-SA-14:25.
804508	279287	February 25, 2015	8-STABLE after Free-BSD-EN-15:01.vt, FreeBSD-EN-15:02.openssl, FreeBSD-EN-15:03.freebsd-update, FreeBSD-SA-15:04.igmp, and FreeBSD-SA-15:05.bind.
804509	305736	September 12, 2016	8-STABLE after resolving a deadlock between device_detach() and usbd_do_request_flags(9).

18.6. FreeBSD 7 Versions

Table 18.6. FreeBSD 7 __FreeBSD_version Values

Value	Revision	Date	Release
700000	147925	July 11, 2005	7.0-CURRENT.
700001	148341	July 23, 2005	7.0-CURRENT after bump of all shared library versions that had not been changed since RELENG_5.
700002	149039	August 13, 2005	7.0-CURRENT after credential argument is added to dev_clone event handler.
700003	149470	August 25, 2005	7.0-CURRENT after memmem(3) is added to libc.
700004	151888	October 30, 2005	7.0-CURRENT after solisten(9) kernel arguments are modified to accept a backlog parameter.
700005	152296	November 11, 2005	7.0-CURRENT after IFP2ENADDR() was changed to return a pointer to IF_LLADDR().
700006	152315	November 11, 2005	7.0-CURRENT after addition of if_addr member to struct ifnet and IFP2ENADDR() removal.
700007	153027	December 2, 2005	7.0-CURRENT after incorporating scripts from the local_startup directories into the base rcorder(8).
700008	153107	December 5, 2005	7.0-CURRENT after removal of MNT_NODEV mount option.

Value	Revision	Date	Release
700009	153519	December 19, 2005	7.0-CURRENT after ELF-64 type changes and symbol versioning.
700010	153579	December 20, 2005	7.0-CURRENT after addition of hostb and vgapci drivers, addition of pci_find_extcap(), and changing the AGP drivers to no longer map the aperture.
700011	153936	December 31, 2005	7.0-CURRENT after tv_sec was made time_t on all platforms but Alpha.
700012	154114	January 8, 2006	7.0-CURRENT after ldconfig_local_dirs change.
700013	154269	January 12, 2006	7.0-CURRENT after changes to /etc/rc.d/abi to support /compat/linux/etc/ld.so.cache being a symlink in a readonly filesystem.
700014	154863	January 26, 2006	7.0-CURRENT after pts import.
700015	157144	March 26, 2006	7.0-CURRENT after the introduction of version 2 of hwpmc(4)'s ABI.
700016	157962	April 22, 2006	7.0-CURRENT after addition of fcloseall(3) to libc.
700017	158513	May 13, 2006	7.0-CURRENT after removal of ip6fw.
700018	160386	July 15, 2006	7.0-CURRENT after import of snd_emu10kx.
700019	160821	July 29, 2006	7.0-CURRENT after import of OpenSSL 0.9.8b.
700020	161931	September 3, 2006	7.0-CURRENT after addition of bus_dma_get_tag function
700021	162023	September 4, 2006	7.0-CURRENT after libpcap 0.9.4 and tcpdump 3.9.4 import.
700022	162170	September 9, 2006	7.0-CURRENT after dlsym change to look for a requested symbol both in specified dso and its implicit dependencies.
700023	162588	September 23, 2006	7.0-CURRENT after adding new sound IOCTLs for the OSSv4 mixer API.

Value	Revision	Date	Release
700024	162919	September 28, 2006	7.0-CURRENT after import of OpenSSL 0.9.8d.
700025	164190	November 11, 2006	7.0-CURRENT after the addition of libelf.
700026	164614	November 26, 2006	7.0-CURRENT after major changes on sound sysctls.
700027	164770	November 30, 2006	7.0-CURRENT after the addition of Wi-Spy quirk.
700028	165242	December 15, 2006	7.0-CURRENT after the addition of sctp calls to libc
700029	166259	January 26, 2007	7.0-CURRENT after the GNU gzip(1) implementation was replaced with a BSD licensed version ported from NetBSD.
700030	166549	February 7, 2007	7.0-CURRENT after the removal of IPIP tunnel encapsulation (VIFF_TUNNEL) from the IPv4 multicast forwarding code.
700031	166907	February 23, 2007	7.0-CURRENT after the modification of bus_setup_intr() (newbus).
700032	167165	March 2, 2007	7.0-CURRENT after the inclusion of ipw(4) and iwi(4) firmware.
700033	167360	March 9, 2007	7.0-CURRENT after the inclusion of ncurses wide character support.
700034	167684	March 19, 2007	7.0-CURRENT after changes to how insmntque(), getnewvnode(), and vfs_hash_insert() work.
700035	167906	March 26, 2007	7.0-CURRENT after addition of a notify mechanism for CPU frequency changes.
700036	168413	April 6, 2007	7.0-CURRENT after import of the ZFS filesystem.
700037	168504	April 8, 2007	7.0-CURRENT after addition of CAM 'SG' peripheral device, which implements a subset of Linux SCSI SG passthrough device API.
700038	169151	April 30, 2007	7.0-CURRENT after changing getenv(3), putenv(3), setenv(3) and unsetenv(3) to be POSIX conformant.

Value	Revision	Date	Release
700039	169190	May 1, 2007	7.0-CURRENT after the changes in 700038 were backed out.
700040	169453	May 10, 2007	7.0-CURRENT after the addition of flopen(3) to libutil.
700041	169526	May 13, 2007	7.0-CURRENT after enabling symbol versioning, and changing the default thread library to libthr.
700042	169758	May 19, 2007	7.0-CURRENT after the import of gcc 4.2.0.
700043	169830	May 21, 2007	7.0-CURRENT after bump of all shared library versions that had not been changed since RELENG_6.
700044	170395	June 7, 2007	7.0-CURRENT after changing the argument for vn_open()/VOP_OPEN() from file descriptor index to the struct file *.
700045	170510	June 10, 2007	7.0-CURRENT after changing pam_nologin(8) to provide an account management function instead of an authentication function to the PAM framework.
700046	170530	June 11, 2007	7.0-CURRENT after updated 802.11 wireless support.
700047	170579	June 11, 2007	7.0-CURRENT after adding TCP LRO interface capabilities.
700048	170613	June 12, 2007	7.0-CURRENT after RFC 3678 API support added to the IPv4 stack. Legacy RFC 1724 behavior of the IP_MULTICAST_IF ioctl has now been removed; 0.0.0.0/8 may no longer be used to specify an interface index. Use struct ipmreqn instead.
700049	171175	July 3, 2007	7.0-CURRENT after importing pf from OpenBSD 4.1
(not changed)	171167		7.0-CURRENT after adding IPv6 support for FAST_IPSEC, deleting KAME IPSEC, and renaming FAST_IPSEC to IPSEC.

Value	Revision	Date	Release
700050	171195	July 4, 2007	7.0-CURRENT after converting setenv/putenv/etc. calls from traditional BSD to POSIX.
700051	171211	July 4, 2007	7.0-CURRENT after adding new mmap/lseek/etc syscalls.
700052	171275	July 6, 2007	7.0-CURRENT after moving I4B headers to include/i4b.
700053	172394	September 30, 2007	7.0-CURRENT after the addition of support for PCI domains
700054	172988	October 25, 2007	7.0-STABLE after MFC of wide and single byte ctype separation.
700055	173104	October 28, 2007	7.0-RELEASE, and 7.0-CURRENT after ABI backwards compatibility to the FreeBSD 4/5/6 versions of the PCIOCGETCONF, PCIOCREAD and PCIOCWRITE IOCTLs was MFCed, which required the ABI of the PCIOCGETCONF IOCTL to be broken again
700100	174864	December 22, 2007	7.0-STABLE after 7.0-RELEASE
700101	176111	February 8, 2008	7.0-STABLE after the MFC of m_collapse().
700102	177735	March 30, 2008	7.0-STABLE after the MFC of kdb_enter_why().
700103	178061	April 10, 2008	7.0-STABLE after adding l_sysid to struct flock.
700104	178108	April 11, 2008	7.0-STABLE after the MFC of procstat(1).
700105	178120	April 11, 2008	7.0-STABLE after the MFC of umtx features.
700106	178225	April 15, 2008	7.0-STABLE after the MFC of write(2) support to psm(4).
700107	178353	April 20, 2008	7.0-STABLE after the MFC of F_DUP2FD command to fcntl(2).
700108	178783	May 5, 2008	7.0-STABLE after some lockmgr(9) changes, which makes it necessary to include sys/lock.h to use lockmgr(9).

Value	Revision	Date	Release
700109	179367	May 27, 2008	7.0-STABLE after MFC of the memrchr(3) function.
700110	181328	August 5, 2008	7.0-STABLE after MFC of kernel NFS lockd client.
700111	181940	August 20, 2008	7.0-STABLE after addition of physically contiguous jumbo frame support.
700112	182294	August 27, 2008	7.0-STABLE after MFC of kernel DTrace support.
701000	185315	November 25, 2008	7.1-RELEASE
701100	185302	November 25, 2008	7.1-STABLE after 7.1-RE-LEASE.
701101	187023	January 10, 2009	7.1-STABLE after strndup(3) merge.
701102	187370	January 17, 2009	7.1-STABLE after cpuctl(4) support added.
701103	188281	February 7, 2009	7.1-STABLE after the merge of multi-/no-IPv4/v6 jails.
701104	188625	February 14, 2009	7.1-STABLE after the store of the suspension owner in the struct mount, and introduction of vfs_susp_clean method into the struct vfsops.
701105	189740	March 12, 2009	7.1-STABLE after the incompatible change to the kern.ipc.shmsegs sysctl to allow allocating larger SysV shared memory segments on 64bit architectures.
701106	189786	March 14, 2009	7.1-STABLE after the merge of a fix for POSIX semaphore wait operations.
702000	191099	April 15, 2009	7.2-RELEASE
702100	191091	April 15, 2009	7.2-STABLE after 7.2-RE-LEASE.
702101	192149	May 15, 2009	7.2-STABLE after ichsmb(4) was changed to use left-adjusted slave addressing to match other SMBus controller drivers.
702102	193020	May 28, 2009	7.2-STABLE after MFC of the fdopendir(3) function.
702103	193638	June 06, 2009	7.2-STABLE after MFC of PmcTools.

Value	Revision	Date	Release
702104	195694	July 14, 2009	7.2-STABLE after MFC of the closefrom(2) system call.
702105	196006	July 31, 2009	7.2-STABLE after MFC of the SYSVIPC ABI change.
702106	197198	September 14, 2009	7.2-STABLE after MFC of the x86 PAT enhancements and addition of d_mmap_single() and the scatter/gather list VM object type.
703000	203740	February 9, 2010	7.3-RELEASE
703100	203742	February 9, 2010	7.3-STABLE after 7.3-RELEASE.
704000	216647	December 22, 2010	7.4-RELEASE
704100	216658	December 22, 2010	7.4-STABLE after 7.4-RELEASE.
704101	221318	May 2, 2011	7.4-STABLE after the gcc MFC in rev 221317.

18.7. FreeBSD 6 Versions

Table 18.7. FreeBSD 6 __FreeBSD_version Values

Value	Revision	Date	Release
600000	133921	August 18, 2004	6.0-CURRENT
600001	134396	August 27, 2004	6.0-CURRENT after permanently enabling PFIL_HOOKS in the kernel.
600002	134514	August 30, 2004	6.0-CURRENT after initial addition of ifi_epoch to struct if_data. Backed out after a few days. Do not use this value.
600003	134933	September 8, 2004	6.0-CURRENT after the re-addition of the ifi_epoch member of struct if_data.
600004	135920	September 29, 2004	6.0-CURRENT after addition of the struct inpcb argument to the pfil API.
600005	136172	October 5, 2004	6.0-CURRENT after addition of the "-d DESTDIR" argument to newsyslog.
600006	137192	November 4, 2004	6.0-CURRENT after addition of glibc style strftime(3) padding options.

Value	Revision	Date	Release
600007	138760	December 12, 2004	6.0-CURRENT after addition of 802.11 framework updates.
600008	140809	January 25, 2005	6.0-CURRENT after changes to VOP_*VOBJECT() functions and introduction of MNTK_MPSAFE flag for Giantfree filesystems.
600009	141250	February 4, 2005	6.0-CURRENT after addition of the cpufreq framework and drivers.
600010	141394	February 6, 2005	6.0-CURRENT after importing OpenBSD's nc(1).
600011	141727	February 12, 2005	6.0-CURRENT after removing semblance of SVID2 matherr() support.
600012	141940	February 15, 2005	6.0-CURRENT after increase of default thread stacks' size.
600013	142089	February 19, 2005	6.0-CURRENT after fixes in <src/include/stdbool.h> and <src/sys/i386/include/_types.h> for using the GCC-compatibility of the Intel C/C++ compiler.
600014	142184	February 21, 2005	6.0-CURRENT after EOVERFLOW checks in vswprintf(3) fixed.
600015	142501	February 25, 2005	6.0-CURRENT after changing the struct if_data member, ifi_epoch, from wall clock time to uptime.
600016	142582	February 26, 2005	6.0-CURRENT after LC_CTYPE disk format changed.
600017	142683	February 27, 2005	6.0-CURRENT after NLS catalogs disk format changed.
600018	142686	February 27, 2005	6.0-CURRENT after LC_COLLATE disk format changed.
600019	142752	February 28, 2005	Installation of acpica includes into /usr/include.
600020	143308	March 9, 2005	Addition of MSG_NOSIGNAL flag to send(2) API.
600021	143746	March 17, 2005	Addition of fields to cdevsw
600022	143901	March 21, 2005	Removed gtar from base system.

Value	Revision	Date	Release
600023	144980	April 13, 2005	LOCAL_CREDS, LOCAL_CONNWAIT socket options added to unix(4).
600024	145565	April 19, 2005	hwpmc(4) and related tools added to 6.0-CURRENT.
600025	145565	April 26, 2005	struct icmphdr added to 6.0-CURRENT.
600026	145843	May 3, 2005	pf updated to 3.7.
600027	145966	May 6, 2005	Kernel libalias and ng_nat introduced.
600028	146191	May 13, 2005	POSIX ttyname_r(3) made available through unistd.h and libc.
600029	146780	May 29, 2005	6.0-CURRENT after libpcap updated to v0.9.1 alpha 096.
600030	146988	June 5, 2005	6.0-CURRENT after importing NetBSD's if_bridge(4).
600031	147256	June 10, 2005	6.0-CURRENT after struct ifnet was broken out of the driver softcs.
600032	147898	July 11, 2005	6.0-CURRENT after the import of libpcap v0.9.1.
600033	148388	July 25, 2005	6.0-STABLE after bump of all shared library versions that had not been changed since RELENG_5.
600034	149040	August 13, 2005	6.0-STABLE after credential argument is added to dev_clone event handler. 6.0-RELEASE.
600100	151958	November 1, 2005	6.0-STABLE after 6.0-RELEASE
600101	153601	December 21, 2005	6.0-STABLE after incorporating scripts from the local_startup directories into the base rcorder(8).
600102	153912	December 30, 2005	6.0-STABLE after updating the ELF types and constants.
600103	154396	January 15, 2006	6.0-STABLE after MFC of pidfile(3) API.
600104	154453	January 17, 2006	6.0-STABLE after MFC of ldconfig_local_dirs change.
600105	156019	February 26, 2006	6.0-STABLE after NLS catalog support of csh(1).
601000	158330	May 6, 2006	6.1-RELEASE

Value	Revision	Date	Release
601100	158331	May 6, 2006	6.1-STABLE after 6.1-RE-LEASE.
601101	159861	June 22, 2006	6.1-STABLE after the import of csup.
601102	160253	July 11, 2006	6.1-STABLE after the iwi(4) update.
601103	160429	July 17, 2006	6.1-STABLE after the resolver update to BIND9, and exposure of reentrant version of netdb functions.
601104	161098	August 8, 2006	6.1-STABLE after DSO (dynamic shared objects) support has been enabled in OpenSSL.
601105	161900	September 2, 2006	6.1-STABLE after 802.11 fixups changed the api for the IEEE80211_IOC_STA_INFO ioctl.
602000	164312	November 15, 2006	6.2-RELEASE
602100	162329	September 15, 2006	6.2-STABLE after 6.2-RE-LEASE.
602101	165122	December 12, 2006	6.2-STABLE after the addition of Wi-Spy quirk.
602102	165596	December 28, 2006	6.2-STABLE after pci_find_extcap() addition.
602103	166039	January 16, 2007	6.2-STABLE after MFC of dlsym change to look for a requested symbol both in specified dso and its implicit dependencies.
602104	166314	January 28, 2007	6.2-STABLE after MFC of ng_deflate(4) and ng_pred1(4) netgraph nodes and new compression and encryption modes for ng_ppp(4) node.
602105	166840	February 20, 2007	6.2-STABLE after MFC of BSD licensed version of gzip(1) ported from Net-BSD.
602106	168133	March 31, 2007	6.2-STABLE after MFC of PCI MSI and MSI-X support.
602107	168438	April 6, 2007	6.2-STABLE after MFC of ncurses 5.6 and wide character support.
602108	168611	April 11, 2007	6.2-STABLE after MFC of CAM 'SG' peripheral device, which implements a

Value	Revision	Date	Release
			subset of Linux SCSI SG passthrough device API.
602109	168805	April 17, 2007	6.2-STABLE after MFC of readline 5.2 patchset 002.
602110	169222	May 2, 2007	6.2-STABLE after MFC of pmap_invalidate_cache(), pmap_change_attr(), pmap_mapbios(), pmap_mapdev_attr(), and pmap_unmapbios() for amd64 and i386.
602111	170556	June 11, 2007	6.2-STABLE after MFC of BOP_BDFLUSH and caused breakage of the filesystem modules KBI.
602112	172284	September 21, 2007	6.2-STABLE after libutil(3) MFC's.
602113	172986	October 25, 2007	6.2-STABLE after MFC of wide and single byte ctype separation. Newly compiled binary that references to ctype.h may require a new symbol, _mb_sb_limit, which is not available on older systems.
602114	173170	October 30, 2007	6.2-STABLE after ctype ABI forward compatibility restored.
602115	173794	November 21, 2007	6.2-STABLE after back out of wide and single byte ctype separation.
603000	173897	November 25, 2007	6.3-RELEASE
603100	173891	November 25, 2007	6.3-STABLE after 6.3-RELEASE.
(not changed)	174434	December 7, 2007	6.3-STABLE after fixing multibyte type support in bit macro.
603102	178459	April 24, 2008	6.3-STABLE after adding l_sysid to struct flock.
603103	179367	May 27, 2008	6.3-STABLE after MFC of the memrchr(3) function.
603104	179810	June 15, 2008	6.3-STABLE after MFC of support for :u variable modifier in make(1).
604000	183583	October 4, 2008	6.4-RELEASE
604100	183584	October 4, 2008	6.4-STABLE after 6.4-RELEASE.

18.8. FreeBSD 5 Versions

Table 18.8. FreeBSD 5 __FreeBSD_version Values

Value	Revision	Date	Release
500000	58009	March 13, 2000	5.0-CURRENT
500001	59348	April 18, 2000	5.0-CURRENT after adding addition ELF header fields, and changing our ELF binary branding method.
500002	59906	May 2, 2000	5.0-CURRENT after kld metadata changes.
500003	60688	May 18, 2000	5.0-CURRENT after buf/bio changes.
500004	60936	May 26, 2000	5.0-CURRENT after binutils upgrade.
500005	61221	June 3, 2000	5.0-CURRENT after merging libxpg4 code into libc and after TASKQ interface introduction.
500006	61500	June 10, 2000	5.0-CURRENT after the addition of AGP interfaces.
500007	62235	June 29, 2000	5.0-CURRENT after Perl upgrade to 5.6.0
500008	62764	July 7, 2000	5.0-CURRENT after the update of KAME code to 2000/07 sources.
500009	63154	July 14, 2000	5.0-CURRENT after ether_ifattach() and ether_ifdetach() changes.
500010	63265	July 16, 2000	5.0-CURRENT after changing mtree defaults back to original variant, adding -L to follow symlinks.
500011	63459	July 18, 2000	5.0-CURRENT after kqueue API changed.
500012	65353	September 2, 2000	5.0-CURRENT after setproctitle(3) moved from libutil to libc.
500013	65671	September 10, 2000	5.0-CURRENT after the first SMPng commit.
500014	70650	January 4, 2001	5.0-CURRENT after <sys/select.h> moved to <sys/selinfo.h>.
500015	70894	January 10, 2001	5.0-CURRENT after combining libgcc.a and libgcc_r.a, and associated GCC linkage changes.
500016	71583	January 24, 2001	5.0-CURRENT after change allowing libc and libc_r to

Value	Revision	Date	Release
			be linked together, deprecating -pthread option.
500017	72650	February 18, 2001	5.0-CURRENT after switch from struct ucred to struct xucred to stabilize kernel-exported API for mountd et al.
500018	72975	February 24, 2001	5.0-CURRENT after addition of CPUTYPE make variable for controlling CPU-specific optimizations.
500019	77937	June 9, 2001	5.0-CURRENT after moving machine/ioctl_fd.h to sys/fdcio.h
500020	78304	June 15, 2001	5.0-CURRENT after locale names renaming.
500021	78632	June 22, 2001	5.0-CURRENT after Bzip2 import. Also signifies removal of S/Key.
500022	83435	July 12, 2001	5.0-CURRENT after SSE support.
500023	83435	September 14, 2001	5.0-CURRENT after KSE Milestone 2.
500024	84324	October 1, 2001	5.0-CURRENT after d_thread_t, and moving UUCP to ports.
500025	84481	October 4, 2001	5.0-CURRENT after ABI change for descriptor and creds passing on 64 bit platforms.
500026	84710	October 9, 2001	5.0-CURRENT after moving to XFree86 4 by default for package builds, and after the new libc strnstr() function was added.
500027	84743	October 10, 2001	5.0-CURRENT after the new libc strcasestr() function was added.
500028	87879	December 14, 2001	5.0-CURRENT after the userland components of smbfs were imported.
(not changed)			5.0-CURRENT after the new C99 specific-width integer types were added.
500029	89938	January 29, 2002	5.0-CURRENT after a change was made in the return value of sendfile(2).

Value	Revision	Date	Release
500030	90711	February 15, 2002	5.0-CURRENT after the introduction of the type fflags_t, which is the appropriate size for file flags.
500031	91203	February 24, 2002	5.0-CURRENT after the usb structure element rename.
500032	92453	March 16, 2002	5.0-CURRENT after the introduction of Perl 5.6.1.
500033	93722	April 3, 2002	5.0-CURRENT after the sendmail_enable rc.conf(5) variable was made to take the value NONE.
500034	95831	April 30, 2002	5.0-CURRENT after mtx_init() grew a third argument.
500035	96498	May 13, 2002	5.0-CURRENT with Gcc 3.1.
500036	96781	May 17, 2002	5.0-CURRENT without Perl in /usr/src
500037	97516	May 29, 2002	5.0-CURRENT after the addition of dlfunc(3)
500038	100591	July 24, 2002	5.0-CURRENT after the types of some struct sockbuf members were changed and the structure was reordered.
500039	102757	September 1, 2002	5.0-CURRENT after GCC 3.2.1 import. Also after headers stopped using _BSD_FOO_T_ and started using _FOO_T_DECLARED. This value can also be used as a conservative estimate of the start of bzip2(1) package support.
500040	103675	September 20, 2002	5.0-CURRENT after various changes to disk functions were made in the name of removing dependency on disklabel structure internals.
500041	104250	October 1, 2002	5.0-CURRENT after the addition of getopt_long(3) to libc.
500042	105178	October 15, 2002	5.0-CURRENT after Binutils 2.13 upgrade, which included new FreeBSD emulation, vec, and output format.
500043	106289	November 1, 2002	5.0-CURRENT after adding weak pthread_XXX stubs to

Value	Revision	Date	Release
			libc, obsoleting libXThrStub.so. 5.0-RELEASE.
500100	109405	January 17, 2003	5.0-CURRENT after branching for RELENG_5_0
500101	111120	February 19, 2003	<sys/dkstat.h> is empty. Do not include it.
500102	111482	February 25, 2003	5.0-CURRENT after the d_mmap_t interface change.
500103	111540	February 26, 2003	5.0-CURRENT after taskqueue_swi changed to run without Giant, and taskqueue_swi_giant added to run with Giant.
500104	111600	February 27, 2003	cdevsw_add() and cdevsw_remove() no longer exists. Appearance of MAJOR_AUTO allocation facility.
500105	111864	March 4, 2003	5.0-CURRENT after new cdevsw initialization method.
500106	112007	March 8, 2003	devstat_add_entry() has been replaced by devstat_new_entry()
500107	112288	March 15, 2003	Devstat interface change; see sys/sys/param.h 1.149
500108	112300	March 15, 2003	Token-Ring interface changes.
500109	112571	March 25, 2003	Addition of vm_paddr_t.
500110	112741	March 28, 2003	5.0-CURRENT after realpath(3) has been made thread-safe
500111	113273	April 9, 2003	5.0-CURRENT after usbhid(3) has been synced with NetBSD
500112	113597	April 17, 2003	5.0-CURRENT after new NSS implementation and addition of POSIX.1 getpw*_r, getgr*_r functions
500113	114492	May 2, 2003	5.0-CURRENT after removal of the old rc system.
501000	115816	June 4, 2003	5.1-RELEASE.
501100	115710	June 2, 2003	5.1-CURRENT after branching for RELENG_5_1.
501101	117025	June 29, 2003	5.1-CURRENT after correcting the semantics of sig-

Value	Revision	Date	Release
			timedwait(2) and sigwait-info(2).
501102	117191	July 3, 2003	5.1-CURRENT after adding the lockfunc and lockfuncarg fields to bus_dma_tag_create(9).
501103	118241	July 31, 2003	5.1-CURRENT after GCC 3.3.1-pre 20030711 snapshot integration.
501104	118511	August 5, 2003	5.1-CURRENT 3ware API changes to twe.
501105	119021	August 17, 2003	5.1-CURRENT dynamically-linked /bin and /sbin support and movement of libraries to /lib.
501106	119881	September 8, 2003	5.1-CURRENT after adding kernel support for Coda 6.x.
501107	120180	September 17, 2003	5.1-CURRENT after 16550 UART constants moved from `<dev/sio/sioreg.h>` to `<dev/ic/ns16550.h>`. Also when libmap functionality was unconditionally supported by rtld.
501108	120386	September 23, 2003	5.1-CURRENT after PFIL_HOOKS API update
501109	120503	September 27, 2003	5.1-CURRENT after adding kiconv(3)
501110	120556	September 28, 2003	5.1-CURRENT after changing default operations for open and close in cdevsw
501111	121125	October 16, 2003	5.1-CURRENT after changed layout of cdevsw
501112	121129	October 16, 2003	5.1-CURRENT after adding kobj multiple inheritance
501113	121816	October 31, 2003	5.1-CURRENT after the if_xname change in struct ifnet
501114	122779	November 16, 2003	5.1-CURRENT after changing /bin and /sbin to be dynamically linked
502000	123198	December 7, 2003	5.2-RELEASE
502010	126150	February 23, 2004	5.2.1-RELEASE
502100	123196	December 7, 2003	5.2-CURRENT after branching for RELENG_5_2
502101	123677	December 19, 2003	5.2-CURRENT after __cxa_atexit/__cxa_finalize

Value	Revision	Date	Release
			functions were added to libc.
502102	125236	January 30, 2004	5.2-CURRENT after change of default thread library from libc_r to libpthread.
502103	126083	February 21, 2004	5.2-CURRENT after device driver API megapatch.
502104	126208	February 25, 2004	5.2-CURRENT after getopt_long_only() addition.
502105	126644	March 5, 2004	5.2-CURRENT after NULL is made into ((void *)0) for C, creating more warnings.
502106	126757	March 8, 2004	5.2-CURRENT after pf is linked to the build and install.
502107	126819	March 10, 2004	5.2-CURRENT after time_t is changed to a 64-bit value on sparc64.
502108	126891	March 12, 2004	5.2-CURRENT after Intel C/C++ compiler support in some headers and execve(2) changes to be more strictly conforming to POSIX.
502109	127312	March 22, 2004	5.2-CURRENT after the introduction of the bus_alloc_resource_any API
502110	127475	March 27, 2004	5.2-CURRENT after the addition of UTF-8 locales
502111	128144	April 11, 2004	5.2-CURRENT after the removal of the getvfsent(3) API
502112	128182	April 13, 2004	5.2-CURRENT after the addition of the .warning directive for make.
502113	130057	June 4, 2004	5.2-CURRENT after ttyioctl() was made mandatory for serial drivers.
502114	130418	June 13, 2004	5.2-CURRENT after import of the ALTQ framework.
502115	130481	June 14, 2004	5.2-CURRENT after changing sema_timedwait(9) to return 0 on success and a non-zero error code on failure.
502116	130585	June 16, 2004	5.2-CURRENT after changing kernel dev_t to be pointer to struct cdev *.

Value	Revision	Date	Release
502117	130640	June 17, 2004	5.2-CURRENT after changing kernel udev_t to dev_t.
502118	130656	June 17, 2004	5.2-CURRENT after adding support for CLOCK_VIRTUAL and CLOCK_PROF to clock_gettime(2) and clock_getres(2).
502119	130934	June 22, 2004	5.2-CURRENT after changing network interface cloning overhaul.
502120	131429	July 2, 2004	5.2-CURRENT after the update of the package tools to revision 20040629.
502121	131883	July 9, 2004	5.2-CURRENT after marking Bluetooth code as non-i386 specific.
502122	131971	July 11, 2004	5.2-CURRENT after the introduction of the KDB debugger framework, the conversion of DDB into a backend and the introduction of the GDB backend.
502123	132025	July 12, 2004	5.2-CURRENT after change to make VFS_ROOT take a struct thread argument as does vflush. Struct kinfo_proc now has a user data pointer. The switch of the default X implementation to xorg was also made at this time.
502124	132597	July 24, 2004	5.2-CURRENT after the change to separate the way ports rc.d and legacy scripts are started.
502125	132726	July 28, 2004	5.2-CURRENT after the backout of the previous change.
502126	132914	July 31, 2004	5.2-CURRENT after the removal of kmem_alloc_pageable() and the import of gcc 3.4.2.
502127	132991	August 2, 2004	5.2-CURRENT after changing the UMA kernel API to allow ctors/inits to fail.
502128	133306	August 8, 2004	5.2-CURRENT after the change of the vfs_mount signature as well as global replacement of PRISON_ROOT with

Value	Revision	Date	Release
			SUSER_ALLOWJAIL for the suser(9) API.
503000	134189	August 23, 2004	5.3-BETA/RC before the pfil API change
503001	135580	September 22, 2004	5.3-RELEASE
503100	136595	October 16, 2004	5.3-STABLE after branching for RELENG_5_3
503101	138459	December 3, 2004	5.3-STABLE after addition of glibc style strftime(3) padding options.
503102	141788	February 13, 2005	5.3-STABLE after Open-BSD's nc(1) import MFC.
503103	142639	February 27, 2005	5.4-PRERELEASE after the MFC of the fixes in <src/include/stdbool.h> and <src/sys/i386/include/_types.h> for using the GCC-compatibility of the Intel C/C++ compiler.
503104	142835	February 28, 2005	5.4-PRERELEASE after the MFC of the change of ifi_epoch from wall clock time to uptime.
503105	143029	March 2, 2005	5.4-PRERELEASE after the MFC of the fix of EOVER-FLOW check in vswprintf(3).
504000	144575	April 3, 2005	5.4-RELEASE.
504100	144581	April 3, 2005	5.4-STABLE after branching for RELENG_5_4
504101	146105	May 11, 2005	5.4-STABLE after increasing the default thread stack-sizes
504102	504101	June 24, 2005	5.4-STABLE after the addition of sha256
504103	150892	October 3, 2005	5.4-STABLE after the MFC of if_bridge
504104	152370	November 13, 2005	5.4-STABLE after the MFC of bsdiff and portsnap
504105	154464	January 17, 2006	5.4-STABLE after MFC of ld-config_local_dirs change.
505000	158481	May 12, 2006	5.5-RELEASE.
505100	158482	May 12, 2006	5.5-STABLE after branching for RELENG_5_5

18.9. FreeBSD 4 Versions

Table 18.9. FreeBSD 4 __FreeBSD_version Values

Value	Revision	Date	Release
400000	43041	January 22, 1999	4.0-CURRENT after 3.4 branch
400001	44177	February 20, 1999	4.0-CURRENT after change in dynamic linker handling
400002	44699	March 13, 1999	4.0-CURRENT after C++ constructor/destructor order change
400003	45059	March 27, 1999	4.0-CURRENT after functioning dladdr(3)
400004	45321	April 5, 1999	4.0-CURRENT after __deregister_frame_info dynamic linker bug fix (also 4.0-CURRENT after EGCS 1.1.2 integration)
400005	46113	April 27, 1999	4.0-CURRENT after suser(9) API change (also 4.0-CURRENT after newbus)
400006	47640	May 31, 1999	4.0-CURRENT after cdevsw registration change
400007	47992	June 17, 1999	4.0-CURRENT after the addition of so_cred for socket level credentials
400008	48048	June 20, 1999	4.0-CURRENT after the addition of a poll syscall wrapper to libc_r
400009	48936	July 20, 1999	4.0-CURRENT after the change of the kernel's dev_t type to struct specinfo pointer
400010	51649	September 25, 1999	4.0-CURRENT after fixing a hole in jail(2)
400011	51791	September 29, 1999	4.0-CURRENT after the sigset_t datatype change
400012	53164	November 15, 1999	4.0-CURRENT after the cutover to the GCC 2.95.2 compiler
400013	54123	December 4, 1999	4.0-CURRENT after adding pluggable linux-mode ioctl handlers
400014	56216	January 18, 2000	4.0-CURRENT after importing OpenSSL
400015	56700	January 27, 2000	4.0-CURRENT after the C++ ABI change in GCC 2.95.2 from -fvtable-thunks to -

Value	Revision	Date	Release
			fno-vtable-thunks by default
400016	57529	February 27, 2000	4.0-CURRENT after importing OpenSSH
400017	58005	March 13, 2000	4.0-RELEASE
400018	58170	March 17, 2000	4.0-STABLE after 4.0-RELEASE
400019	60047	May 5, 2000	4.0-STABLE after the introduction of delayed checksums.
400020	61262	June 4, 2000	4.0-STABLE after merging libxpg4 code into libc.
400021	62820	July 8, 2000	4.0-STABLE after upgrading Binutils to 2.10.0, ELF branding changes, and tcsh in the base system.
410000	63095	July 14, 2000	4.1-RELEASE
410001	64012	July 29, 2000	4.1-STABLE after 4.1-RELEASE
410002	65962	September 16, 2000	4.1-STABLE after setprocitle(3) moved from libutil to libc.
411000	66336	September 25, 2000	4.1.1-RELEASE
411001			4.1.1-STABLE after 4.1.1-RELEASE
420000	68066	October 31, 2000	4.2-RELEASE
420001	70895	January 10, 2001	4.2-STABLE after combining libgcc.a and libgcc_r.a, and associated GCC linkage changes.
430000	73800	March 6, 2001	4.3-RELEASE
430001	76779	May 18, 2001	4.3-STABLE after wint_t introduction.
430002	80157	July 22, 2001	4.3-STABLE after PCI powerstate API merge.
440000	80923	August 1, 2001	4.4-RELEASE
440001	85341	October 23, 2001	4.4-STABLE after d_thread_t introduction.
440002	86038	November 4, 2001	4.4-STABLE after mount structure changes (affects filesystem klds).
440003	88130	December 18, 2001	4.4-STABLE after the userland components of smbfs were imported.
450000	88271	December 20, 2001	4.5-RELEASE

Value	Revision	Date	Release
450001	91203	February 24, 2002	4.5-STABLE after the usb structure element rename.
450002	92151	March 12, 2002	4.5-STABLE after locale changes.
450003			(Never created)
450004	94840	April 16, 2002	4.5-STABLE after the sendmail_enable rc.conf(5) variable was made to take the value NONE.
450005	95555	April 27, 2002	4.5-STABLE after moving to XFree86 4 by default for package builds.
450006	95846	May 1, 2002	4.5-STABLE after accept filtering was fixed so that is no longer susceptible to an easy DoS.
460000	97923	June 21, 2002	4.6-RELEASE
460001	98730	June 21, 2002	4.6-STABLE sendfile(2) fixed to comply with documentation, not to count any headers sent against the amount of data to be sent from the file.
460002	100366	July 19, 2002	4.6.2-RELEASE
460100	98857	June 26, 2002	4.6-STABLE
460101	98880	June 26, 2002	4.6-STABLE after MFC of `sed -i'.
460102	102759	September 1, 2002	4.6-STABLE after MFC of many new pkg_install features from the HEAD.
470000	104655	October 8, 2002	4.7-RELEASE
470100	104717	October 9, 2002	4.7-STABLE
470101	106732	November 10, 2002	Start generated _std{in,out,err}p references rather than _sF. This changes std{in,out,err} from a compile time expression to a runtime one.
470102	109753	January 23, 2003	4.7-STABLE after MFC of mbuf changes to replace m_aux mbufs by m_tag's
470103	110887	February 14, 2003	4.7-STABLE gets OpenSSL 0.9.7
480000	112852	March 30, 2003	4.8-RELEASE
480100	113107	April 5, 2003	4.8-STABLE

Value	Revision	Date	Release
480101	115232	May 22, 2003	4.8-STABLE after realpath(3) has been made thread-safe
480102	118737	August 10, 2003	4.8-STABLE 3ware API changes to twe.
490000	121592	October 27, 2003	4.9-RELEASE
490100	121593	October 27, 2003	4.9-STABLE
490101	124264	January 8, 2004	4.9-STABLE after e_sid was added to struct kinfo_e-proc.
490102	125417	February 4, 2004	4.9-STABLE after MFC of libmap functionality for rtld.
491000	129700	May 25, 2004	4.10-RELEASE
491100	129918	June 1, 2004	4.10-STABLE
491101	133506	August 11, 2004	4.10-STABLE after MFC of revision 20040629 of the package tools
491102	137786	November 16, 2004	4.10-STABLE after VM fix dealing with unwiring of fictitious pages
492000	138960	December 17, 2004	4.11-RELEASE
492100	138959	December 17, 2004	4.11-STABLE
492101	157843	April 18, 2006	4.11-STABLE after adding libdata/ldconfig directories to mtree files.

18.10. FreeBSD 3 Versions

Table 18.10. FreeBSD 3 `__FreeBSD_version` Values

Value	Revision	Date	Release
300000	22917	February 19, 1996	3.0-CURRENT before mount(2) change
300001	36283	September 24, 1997	3.0-CURRENT after mount(2) change
300002	36592	June 2, 1998	3.0-CURRENT after semctl(2) change
300003	36735	June 7, 1998	3.0-CURRENT after ioctl arg changes
300004	38768	September 3, 1998	3.0-CURRENT after ELF conversion
300005	40438	October 16, 1998	3.0-RELEASE
300006	40445	October 16, 1998	3.0-CURRENT after 3.0-RELEASE

Value	Revision	Date	Release
300007	43042	January 22, 1999	3.0-STABLE after 3/4 branch
310000	43807	February 9, 1999	3.1-RELEASE
310001	45060	March 27, 1999	3.1-STABLE after 3.1-RELEASE
310002	45689	April 14, 1999	3.1-STABLE after C++ constructor/destructor order change
320000			3.2-RELEASE
320001	46742	May 8, 1999	3.2-STABLE
320002	50563	August 29, 1999	3.2-STABLE after binary-incompatible IPFW and socket changes
330000	50813	September 2, 1999	3.3-RELEASE
330001	51328	September 16, 1999	3.3-STABLE
330002	53671	November 24, 1999	3.3-STABLE after adding mkstemp(3) to libc
340000	54166	December 5, 1999	3.4-RELEASE
340001	54730	December 17, 1999	3.4-STABLE
350000	61876	June 20, 2000	3.5-RELEASE
350001	63043	July 12, 2000	3.5-STABLE

18.11. FreeBSD 2.2 Versions

Table 18.11. FreeBSD 2.2 __FreeBSD_version Values

Value	Revision	Date	Release
220000	22918	February 19, 1997	2.2-RELEASE
(not changed)			2.2.1-RELEASE
(not changed)			2.2-STABLE after 2.2.1-RELEASE
221001	24941	April 15, 1997	2.2-STABLE after texinfo-3.9
221002	25325	April 30, 1997	2.2-STABLE after top
222000	25851	May 16, 1997	2.2.2-RELEASE
222001	25921	May 19, 1997	2.2-STABLE after 2.2.2-RELEASE
225000	30053	October 2, 1997	2.2.5-RELEASE
225001	31300	November 20, 1997	2.2-STABLE after 2.2.5-RELEASE
225002	32019	December 27, 1997	2.2-STABLE after ldconfig -R merge
226000	34445	March 24, 1998	2.2.6-RELEASE
227000	37803	July 21, 1998	2.2.7-RELEASE

Value	Revision	Date	Release
227001	37809	July 21, 1998	2.2-STABLE after 2.2.7-RELEASE
227002	39489	September 19, 1998	2.2-STABLE after semctl(2) change
228000	41403	November 29, 1998	2.2.8-RELEASE
228001	41418	November 29, 1998	2.2-STABLE after 2.2.8-RELEASE

Note

Note that 2.2-STABLE sometimes identifies itself as "2.2.5-STABLE" after the 2.2.5-RELEASE. The pattern used to be year followed by the month, but we decided to change it to a more straightforward major/minor system starting from 2.2. This is because the parallel development on several branches made it infeasible to classify the releases merely by their real release dates. Do not worry about old -CURRENTs; they are listed here just for reference.

18.12. FreeBSD 2 Before 2.2-RELEASE Versions

Table 18.12. FreeBSD 2 Before 2.2-RELEASE __FreeBSD_version Values

Value	Revision	Date	Release
119411			2.0-RELEASE
199501	7153	March 19, 1995	2.1-CURRENT
199503	7310	March 24, 1995	2.1-CURRENT
199504	7704	April 9, 1995	2.0.5-RELEASE
199508	10297	August 26, 1995	2.2-CURRENT before 2.1
199511	12189	November 10, 1995	2.1.0-RELEASE
199512	12196	November 10, 1995	2.2-CURRENT before 2.1.5
199607	17067	July 10, 1996	2.1.5-RELEASE
199608	17127	July 12, 1996	2.2-CURRENT before 2.1.6
199612	19358	November 15, 1996	2.1.6-RELEASE
199612			2.1.7-RELEASE